The New York Times

EASY TO NOT-SO-EASY CROSSWORD PUZZLE OMNIBUS VOLUME 4

200 Monday–Saturday Crosswords from the Pages of *The New York Times*

Edited by Will Shortz

ST. MARTIN'S GRIFFIN ☙ NEW YORK

THE NEW YORK TIMES EASY TO NOT-SO-EASY CROSSWORD PUZZLE OMNIBUS VOLUME 4.
Copyright © 2010 by The New York Times Company. All rights reserved.
Printed in the United States of America. For information, address
St. Martin's Press, 175 Fifth Avenue, New York, N.Y. 10010.

www.stmartins.com

All of the puzzles that appear in this work were originally published in *The New York Times*
from January 1, 2004, to September 9, 2004. Copyright © 2004 by
The New York Times Company. All rights reserved. Reprinted by permission.

ISBN 978-0-312-60825-5

10   9   8   7   6

The New York Times

EASY TO NOT-SO-EASY CROSSWORD PUZZLE
OMNIBUS VOLUME 4

ACROSS

1 Unwanted e-mail
5 Top spot
9 Stupid jerk
14 Attire for Caesar
15 Get-out-of-jail money
16 Toward the back
17 Writer Waugh
18 "Coffee, Tea ___?" (1960's best seller)
19 Light bulb holders
20 "Vanilla Sky" actress
23 Young 'un
24 "I Like ___" You
25 Carryall
29 Dead-on
31 How often Santa checks his list
33 Pie ___ mode
34 "I found it!"
36 Tic-tac-toe win
37 One who's closemouthed
38 Maiden voyage preceder
43 City near Osaka
44 Live
45 "___ the ramparts . . ."
46 Human's cousin
47 Old-time oath
49 1960's tripper Timothy
53 Best Picture of 1997
55 3 on a sundial
57 Grassy area
58 Ballpark maintenance groups
61 Pulitzer winner ___ Jefferson
64 Unaccompanied
65 Bush's ___ of Evil
66 Be of use
67 Swear
68 Nothing more than
69 Crown sparkler
70 Zany Martha
71 Waterfront walkway

DOWN

1 Paper clip alternative
2 Medieval weapon
3 Meeting plan
4 Nutmeg spice
5 "You can't judge ___ by its cover"
6 Wall-to-wall installation
7 Charades player
8 November event
9 Military action?
10 Fad
11 Skirt stitching
12 Atlas page
13 Hosp. areas
21 Supple
22 Highly ornate
26 "___ Ha'i"
27 "Oh, woe!"
28 Charades, e.g.
30 Wedding reception centerpiece
32 Impressed, and how!
35 Slowly, to a conductor
37 Medical breakthrough
38 It's played with a deck of 32 cards
39 Arizona Indian
40 Aid in crime
41 Delphic
42 Thing from the past
47 Sign up
48 Actor Poitier
50 Soviet leader ___ Kosygin
51 Provide with new cable
52 Late P.L.O. head Arafat
54 Texas A&M athlete
56 Grenoble's river
59 Popular PBS science series
60 Interstate exit
61 Rank below Lt. Col.
62 "___ Maria"
63 Like crunchy carrots

by Allan E. Parrish

ACROSS

1 Birds' homes
6 Order (around)
10 Quaint cry of shock
14 Not bottled, as beer
15 Choir voice
16 Knot
17 Writer ___ Rogers St. Johns
18 Nay opposers
19 Coin opening
20 Nursery rhyme bakery item
23 Rap's Dr. ___
24 Theater alert
25 More down and out
27 Omaha's home: Abbr.
30 Burden
33 Letters and packages
34 Make, in arithmetic
35 Reception with open arms
39 Was a passenger
41 Play on the radio
42 Supply-and-demand subj.
43 Tidy Lotto prize
48 Mary ___ cosmetics
49 Sweet Spanish dessert
50 Suffix with kitchen
51 Railroad stop: Abbr.
52 Once-fashionable card game
55 PanAm rival
57 Doctors' org.
58 Scarce consolation
64 Pompeii, e.g., today
66 Writer Ephron
67 Anouk of "La Dolce Vita"
68 Capital NNW of Copenhagen
69 Slaughter of the 1940's–50's Cardinals
70 ___-fatty acid
71 Taking the blue ribbon
72 Fall mo.
73 Elephant groups

DOWN

1 Ark builder
2 Prefix with derm
3 Leave in, as text
4 Bathroom powders
5 Songbird
6 Seabiscuit and Citation, e.g.
7 Barcelona cheers
8 Pierces
9 Flip response to a complaint
10 Naval rank: Abbr.
11 Famous bed tester
12 Love to pieces
13 Keep (from)
21 Mrs. Chaplin
22 Patricia who won an Oscar for "Hud"
26 Backgammon equipment
27 Drug cop
28 Suffix with switch
29 Not the most comfortable place to sleep
31 Russia's ___ Mountains
32 Grin
36 Lawyer's document
37 Palace protector
38 "A Day Without Rain" singer, 2000
40 Singer Fitzgerald
44 Fem. opposite
45 Recites
46 Germany's ___ von Bismarck
47 Educational innovation of the 1960's
52 Tree with pods
53 Entertain
54 By oneself
56 Blazing
59 Let go
60 Play group?
61 Bridge master Sharif
62 Tear
63 "___ of the D'Urbervilles"
65 Word in most of the Commandments

by Kurt Mengel

ACROSS

1 Layers
7 Sound of a lightning bolt
10 Cut the hair of
14 Main argument
15 Frank Sinatra's "___ Fool to Want You"
16 Top-notch
17 Losses, in accounting
18 Charlie Rose's network
19 Serving with chop suey
20 Jonathan Swift pamphlet about Ireland
23 To be given away
24 Court
25 The whole shebang
26 Twisty turn
27 See 29-Across
29 With 27-Across, get hitched
31 Cigarette residue
34 Ukr., once
35 Flight paths
37 Reason for turning down an invitation
41 Capulet rival
42 Stars and Stripes land
43 Ocean
44 Guess: Abbr.
45 Film director Craven
46 Nightwear, for short
49 Helios' Roman counterpart
51 Calf's mother
53 Jai ___
54 2003 teen comedy
59 Practice, as skills
60 Apply
61 Territory
62 In addition
63 Spy novelist Deighton
64 Show clearly

65 Spelling contests
66 "Acid"
67 Caught, as fish

DOWN

1 Machine-gun by plane
2 One's wife, slangily
3 Changes the decor of
4 Actor's whisper
5 Point at the dinner table?
6 Implores
7 Nothin'
8 Olympian repast
9 El ___, Tex.
10 Noel
11 Clark Kent's gal
12 Ancient Peruvian
13 Speed away, with "out"
21 Number of teeth Goofy has
22 Popular discount shoe store
27 Tel Aviv native
28 Worthless part
30 Bandy words
32 Capitol Hill V.I.P.: Abbr.
33 President after F.D.R.
34 Drunkard
35 Get better, as wine
36 Drs.' group
37 Afternoons and evenings, briefly
38 Caviar
39 Kinda
40 Wackos
45 Internet start-up?
46 Flexible
47 Actress Rule
48 Like finished contracts
50 Nabisco cookies
52 Continuously
53 Come clean
54 Ishmael's captain
55 Spy
56 Select
57 First lady's residence
58 Hawk's opposite

by Zach Jesse

ACROSS

1 Manila envelope closer
6 Computer screen image
10 "Spare tire"
14 Dominican Republic neighbor
15 Italia's capital
16 Interlude
17 Luggage clip-on
18 "Amo, amas, ___ . . ."
19 Prod
20 It made Leary bleary
22 Rizzuto of the 1940's–50's Yankees
24 Fire, as from a job
25 Unruffled
28 Laid on generously
30 Tot's wheels
32 Hwy. mishap respondent
33 Med school subj.
34 Driveway occupant
36 Becomes a domehead
40 Skirt that shows off legs
41 Pasture
43 Forsaken
44 Fossil fuel blocks
46 Harry Potter's lightning bolt, e.g.
47 Suffix with buck
48 Piercing site
50 Exceed the bounds of
52 Summary holder?
56 With resolute spirit
57 WSW's opposite
58 Party for lei wearers
59 ___ Lanka
60 ___ Jay Lerner of Lerner & Loewe
62 Jolt
64 Jazz's James and Jones

68 Fall's opposite
69 Sea eagle
70 System utilizing grates
71 Editor's mark
72 Space capsule insignia
73 Rulers before Lenin

DOWN

1 Greek X
2 Boy
3 River island
4 Downers?
5 Farm pen
6 Tax deferral means: Abbr.
7 Connectors?
8 Nebraska city
9 Not an emigré
10 Winter ailment
11 Leave in the ___
12 Pond growths
13 Mix
21 Joe that won't keep you up
23 Arm or leg
25 Envelope sticker
26 Bert's Muppet pal
27 Late Princess of Wales
29 Uppers?
31 San ___ Obispo, Calif.
35 Norway's patron saint

37 Peter of "Casablanca"
38 Slobber
39 Like a winter wonderland
42 Wine residue
45 Comedian Mort
49 Sandwich with sauerkraut
51 Least seen
52 Closes in on
53 Dark
54 Pull one's leg
55 Mrs. Bush
61 Volleyball equipment
63 Small coal size
65 Intl. flier, once
66 ___ Lingus
67 Last year's jrs.

by Patrick Merrell

ACROSS

1 Homebuilder's strip
5 Bruins of the Pac 10
9 Unflashy
14 "Can you hear me? . . . hear me? . . . hear me?"
15 Horse in a 60's sitcom
16 Ralph __ Emerson
17 "What a shame!"
18 Laser light
19 Go in
20 Overly florid writing
23 Acorn maker
24 Before, to Byron
25 Recharges one's batteries, so to speak
27 Bucky Beaver's toothpaste, in old ads
31 Switchblade
33 Weapons of __ destruction
37 Pesos
39 Prefix with metric or tonic
40 Author Ferber
41 1951 Alec Guinness film, with "The"
44 City west of Tulsa
45 Night before
46 Go on Social Security, maybe
47 One-and-only
48 Mouth off to
50 September bloom
51 Frisbee, e.g.
53 Some univ. instructors
55 "I knew it!"
58 The 1890's
64 Reaction to the Beatles, once
66 Flying: Prefix
67 Pitch
68 "Git __ Little Dogies"
69 Section of seats
70 58-Across and others
71 "Death Be Not Proud" poet John
72 North Carolina college
73 Hourly pay

DOWN

1 __ year (2004, e.g.)
2 Legal rights grp.
3 In that direction, to a whaler
4 The "H" in "M*A*S*H": Abbr.
5 Brownish
6 Thin pancakes
7 "All in the Family" producer Norman
8 Call on the carpet
9 Clean the carpet
10 Brownish
11 Choir voice
12 Notion
13 Social misfit
21 Memorize
22 __-faire
26 Gets the lead out?
27 Runs in neutral
28 Upright or baby grand
29 Blacksmith's block
30 Had to have
32 Root beer brand
34 Fess up to
35 Sound of slumber
36 Cavalry blade
38 Texas oil city
42 Clear out, as before a hurricane
43 Renter's paper
49 Alternative to mono
52 Likeness
54 Decorate
55 "Diary of __ Housewife" (1970 film)
56 Angel's headwear
57 Unattributed: Abbr.
59 Bridal wear
60 Grind with the teeth
61 Distinctive quality
62 Quarter-mile race, e.g.
63 In addition
65 Holiday __

by Gregory E. Paul

ACROSS

1 People who make you yawn
6 Tibetan monk
10 British fellow
14 Crème de la crème
15 Had payments due
16 Part of a Valentine bouquet
17 Greek marketplace
18 Glenn Miller's "In the ___"
19 Leave out
20 Testifier in a court case
23 Sea eagles
24 "___ will be done . . ."
25 Event with floats
29 Female in a pride
33 Hebrew prophet
34 Be enraptured
36 Animal that beats its chest
37 Pleasant excursion
41 Golf peg
42 Abominates
43 Gillette razor
44 Regards highly
46 Mother of Joseph
48 Wayne film "___ Bravo"
49 Prayer's end
51 Top of a tall building, maybe
59 After-bath powder
60 Fed chairman Greenspan
61 Harold who composed "Over the Rainbow"
62 Gait faster than a walk
63 Film part
64 Cotton thread
65 Disastrous marks for a gymnast
66 Gardener's spring purchase
67 Outpouring

DOWN

1 Smile widely
2 Korbut of the 1972 Olympics
3 Very funny person
4 Raison d'___
5 Charred
6 Fictional salesman Willy
7 M.P.'s hunt them
8 Pussy's cry
9 Building wing
10 Actor Hume
11 Where the heart is, they say
12 Sale tag caution
13 Dogs, but rarely hogs
21 Anger
22 Daring bikini
25 Stickum
26 French girlfriends
27 Synonym man
28 Cigarette's end
29 Colleague of Clark at The Daily Planet
30 Our planet
31 Steeple
32 Flower part
34 Film designers' designs
35 Tiny
38 Not our
39 Tea urns
40 Tic-___-toe
45 Builds
46 ___ Speedwagon
47 Chronicles
49 "It is ___ told by an idiot": Macbeth
50 Dug up
51 ___ the Great (10th-century king)
52 Building near a silo
53 ___ gin fizz
54 ___ vera
55 What icicles do
56 Lohengrin's love
57 Boston cager, informally
58 Leg's middle

by Robert Dillman

ACROSS

1 Chances
5 Wires on a bicycle wheel
11 Tavern
14 In ___ of (substituting for)
15 One of Jerry's pals on "Seinfeld"
16 Down Under bird
17 Bejeweled president?
19 Mo. of Presidents' Day
20 "Much ___ About Nothing"
21 Dine
22 Planet
24 Pale, aging president?
28 Most elderly
31 Hang around for
32 Place to store valuables
33 Hair colorer
34 ___ and hearty
38 Devoted follower
40 Demolisher
42 More's opposite
43 Opening for a tab
45 Zeal
46 Burning up
48 Disinfects
49 Comic president?
53 Wheel turners
54 Tint
55 Historic period
58 Compete (for)
59 Hirsute president?
64 Mont Blanc, e.g.
65 Money earned
66 Communicate by hand
67 Tennis court divider
68 Check receivers
69 Neighborhood

DOWN

1 Gymnast Korbut
2 Stopped working, as an engine
3 Showroom model
4 Total
5 Trigonometric ratio
6 Ancient Greek thinker
7 Paddle
8 Set of tools
9 WSW's reverse
10 Composer Rachmaninoff
11 Obscure
12 Tiny creature
13 "American Idol" winner ___ Studdard
18 Frothy
23 One using lots of soap
24 Object of a dowser's search
25 Reclined
26 Lived
27 Like hen's teeth
28 The White House's ___ Office
29 Delicate fabric
30 Performing twosomes
33 "We love to fly, and it shows" airline
35 Alan of "M*A*S*H"
36 Ponce de ___
37 Goofs
39 Nicholas I or II
41 Appraiser
44 "___ the land of the free . . ."
47 Send again
48 Slides
49 From Jakarta, e.g.
50 Kick out of the country
51 Snoozed
52 Lemon ___ (herb)
55 Kuwaiti ruler
56 Fury
57 "___ and the King of Siam"
60 Santa ___ winds
61 Wintry
62 Shad product
63 Land between Can. and Mex.

by Charles Barasch

ACROSS

1 Shade trees
5 Consent (to)
10 Baby bottle contents
14 "See you later!"
15 Senior dances
16 Assert
17 Flimflam
19 Roman cloak
20 ___ of a kind
21 Warp-resistant wood
22 Temptress
23 One who went to tell the king the sky was falling
26 Not just ask
29 Commotions
30 Family data
31 Juicy tropical fruit
33 Watering hole
36 Perform a dance with a shake
40 WNW's opposite
41 Hackneyed
42 Wall Street inits.
43 Wearisome one
44 Archipelago parts
46 Some messing around
49 Narrative
51 The "A" of ABM
52 Just great
55 Royal attendant
56 Mishmash
59 Asia's shrinking ___ Sea
60 County north of San Francisco
61 Where a stream may run
62 Lots of
63 Clay pigeon shoot
64 Final word

DOWN

1 Talk back?
2 Big cat
3 Nutmeg relative
4 Not worth a ___
5 Tack on
6 Bad pun response
7 Having lots of ups and downs
8 Cousin of an ostrich
9 Road curve
10 Morning prayers
11 Off-white
12 Theater section
13 Skating champ Michelle
18 British gun
22 Busybody
23 Dish of leftovers
24 Group of jurors
25 Jittery
26 Florida's Miami-___ County
27 Selves
28 Apportion, with "out"
31 Miser's hoarding
32 Alias
33 ___ terrier
34 Nuisance
35 One side of a vote
37 Jet black
38 "Listen!"
39 Exclusively
43 By the skin of one's teeth
44 Purpose
45 Omit
46 Title colonel in a 1960's sitcom
47 Military chaplain
48 Actress Dickinson
49 Unsolicited e-mail
50 "Gone With the Wind" estate
52 Man cast out of paradise
53 Girl-watch, e.g.
54 Sharp
56 ___ Pinafore
57 Acorn's source
58 Reproductive cells

by Anne Garelick

ACROSS

1 Continental currency
5 Give off
9 Assumed name
14 Jazz's Kenton
15 Go (over) carefully
16 Officer's shield
17 Easy wins
19 With 62-Across, a possible title for this puzzle
20 Long sandwich
21 Regarding
23 Word after ready or petty
24 Web addresses, for short
26 List-ending abbr.
28 Young hospital helpers
33 Capone and Capp
34 Always, poetically
35 Predicament
37 Where a car may end up after an accident
40 Have dinner
42 Talent
43 Says "cheese"
45 Part of a baseball uniform
47 Tic-___-toe
48 Credits for doing nice things
52 The writing ___ the wall
53 Choir voice
54 Play parts
57 Fishhook feature
59 Corporate money managers: Abbr.
62 See 19-Across
64 Some USA Today graphics
67 The "V" of VCR
68 "Good grief!"
69 "Uh-huh"
70 Snoozer's sound
71 Old salts
72 Italia's capital

DOWN

1 PC key
2 The Beehive State
3 Yard tool
4 Small winning margin, in baseball
5 Ecol. watchdog
6 Baked beans ingredient
7 Bothers
8 Teacher, at times
9 Middle muscles, for short
10 Legal assistant
11 Brainstorm
12 Mellows, as wine
13 Adam's third
18 Basic dictionary entry
22 Soul singer Redding
25 Caustic substance
27 Rental units: Abbr.
28 Get to the top of
29 Up and about
30 It may be called on the battlefield
31 Singer Bonnie
32 "___ Marner"
33 Computer pop-ups
36 R.N.'s forte
38 Religious site
39 Chops
41 Goldilocks sat in his chair
44 Snooty person
46 Campaigner, in brief
49 All worked up
50 Hankering
51 "That's cheating!"
54 Ones heading for the hills?: Abbr.
55 Nickel or dime
56 Commotion
58 Latvia's capital
60 Approximately
61 Flower stalk
63 Tiller's tool
65 S. & L. offerings
66 Baltic or Bering

by Gail Grabowski

ACROSS

1 Fed. food inspectors
5 Raindrop sound
9 Songwriters' grp.
14 Lecherous look
15 Cleveland cagers, briefly
16 Weigher
17 Co-star of 36-Down
19 Jabs
20 It's heard on the grapevine
21 I. M. Pei, for one
23 Red flag, e.g.
24 Lyricist Lorenz ___
25 See 41-Down
29 Online film maker
33 Star of 36-Down
38 Stallone title role
39 Out of port
40 January in Juárez
42 "___ delighted!"
43 Brouhahas
45 Co-star of 36-Down
47 Knock over
49 Fencing blade
50 The "Y" of B.Y.O.B.
52 Barge's route
57 100% incorrect
62 Whooping ___
63 50's candidate Stevenson
64 Setting for 36-Down
66 ___ breath (flower)
67 "Guilty" or "not guilty"
68 Flex
69 Boffo show
70 Gardener's bagful
71 Counts up

DOWN

1 Part of UHF
2 Capital of South Korea
3 Film director Jonathan
4 Shady spot
5 Alternatives to Macs
6 Syllables in "Deck the Halls"
7 Finished
8 Intimidate, with "out"
9 Person with goals
10 Co-star of 36-Down
11 Wedding reception centerpiece
12 Writer Waugh
13 Exterminator's target
18 Garden products name
22 "Hee ___"
26 ___-inspiring
27 Lois of "Superman"
28 "___ Jacques" (children's song)
30 Naval leader: Abbr.
31 "Dancing Queen" quartet
32 Big name in water faucets
33 Makeshift river conveyance
34 Norway's capital
35 Certain tide
36 TV series that premiered in 1974
37 Cause for a plumber
41 With 25-Across, 50%
44 Molasseslike
46 Muhammad's birthplace
48 Where Switz. is
51 Easy wins
53 Popular Caribbean island
54 Sans clothing
55 Put ___ to (halt)
56 English city NE of Manchester
57 Applies lightly
58 Dutch cheese
59 "Duchess of ___" (Goya work)
60 Cairo's river
61 Elation
65 Mouthful of gum

by Allan E. Parrish

ACROSS

1 Opposite of highs
5 Big stingers
10 Concert blasters
14 Hawaiian island
15 Maximum poker bet
16 Bob who lost to Bill Clinton
17 Warner's statement after the fact
19 "Roots" author Haley
20 "Julius Caesar," e.g.
22 ___-fi
23 Bird's home
24 Fire leftover
27 Eve's predecessor
30 Tortilla chip dip
34 Fateful day in a 20-Across
38 Ringer
39 Not so good
40 Egg: Prefix
41 Baseball hit just beyond the infield
42 Bard of ___
43 Fateful day in a 20-Across
45 Pays a landlord
47 Require
48 "I get it!"
49 Guys-only
52 Cry to a mouse
54 "Et tu, Brute? Then fall, Caesar!," e.g.
62 Building beam
63 One who warned Caesar
64 Bronx cheer
65 Golfer Palmer, familiarly
66 Liberals, with "the"
67 ___-bitsy
68 Fabric colorers
69 Schnauzer in Dashiell Hammett books

DOWN

1 ___ Lane, admirer of Superman
2 Inauguration Day recital
3 Command to a horse
4 Broods
5 Land next to a road
6 Crooked
7 Turn on a pivot
8 Resident near the Leaning Tower
9 Make a nighttime ruckus
10 Not limited to one use
11 Gangster's gal
12 Defendant's declaration at an arraignment
13 Alluring
18 The 60's or 70's, e.g.
21 Road section requiring caution
24 Battling
25 Rudely push
26 Long-billed wader
28 ___ this minute
29 "The Jeffersons" theme "___ On Up"
31 Hotelier Helmsley
32 Laziness
33 Omega's opposite
35 Feels no remorse
36 Drum accompanier
37 John Philip Sousa offering
41 Moistens with droplets
43 "Little Women" family name
44 Grows chewers
46 VW predecessors?
50 Syrian president
51 "Mine eyes have seen the ___ . . ."
53 Australian "bear"
54 Land SW of Samoa
55 Assist in crime
56 Fannie ___ (securities)
57 Top-notch
58 Mix (up)
59 Deli loaves
60 Adept
61 Sp. miss

by Patrick Merrell

ACROSS

1 1953 Leslie Caron title role
5 Water pitcher
9 Companion for Snow White
14 Garden of ___
15 Bad habit
16 At the proper time
17 Meteorologist's favorite movie of 1939?
20 Longtime buddy
21 Metals from the earth
22 Drunk's problem
23 One of the Jackson 5
25 Quaker ___
27 "Pow!"
30 "___ the night before Christmas . . ."
32 Lumberjack's "Heads up!"
36 Lotion ingredient
38 "Now it all makes sense!"
40 Dinero
41 Meteorologist's favorite movie of 1952?
44 Tennis champ Chris
45 London district
46 Jazz singer ___ James
47 Dislike with a passion
49 Writer Philip
51 "Game, ___, match!"
52 Kite part
54 Trade
56 Co. that merged with Time Warner
59 Consider
61 Meeting schedule
65 Meteorologist's favorite movie of 2000?
68 Miss America's crown
69 Scotch ___
70 Forest unit
71 Sing in the Alps
72 Speak unclearly
73 [Been there, done that]

DOWN

1 Toy block company
2 TV's "American ___"
3 Give temporarily
4 Bumbling
5 Easily-blamed alter ego
6 Mental quickness
7 Canyon effect
8 Fashionably outdated
9 Chills in the cooler
10 ESE's reverse
11 Etching liquid
12 Little squirt
13 Government agents
18 "Hold on!"
19 Miami basketball team
24 Desert resting place
26 Campfire treat popular with Scouts
27 ___ on a true story
28 Full of energy
29 "Water Lilies" painter Claude
31 Mexican mister
33 Marina sights
34 Cream of the crop
35 Charged
37 Everglades wader
39 Cultural values
42 Words with a handshake
43 Deep trouble
48 Seating level
50 Crones
53 About half of all turns
55 Trifling
56 Lawyer: Abbr.
57 Birthplace of seven U.S. presidents
58 Its symbol is Pb
60 Breakfast, lunch or dinner
62 Author Ephron
63 Sketched
64 "You can say that again!"
66 Opposite of post-
67 PC core: Abbr.

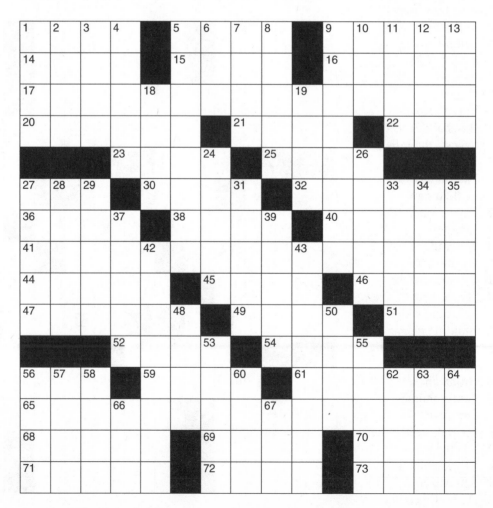

by Kyle Mahowald

ACROSS

1 Apple computers
5 1:00, e.g.
9 Eye color
14 Hideous
15 In ___ (actual)
16 New York's ___ Fisher Hall
17 Time for a Wild West shootout
18 "Excuse me . . ."
19 Pointing device
20 Fancy term for a 36-Across
23 Hornswoggled
24 Tetley product
25 Regretted
26 London's Big ___
27 Shopping place
28 Quick punch
31 Self-evident truth
34 ___ fide
35 Coke or Pepsi
36 Puzzling person?
39 Goldie of "Laugh-In" fame
40 Party giver
41 Atlas blow-up
42 Needle hole
43 Yappy dog, briefly
44 Colorado native
45 Kodak product
46 Explosive letters
47 Put down, slangily
50 Fancy term for a 36-Across
54 Secluded valleys
55 Actress Winslet
56 Stage part
57 W.W. II vessel
58 Split personalities?
59 Think tank output
60 Hairy-chested
61 Edges
62 Work station

DOWN

1 Chew (on)
2 Ancient marketplace
3 Cirrus or cumulus
4 Lip-___ (not really sing)
5 Realm for St. Peter
6 Actor Milo
7 One who takes drugs, e.g.
8 "The Night Watch" painter
9 Tiny village
10 Steer clear of
11 Mount Olympus chief
12 Formerly, once
13 Caustic substance
21 Tabloid twosomes

22 Surrounding glows
26 Cap'n's mate
27 Samuel with a code
28 Scribbles (down)
29 Cream ingredient
30 Quarterback Starr
31 Flu symptom
32 Picture of health?
33 "___ Russia $1200" (Bob Hope book)
34 Gambling professional
35 Art movie theater
37 Overcome utterly
38 "Same here!"
43 Boar's abode
44 Except if
45 Important exam
46 ___ pole

47 Electron tube
48 Cruise stopovers
49 T-bone, e.g.
50 Site of Napoleon's exile
51 Light on Broadway
52 Prepare for takeoff
53 Lines on a radar screen
54 Doublemint, e.g.

by Barry Silk

14 MONDAY

ACROSS

1 Tough spots
  to get out of
5 City leader
10 Ego
14 Old radio word
  for the letter O
15 "___ there yet?"
16 Half a sextet
17 Charlton Heston
  epic, with "The"
20 Ratfink
21 Ray of
  the Kinks
22 Essential
25 Witherspoon of
  "Legally Blonde"
26 "Holy smokes!"
29 Marked, as a
  survey square
31 Whodunit
  board game
32 New Guinea
  native
34 C.E.O.'s degree
37 Home for Pooh
  and Tigger
40 Baseballer Mel
41 Large system of
  newsgroups
42 Smog
43 Unappetizing
  dishes
44 Try to pick up,
  as at a bar
45 Laissez-___
48 Join forces (with)
51 Popular Honda
53 Runs full speed
57 Chain in the upper
  St. Lawrence River
60 Ages and ages
61 False move
62 Jazzy improv style
63 One bit of
  medicine
64 Hot dog
  picker-upper
65 Amerada ___ (oil
  giant)

DOWN

1 Writes (down)
2 Assist in
  wrongdoing
3 Pre-stereo sound
4 Supported,
  as a motion
5 Mrs. Eisenhower
6 Like gunmen
  and octopuses
7 Nay's opposite
8 Possess
9 Foxx of "Sanford
  and Son"
10 Filmmaker Spielberg
11 Bert's roommate on
  "Sesame Street"
12 Reduced-calorie
  beers
13 "All That Jazz"
  choreographer Bob
18 Bullfight cheers
19 Corps member
23 Wide area
24 Two of cards
26 Sound in a big,
  empty room
27 Excess supply
28 Uncle's partner
30 It's thrown at
  a bull's-eye
32 Mexican money
33 Good (at)
34 Castle encircler
35 Old TV clown
36 Chief Yemeni port
38 Kings and
  queens
39 Auto accident
  injury
43 Complain
44 Hockey great
  Bobby
45 Destined
46 Sound preceding
  "God bless"
47 Desktop pictures
49 Growing older
50 Sail supports
52 Loony
54 Formerly
55 Some handhelds:
  Abbr.
56 Speedy fliers,
  for short
58 Modern: Prefix
59 Kipling's "Gunga ___"

by Jim Hyres

Teresa Kraft 11-15-21

ACROSS

1 Subdued color
7 Lift in Aspen
11 Height: Abbr.
14 Title girl in Kay Thompson books
15 "Othello" villain
16 Pastoral place
17 Golf locale
19 Prohibit
20 Letters on a Cardinal's cap
21 Rock musician Brian
22 Diving board's part of a swimming pool
24 Ambles (along)
27 Johnson of "Laugh-In"
28 Thom ___ shoes
30 Extremely low, as prices
34 Strokes on a green
36 Game authority
37 Brays
40 Views, as through binoculars
44 Online correspondence
46 Quick bite
47 Informal group discussion
52 Choir voice
53 Roundish
54 Walks about looking for prey
56 Frog's seat
60 Figure skater Midori
61 ___ Lingus
64 On the ___ (fleeing)
65 Pivoting span on a river
68 Summer in Montréal
69 Encl. with a manuscript
70 Give, as duties
71 One side in checkers
72 Little 'un
73 Tyrannical leader

DOWN

1 Chest muscles, briefly
2 Tremendously
3 One's special person in life
4 ___ Lizzie (Model T)
5 ___ Park, Colo.
6 Loewe's partner on Broadway
7 The first O of O-O-O
8 Like Yul Brynner or Telly Savalas
9 Tropical fever
10 Justice's attire
11 Queen Victoria's prince
12 Shack
13 Two-trailer rig
18 Toy that does tricks
23 Fatherly
25 Furtively
26 Jr. high, e.g.
28 Speedometer letters
29 Billiards rod
31 Keystone officer
32 Automatic tournament advance
33 Bullring hurrahs
35 Identical
38 "What ___ I saying?"
39 ___-boom-bah
41 Spicy chip topping
42 Malfunction, with "up"
43 Bout ender, for short
45 Place for gloss
47 Hair salon item
48 Fly
49 Picked up stealthily
50 It goes on a photocopier: Abbr.
51 "Pretty good!"
55 Poorer
57 "Hey, you!"
58 Not at home
59 Part of the spine
62 Frozen waffle brand
63 Apartment payment
66 Previously named
67 Magazine no.

by Gail Grabowski

Grid solution:

1 P	2 A	3 S	4 T	5 E	6 L		7 T	8 B	9 A	10 R		11 A	12 L	13 T
14 E	L	O	I	S	E		15 I	A	G	O		16 L	E	A
17 C	O	U	N	T	R	18 Y	C	L	U	B		19 B	A	N
20 S	T	L		21 E	N	O		22 D	E	E	23 P	E	N	D
			24 M	O	S	E	Y	S		26		27 A	R	T	E
28 M	29 C	A	N		30 R	O	C	K	31 B	32 O	33 T	T	O	M
34 P	U	T	T	S		36 H	O	Y	L	E			
37 H	E	E	H	A	38 W	39 S		40 P	E	E	R	41 S	42 A	43 T
			44 E	M	A	I	L		45		46 S	N	A	C	K
47 R	48 A	49 P	S	E	S	S	I	O	50 N	51	52 A	L	T	O
53 O	V	A	L			54 P	R	O	55 W	L	S		
56 L	I	L	Y	57 P	58 A	59 D		60 I	T	O		61 A	62 E	63 R
64 L	A	M		65 S	W	I	66 N	G	B	R	67 I	D	G	E
68 E	T	E		69 S	A	S	E		70 A	S	S	I	G	N
71 R	E	D		72 T	Y	K	E		73 D	E	S	P	O	T

ACROSS

1 Timber wolf
5 Gymnast Comaneci
10 Little tricksters
14 Grad
15 Addicts
16 One who nabs 15-Across
17 Nothing more than
18 Eats elegantly
19 French cheese
20 Like some Christians
22 Four-door
23 Do cross-country
24 When the stomach starts grumbling
26 Air conditioner capacity, for short
29 Co. name completer
31 Boar's mate
32 Not behaving conservatively
39 Genesis garden
40 French sea
41 Dublin's land
42 Not just gone
47 ___ Jima
48 Science guy Bill
49 CD predecessors
50 Does a U-turn
55 Place to relax
57 Enlighten
58 Utterance that sums up 20-, 32- and 42-Across
63 Misshapen citrus
64 Chicago airport
65 "A Clockwork Orange" protagonist
66 Unload, as stock
67 Voting machine part
68 5,280 feet
69 Dutch cheese
70 Clothe
71 Quaker ___

DOWN

1 Gentle animal
2 Toast spread
3 Famous duelist
4 Black cats, traditionally speaking
5 Prodding
6 One side of the Urals
7 Overalls material
8 "Me, Myself & ___" (2000 flick)
9 Ninny
10 Not on one side or the other
11 ___ Gras
12 Trojan War king
13 Verona, in "Romeo and Juliet"
21 Related
22 ___ gin fizz
25 Arson aftermath
26 Ran, as colors
27 Seashore washer
28 Eye layer
30 Deep sleep
33 Sundance entry, informally
34 Actor Beatty
35 1982 Disney film
36 Use a rotary phone
37 Basic of golf instruction
38 Lampreys, e.g.
43 Twisted
44 Letters of distress
45 Dish sometimes served "on the half-shell"
46 Officials elected for two yrs.
50 Employ again
51 Nosed (out)
52 Mediterranean estate
53 Old-fashioned anesthetic
54 Trim
56 Site of an 1836 massacre
59 Son of Zeus
60 Russian gold medalist ___ Kulik
61 Had emotions
62 Alimony receivers
64 On in years

by Michael Doran

ACROSS

1 Casino game
5 Symbol on a "one way" sign
10 Numbered musical work
14 Patron saint of Norway
15 "Yeah"
16 Prefix with physical
17 Homeless child
18 Mother ___ stories
19 Checkbook record
20 Mother in a 1960s sitcom
23 Web address: Abbr.
24 Naturalness
25 Sen. Feinstein
27 Go away
30 Mississippi city
32 Arkansas's ___ Mountains
33 Be in harmony (with)
34 Diner sign
37 Vessel for ashes
38 Thirst quenchers
41 Poker prize
42 Historical
44 Pinnacle
45 Port-au-Prince's land
47 It's a bore
49 Los Angeles baseballer
50 Golden period
52 Drop of sweat
53 "Hold On Tight" band
54 1965 Natalie Wood title role
60 Emcee's need
62 Big African critter
63 Opposite of 15-Across
64 France's Cote d'
65 Fund contributor
66 Laced up
67 Partner of rank and serial number

68 Gushes
69 Lyric poems

DOWN

1 Chickens and turkeys
2 Jai ___
3 Train transport
4 Extended slump
5 Month without a national holiday
6 River of Lyon
7 Greek R's
8 Un-elect
9 Apple-polisher
10 Meditative sounds
11 Merrie Melodies "co-star"
12 Reversal
13 Valuable fur

21 Pre-euro German money
22 ___ Bravo
26 Paul Bunyan's tool
27 Arrange, as the hair
28 Book before Nehemiah
29 "Li'l Abner" mother
30 Gang member, maybe
31 Wild goat
33 Make sport of
35 Lug
36 Recipe direction
39 Holders of referee whistles
40 River hazard
43 Small amount
46 Extend, as a house

48 Roll of bills
49 Styles
50 Charles Atlas, for one
51 "My Fair Lady" lady
52 Already
55 Breakfast restaurant chain
56 Trig function
57 Empty space
58 Fencing blade
59 Wines that aren't whites
61 Afore

by Merle Baker

ACROSS

1 Did laps in a pool
5 Foolhardy
9 "She loves me …she loves me not" flower
14 "Horrors!"
15 "Cómo ___ usted?"
16 Blast from the past
17 Spick-and-span
18 Genesis twin
19 F.B.I. worker
20 Achieve initial success
23 Singletons
24 Bullfight cheer
25 Suffix with lion
28 Oar-powered ship
31 Like a fiddle
34 "Scratch and win" game
36 Pub brew
37 Sweep under the rug
38 Estimates
42 Intl. oil group
43 Take to court
44 Use crib notes
45 Cheyenne's locale: Abbr.
46 Kind of underwear
49 Foxy
50 "___ Drives Me Crazy" (Fine Young Cannibals hit)
51 Western tribe
53 Completely mistaken
60 Improperly long sentence
61 Risk-free
62 Number not on a grandfather clock
63 Space shuttle gasket
64 With warts and all
65 Elm or elder
66 ___ Park, Colo.
67 Camper's cover
68 Hankerings

DOWN

1 Spiritual, e.g.
2 Cry on a roller coaster
3 Med. school class
4 E pluribus unum, for instance
5 "___ Madness" (1936 antidrug film)
6 Whence St. Francis
7 Night twinkler
8 Düsseldorf dwelling
9 Within one's power
10 Pond buildup
11 March 15, e.g.
12 Trig term
13 "Are we there ___?"
21 In first place
22 Marisa of "My Cousin Vinny"
25 Arm joint
26 Unrinsed, maybe
27 Fifth-century pope
29 Autumn yard worker
30 Santa's little helper
31 Pink-slips
32 Perfect
33 Short-tempered
35 Nurse's skill, for short
37 "What'd you say?"
39 Gray
40 Feel sorry about
41 Symbol at the head of a musical staff
46 First ___ first
47 Breakfast bread
48 Swear (to)
50 Masonry
52 Nearing retirement age, maybe
53 Yours and mine
54 The "U" in I.C.U.
55 Future atty.'s exam
56 Facilitate
57 Dublin's land
58 Legal claim
59 Goes kaput
60 Salmon eggs

by Gregory E. Paul

ACROSS

1 Likely
4 Hot dish with beans
9 Bridge maven Charles
14 Justice Sandra ___ O'Connor
15 Appealingly shocking
16 Licorice flavoring
17 Antique auto
19 Frank of rock's Mothers of Invention
20 Vegetable oil component
21 The "S" of CBS
23 Black currant
25 Humiliated
29 Tea server's question
33 Out of one's mind
36 Van Susteren of Fox News
37 Alternative to a nail
38 "That's ___!" (angry denial)
40 Conductor's stick
42 Long-eared hopper
43 Neuters
45 Danger
47 Fashion inits.
48 Cause of an out
51 Refuses
52 Smoothed
56 Drops
60 Baghdad resident
61 ___ Mongolia
64 Small frosted cake
66 Item confiscated at an airport
67 Goofy
68 Wrestler's locale
69 Seasoned sailors
70 Parachute pulls
71 They: Fr.

DOWN

1 ___ committee
2 Newswoman Zahn
3 Varieties
4 Asexual reproduction
5 Where spokes meet
6 Showy flower
7 Showy flower
8 "Beware the ___..."
9 Park shelters
10 Parading...or a hint to this puzzle's theme
11 ___ Van Winkle
12 Psychic's claim
13 Educator's org.
18 Japanese soup
22 Punch out, as Morse code
24 Kosovo war participant
26 Not stay on the path
27 Pitchers
28 Wooden pin
30 Bounded
31 Absolute
32 New Zealand native
33 A brig has two
34 ___ male (top dog)
35 Locked book
39 Command to people who are 10-Down
41 "Just do it" sloganeer
44 Gentlemen of España
46 An original tribe of Israel
49 Scatter, as seeds
50 Feudal figure
53 Ashley's country-singing mother
54 Sweet'N Low rival
55 Mud, dust and grime
57 Like "The Lord of the Rings"
58 It's north of Carson City
59 Movie rating unit
61 Approves
62 Spanish article
63 Up to, informally
65 Polit. maverick

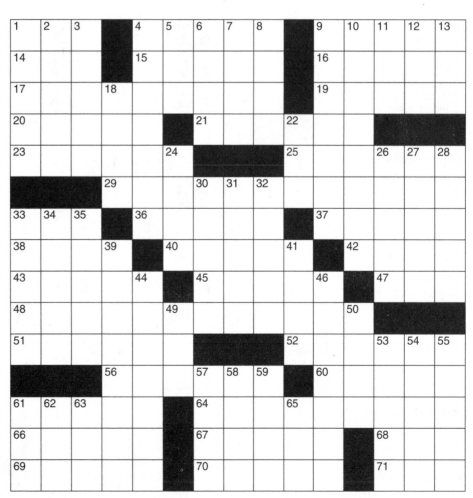

by Joy M. Andrews

ACROSS

1 Boeing 747's and 767's
5 The Monkees' "___ Believer"
8 "Am not!" rejoinder
14 Forced out
16 Wash receptacles
17 With 56-Across, lawyer who argued in 19- and 49-Across
18 Pre-Mexican Indians
19 With 49-Across, noted decision made 5/17/54
21 Buying binge
24 Musical talent
25 Eight: Fr.
26 Stuart queen
29 Went after congers
34 Aged
35 On the briny
36 Curious thing
37 Decision reversed by 19- and 49-Across
40 One sailing under a skull and crossbones
41 Locust or larch
42 Spanish aunt
43 Belgian painter James
44 Chief Justice ___ Warren, majority opinion writer for 19- and 49-Across
45 Rolodex nos.
46 Select, with "for"
48 Stanford-___ test
49 See 19-Across
55 Sitting room
56 See 17-Across
60 Groups of starting players
61 Forebodes
62 Former Vice President Dick
63 Ave. crossers
64 Mary ___ Lincoln

DOWN

1 Stick (out)
2 Book after Galatians: Abbr.
3 Capote, for short
4 Iced dessert
5 Langston Hughes poem
6 Cat's cry
7 Annex: Abbr.
8 Addis ___, Ethiopia
9 Symbol of sharpness
10 "Cómo ___ usted?"
11 Echelon
12 How a lot of modern music is sold
13 Secret W.W. II agcy.
15 Brute
20 Flying geese formation
21 Quaint establishment
22 Arrive, as by car
23 Passengers
26 "___ sow, so shall . . ."
27 Reno's state: Abbr.
28 U.S./Can./Mex. pact
30 University URL ending
31 Pay attention
32 French star
33 Ruler by birth
35 Houston landmark
36 Pitcher Hershiser
38 ___ Paulo, Brazil
39 Go off track
44 And so forth
45 Soldier's helmet, slangily
47 Short-winded
48 Bruce Springsteen, with "the"
49 ___ of office
50 Gratis
51 Flair
52 Concert equipment
53 Pucker-inducing
54 Angers
55 ___-Man (arcade game)
57 Past
58 Was ahead
59 "Acid"

by Ethan Cooper

ACROSS

1 Dreadful, as circumstances
5 One not of high morals
10 Spanish house
14 TV's "American ___"
15 Come back
16 Shakespeare, the Bard of ___
17 1970 Richard Thomas film adapted from a Richard Bradford novel
20 Mao ___-tung
21 Hula shakers
22 To no ___ (uselessly)
23 Outlaws
24 Wall Street business
26 Jumped
29 Long baths
30 Ayatollah's land
31 Kunta ___ of "Roots"
32 Duo
35 1975 Al Pacino film
39 Lamb's mother
40 Landlord payments
41 Shrek, for one
42 Slight hangups
43 Reveries
45 Oilless paint
48 Cure
49 Lily family plants
50 Arias, usually
51 King topper
54 1941 Priscilla Lane film whose title was a #1 song
58 Advance, as money
59 Lollapalooza
60 Bridle strap
61 Football positions
62 "I'm innocent!"
63 Poet ___ St. Vincent Millay

DOWN

1 Earth
2 Midmonth date
3 Was transported
4 Raised railroads
5 Difficult
6 Harvests
7 Intermissions separate them
8 Silent
9 ___-am (sports competition)
10 Sail material
11 Birdlike
12 ___ boom
13 Corner
18 Mongol title
19 Fouler
23 Wedding reception staple
24 Type assortments
25 "I can't believe ___..." (old ad catchphrase)
26 Lateral part
27 Ship's front
28 Fury
29 Sorts (through)
31 Australian hopper, for short
32 "Gladiator" garment
33 Fish bait
34 Halves of a 32-Across
36 James of "Gunsmoke"
37 Wine vintage
38 Christmas song
42 Zips (along)
43 X out
44 Cause for umbrellas
45 Billiards furniture
46 Actress Burstyn
47 Knoll
48 Yawn-inducing
50 Yards rushing, e.g.
51 Elderly
52 Goatee site
53 Sicilian volcano
55 Son of, in Arabic names
56 Recent: Prefix
57 Fury

by Frederick J. Healy

ACROSS

1 True-blue
6 Toy gun poppers
10 Smooch
14 "Good Night" girl of song
15 Arthur ___ Stadium in Queens
16 Peak
17 River triangle
18 Signify
19 Horn's sound
20 Logic
23 ___ capita
24 Buffalo's lake
25 Money in the bank, e.g.
30 Declare
33 Seizes without authority
34 Old what's-___-name
35 George W. Bush's alma mater
36 Michael who starred in "Dirty Rotten Scoundrels"
37 Snorkeling accessory
38 Wolf calls
39 Broadway hit with 7,000+ performances
40 With it
41 Immobilize
42 Swelling reducer
43 Highway stops
45 Ritzy
46 Little rascal
47 Question of concern, with a hint to 20-, 25- and 43-Across
54 Corner square in Monopoly
55 Den
56 Unsophisticated
57 Loafing
58 Dublin's home
59 Lyrics accompany them
60 2000 "subway series" losers
61 Toy used on hills
62 Commence

DOWN

1 Eyeball covers
2 Nabisco cookie
3 Shout
4 Against
5 Weapon in the game of Clue
6 Tripod topper
7 On the open water
8 Adds gradually
9 Mexican misters
10 Couric of CBS News
11 Computer symbol
12 Haze
13 Movie backdrop
21 Commies
22 Tiny criticism
25 Emmy-winner (finally!) Susan
26 Author ___ Bashevis Singer
27 Truly
28 Vases
29 Harbor sights
30 Took care of
31 Totally tired
32 Sí and oui
35 Quotable Yank
37 Swerve back and forth, as a car's rear end
38 Very short shorts
40 Big bothers
41 Soccer star Mia
43 Caught
44 In layers
45 Sees a ghost, maybe
47 Walk through water
48 Sword handle
49 Put on the payroll
50 Tightly stretched
51 Turner who sang "I Don't Wanna Fight"
52 At any time
53 Sabbath activity
54 ___-dandy

by Lynn Lempel

ACROSS

1 Literature Nobelist Bellow
5 Slender
9 Gregorian music style
14 Port or claret
15 Left a chair
16 Edmonton hockey player
17 Vicinity
18 Out of the wind
19 Handsome wood design
20 Place to pull in for a meal
23 Seafood in shells
24 Site of one-armed bandits
27 Place for a pig
28 New York ballplayer
29 Ryan of "When Harry Met Sally"
30 Four-star officer: Abbr.
31 F.D.R. radio broadcast
34 As well
37 Responses to a masseur
38 German chancellor ___ von Bismarck
39 Highest-priced boxing ticket
44 It may be served with crumpets
45 Snoop around
46 Old cable inits.
47 "Sesame Street" broadcaster
50 Modern affluent type
52 Teen meeting place
54 Kindly doctor's asset
57 Setting for Theseus and the Minotaur
59 Plumb crazy
60 Skin outbreak
61 Broadcasting
62 Whiskey drink
63 Display
64 Desires
65 Statement figures: Abbr.
66 "Bonanza" brother

DOWN

1 Groups of bees
2 Clear of stale smells
3 Apprehensive
4 Clues, to a detective
5 Movie preview
6 Not change course
7 "Gotcha"
8 Must-have item
9 Just-made-up word
10 Actor/dancer Gregory
11 O.K.
12 Org. that funds exhibits
13 Have a go at
21 Big rig
22 Decorated, as a cake
25 Well-groomed
26 Not fooled by
29 Fail to qualify, as for a team
31 London weather, often
32 That girl
33 Barracks bunk
34 Bohemian
35 In ___ of (replacing)
36 Vegetable in a crisp pod
40 Tarantulas, e.g.
41 Angers
42 Captivates
43 Tennis star Kournikova
47 Pullover raincoat
48 ___ Aires
49 Scatters, as petals
51 Mini, in Marseille
53 Grind, as teeth
55 Rick's love in "Casablanca"
56 Fate
57 It may be put out to pasture
58 Genetic stuff

by Craig Kasper

ACROSS

1 End-of-week cry
5 Makes, as tea
10 Wise ___ owl
14 Folk singer Guthrie
15 Soprano Callas
16 Popular building block
17 1959 Doris Day/Rock Hudson comedy
19 Actress Singer of "Footloose"
20 Victor's entitlement
21 Errors
23 See 24-Across
24 With 23-Across, Neptune, e.g.
26 Back street
27 Clearance item's caveat
29 Wrestler's win
30 Had a bite
31 Disposable pen maker
32 Davenport
33 Church official
37 What a full insurance policy offers
40 Bronze and stainless steel
41 Bed size smaller than full
42 ___ Paul's seafood
43 Spider's prey
44 Conger or moray
45 Mosquito repellent ingredient
46 First lady after Hillary
49 Put two and two together?
50 California's Big ___
51 Evidence in court
53 Tetley competitor
56 Radio tuner
57 Piano player's aid
60 France, under Caesar

61 "___ Doone" (1869 novel)
62 Not us
63 Building additions
64 Vote into office
65 Jekyll's alter ego

DOWN

1 Bugler's evening call
2 Hang on tight?
3 Not according to Mr. Spock
4 Shakespearean volumes
5 Some luxury cars
6 Squealer
7 Time in history
8 "The Flintstones" mother

9 Pseudonym of H. H. Munro
10 Post-danger signal
11 1988 Olympics host
12 Be of one mind
13 Clamorous
18 Outdated
22 Lustrous fabric
24 Go (through), as evidence
25 Made into law
27 "Mamma Mia" pop group
28 Window box location
29 Verse-writing
30 Tablet with ibuprofen
32 Bygone space station
34 Averse to picture-taking

35 Meanie
36 Home in a tree
38 Without any extras
39 Was beholden to
45 University of Minnesota campus site
46 Overhang
47 Like some symmetry
48 Mover's rental
49 Playwright ___ Fugard
50 Uncle ___
52 Ireland, the Emerald ___
53 Ballpark figure?
54 Went out, as a fire
55 Pinnacle
58 Before, in 29-Down
59 Business letter abbr.

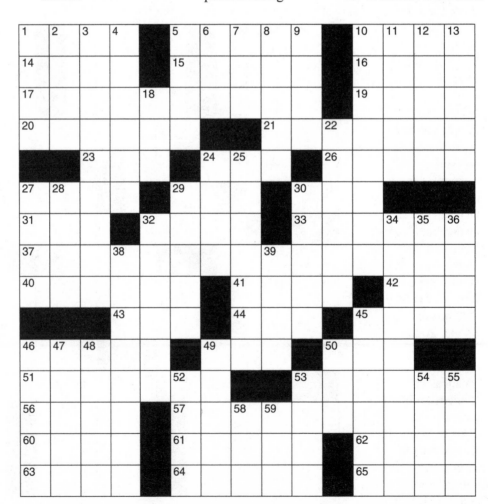

by Craig Kasper

ACROSS

1 Crossword pattern
5 Dinner and a movie, perhaps
9 No longer fresh
14 Prefix with space
15 Sharif of "Funny Girl"
16 Swatch competitor
17 Convention group
18 Sitarist Shankar
19 Christopher of "Superman"
20 Polyester, e.g.
23 Battering device
24 Words before tear or roll
25 Astroturf, e.g.
34 Everest or Ararat
35 Comic strip orphan
36 Country singer Brenda
37 Johnson of "Laugh-In"
38 Vision-related
39 Darn, as socks
40 Lunar New Year
41 Grand Canyon transport
42 Contemptible person
43 Oleomargarine, e.g.
46 Airport monitor abbr.
47 Blonde shade
48 Fake 50, e.g.
57 Throng
58 Banjo-plucking Scruggs
59 Hand lotion ingredient
60 Indy-winning Al, Jr. or Sr.
61 Canal of song
62 It's trapped on laundry day
63 Sirs' counterparts
64 Give temporarily
65 Falls behind

DOWN

1 Chews the fat
2 Depend (on)
3 "Pumping ___"
4 Marxism, for one
5 Starting notes in music
6 Amo, amas, ___ . . .
7 Rikki-Tikki-___
8 Guitarist Clapton
9 Eerie
10 Item of men's jewelry
11 From the United States: Abbr.
12 Jeans purveyor Strauss
13 Business V.I.P.
21 Sword handle
22 ___ acid (B vitamin)
25 Maker of precious violins
26 Composer/author Ned
27 ___-frutti
28 Isle in the Bay of Naples
29 Emcee's spiel
30 Negatively charged particle
31 Alaskan native
32 "Common" thing that's not always common
33 Passover feast
38 Bizarre
39 Closet larvae repellent
41 Does deals without money
42 Earthy desire
44 Bicycle for two
45 Tried to save a sinking boat
48 Buddy
49 One of the O'Neills
50 ___ Major
51 Rod's partner
52 Price of a ride
53 "___ go bragh"
54 Pelvic bones
55 Beyond the end line
56 Answer to "Shall we?"

by Sarah Keller

ACROSS

1 What a surfer rides
5 Do agricultural work
9 Pre-euro German money
14 Violinist Leopold
15 Side squared, for a square
16 When added up
17 Porn classification
19 AM/FM device
20 Rainbow's shape
21 Attractive
23 Nova ___
26 Battle exhortations
27 Followers of the Vatican
29 Dockworker's org.
30 Postponed
31 Driver entitled to free maps, perhaps
37 Sprinted
38 Grp. battling consumer fraud
39 Genetic letters
40 Big shoe request
44 Accumulate
46 Lumberjack's tool
47 Binds, as wounds
49 Sign-making aids
54 Gets the soap off
55 Part of a grandfather clock
56 "Then what . . .?"
57 Handy ___ (good repairmen)
58 English king during the American Revolution
63 Feed, as a fire
64 Jazz's Fitzgerald
65 Horse color
66 Customs
67 Leave in, to a proofreader
68 At the ocean's bottom, as a ship

DOWN

1 Floor application
2 Secondary, as an outlet: Abbr.
3 Annoy
4 Inconsistent
5 Wealthy sort, slangily
6 ___ Ben Canaan of "Exodus"
7 Extend a subscription
8 ___ cum laude
9 Act of God
10 Horrid glances from Charles Grodin?
11 Hub projections
12 Kevin of "A Fish Called Wanda"
13 Wades (through)
18 Stand up
22 Bad, as a prognosis
23 Mold's origin
24 Something not really on Mars
25 Hypothesize
28 Kemo ___ (the Lone Ranger)
32 Pres. Lincoln
33 Help in crime
34 Button material
35 Follow
36 Metal filers
41 Beard named for a Flemish artist
42 Forgives
43 Astronaut Armstrong
44 Imitating
45 Darners
48 Mount where an ark parked
49 Charley horse, e.g.
50 ___-one (long odds)
51 Witch of ___
52 Olympic sleds
53 Refine, as metal
59 Bullring call
60 Debtor's note
61 Writer Fleming
62 It's kept in a pen

by Patrick Merrell

ACROSS

1 Food lover's sense
6 Home for alligators
11 "Open __ 9" (shop sign)
14 Pays to play poker
15 Talk show group
16 Early afternoon hour
17 "Pronto!"
19 Tribe related to the Hopi
20 Historic times
21 Use a hose on, as a garden
23 Rev. William who originated the phrase "a blushing crow"
27 "What so __ we hailed . . ."
29 Singer Don of the Eagles
30 Opt for
31 Parking lot posting
32 Dahl who wrote "Charlie and the Chocolate Factory"
33 Subject of "worship"
36 Sound in a cave
37 Pocketbook
38 Ditty
39 Itsy-bitsy
40 Free-for-all
41 "I do" sayer
42 "Tom __" (#1 Kingston Trio hit)
44 Smashed and grabbed
45 Adds up (to)
47 "__ keepers . . ."
48 Boxing matches
49 Skin soother
50 Sphere
51 "Pronto!"
58 Gibson who was People magazine's first Sexiest Man Alive
59 Hair-raising
60 Dickens's __ Heep
61 "Later!"
62 Coral ridges
63 Shindig

DOWN

1 Bar bill
2 At __ rate
3 Mudhole
4 Golf ball support
5 Ancient Jewish sect
6 Javelin
7 The "W" in V.F.W.
8 Plus
9 "Oh, give __ home . . ."
10 Layered building material
11 "Pronto!"
12 Computer chip company
13 Suspicious
18 Card below a four
22 "The Sound of Music" setting: Abbr.
23 Nagging sort
24 Result of a treaty
25 "Pronto!"
26 Skillet lubricant
27 Moon stage
28 Part in a play
30 Actor Feldman
32 Contest specifications
34 Below
35 Requires
37 Hit with snowballs, say
38 Walked on
40 Loch Ness dweller, they say
41 Studies hard
43 Ump's call
44 Animal with a cub
45 Mushroom cloud maker
46 Amsterdam of "The Dick Van Dyke Show"
47 Goes by jet
49 "__ I care!"
52 Part of a giggle
53 Bad temper
54 __-la-la
55 Atmosphere
56 Turner who led a revolt
57 "__ will be done"

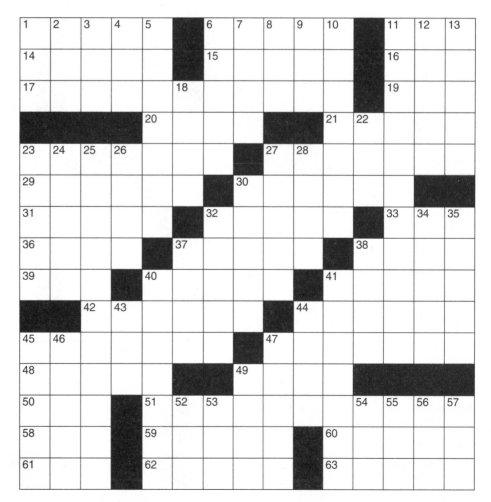

by Gregory E. Paul

ACROSS

1 Big blowout
5 Vehicles with meters
9 Like some committees
14 Charles Lamb's nom de plume
15 Cookie with creme inside
16 Takes a card from the pile
17 Where to order egg salad
18 Flintstone fellow
19 Designer Karan
20 Practically gives away
23 Whole lot
24 Restless
27 Bandleader Shaw
29 Big galoots
31 "Vive le ___!"
32 Faint from rapture
33 Waterless
34 Mulligatawny, for one
35 Starts telling a different story
38 Theme park attraction
39 Bringing up the rear
40 Magician's rods
41 Gallery display
42 One who's suckered
43 Voting districts
44 Pushed snow aside
46 Saucy
47 Prepares to be punished
53 Desperately want
55 Homeboy's turf
56 Hurry up
57 Macho guys
58 English princess
59 River in an Agatha Christie title
60 Apply, as pressure
61 Not the original color
62 Meal in a pot

DOWN

1 People retire to these spots
2 Toward the sheltered side
3 Window feature
4 Dangerous bit of precipitation
5 Morning eyeopener
6 Turn signal
7 Brewski
8 Word after baking or club
9 Extras
10 Speak in a monotone
11 Loiter
12 Part of B.Y.O.B.
13 Jefferson Davis org.
21 David's weapon, in the Bible
22 Soft leather
25 Pings and dings
26 "Holy mackerel!"
27 Spinning
28 Celebrity's upward path
29 Cropped up
30 Pub offering
32 Throw out
33 "On the double!"
34 Bravura performances
36 Escape the detection of
37 Bunch of bees
42 Not half bad
43 Pulled dandelions, say
45 Be indecisive
46 Give a buzz
48 Certain herring
49 Chichi
50 Clubs or hearts
51 Capri, for one
52 Enjoy some gum
53 Friend of Fidel
54 Mystery author Stout

by Nancy Salomon and Kendall Twigg

ACROSS

1 Musical genre pioneered by Bill Haley and His Comets
5 Cove
10 Partner of ready and willing
14 Unattractive tropical fruit
15 Voting site
16 Hit with the fist
17 Sunbather's award?
19 Sandwich fish
20 Still
21 Before, in poetry
22 Interpret without hearing
24 1051 on monuments
25 Edward who wrote "The Owl and the Pussycat"
26 Temples in the Far East
30 Assassinating
33 Old-time actress Massey
34 Join, in woodworking
36 La Paz is its cap.
37 President after Tyler
38 Sun-bleached
39 "___ Ben Adhem," Leigh Hunt poem
40 Finish
41 Duelist Burr
42 Was bright, as the sun
43 Mark for misconduct
45 Gas ratings
47 Kuwaiti leader
48 Sun or planet
49 Depot baggage handlers
52 Actress Joanne
53 Next-to-last Greek letter
56 Wings: Lat.
57 Romantics' awards?
60 1/500 of the Indianapolis 500
61 Have a mad crush on
62 Colorful gem
63 [No bid]
64 Changed direction, as a ship
65 Actor Billy of "Titanic"

DOWN

1 Slippers' color in "The Wizard of Oz"
2 Shrek, for one
3 Blood problem
4 One of the same bloodline
5 Portugal and Spain together
6 Snout
7 Auction unit
8 List-ending abbr.
9 Tickled pink
10 Off course
11 Sad person's award?
12 Moon goddess
13 Old-time exclamation
18 Mrs. F. Scott Fitzgerald
23 Nectar source
24 Neurotic TV detective played by Tony Shalhoub
26 Spoke (up)
27 On one's own
28 Big recording artists' awards?
29 Brainy
30 Dictation taker
31 Nary a soul
32 Affixes (to)
35 Wedding 58-Down
38 Good sportsmanship
39 "Moby-Dick" captain
41 Song for a diva
42 Olympic gymnast Kerri
44 Roasts' hosts
46 ___ beef
49 Entrance to an expressway
50 Director Kazan
51 Scotch's partner
52 Dreadful
53 Insect stage
54 Go across
55 ___ of Man
58 See 35-Down
59 Family relation, for short

by Bernice Gordon

ACROSS

1 Mall component
6 Genesis twin
10 Fly like an eagle
14 Hiker's path
15 Goatee's locale
16 Time for eggnog
17 Having no entryways?
19 A.A.A. recommendations: Abbr.
20 Left on a map
21 How some ham sandwiches are made
22 Letter after theta
23 Disney World attraction
25 Opposite of whole, milkwise
27 "French" dog
30 "I'm ready to leave"
32 Down Under bird
33 Britannica, for one: Abbr.
35 "Thanks, Pierre!"
38 Squeal (on)
39 ___ standstill (motionless)
40 City that Fred Astaire was "flying down to" in a 1933 hit
42 "Dear old" family member
43 Jogs
45 Looks sullen
47 Poetic palindrome
48 Tributary
50 Word before Nevada or Leone
52 Hold back
54 Give a benediction to
56 Ball field covering
57 Motionless
59 Campaign funders, for short
63 Buffalo's lake
64 Having no vision?
66 Submarine danger
67 Number between dos and cuatro
68 Weird
69 Habitual tipplers
70 Gumbo vegetable
71 Modify to particular conditions

DOWN

1 Put in the hold
2 "___ Grit" (John Wayne film)
3 Quaker ___
4 Ran amok
5 Santa's little helper
6 Commercial prefix with Lodge
7 In a moment
8 Bright and breezy
9 Still in the out-box, as mail
10 Injection selection
11 Having no commandment?
12 Prince Valiant's wife
13 Plopped down again
18 Museum guide
24 Delighted
26 Gradual absorption method
27 Saucy
28 Bradley or Sharif
29 Having no typeset letters?
31 Stocking shade
34 Where to watch whales in Massachusetts, with "the"
36 Writer John Dickson ___
37 Inkling
41 "The only thing we have to fear is fear ___": F.D.R.
44 Prairie homes
46 It goes around the world
49 Mississippi River explorer
51 Caught sight of
52 Agenda details
53 The first part missing in the author's name ___ Vargas ___
55 The second part missing in the author's name ___ Vargas ___
58 Istanbul resident
60 Taj Mahal locale
61 Intel product
62 Typesetting mark
65 Poseidon's domain

by Holden Baker

ACROSS

1 Pitches four balls to
6 Cain's brother
10 Insurrectionist Turner and others
14 Not reacting chemically
15 Muse of history
16 Monogram part: Abbr.
17 Pilfer
18 Kitchen gadget that turns
20 "Faster!"
22 No great ___
23 Iced tea flavoring
26 Full complement of fingers
27 Sob
30 Before, in poetry
31 Classic gas brand
34 Composer Rachmaninoff
36 Midsection muscles, for short
37 "Faster!"
40 Knight's title
41 Rat or squirrel
42 Dye containers
43 Western Indian
44 Linear, for short
45 Rope-a-dope boxer
47 Fixes
49 1960s–'70s space program
52 "Faster!"
57 Cramped space
59 Rich cake
60 Primer dog
61 Sharif of film
62 Gives an audience to
63 Band with the 1988 #1 hit "Need You Tonight"
64 Monthly payment
65 Birds by sea cliffs

DOWN

1 Bit of smoke
2 Contrarians
3 Bloodsucker
4 Volcano that famously erupted in 1883
5 Acts of the Apostles writer
6 Bank holdings: Abbr.
7 Dull
8 Mozart's "a"
9 Circle
10 Daughter of a sister, perhaps
11 Ben Stiller's mother
12 Bit of business attire
13 Narrow water passage: Abbr.
19 Washed-out
21 Money for retirement
24 What a satellite may be in
25 Digs with twigs?
27 Kennel club info
28 "Son of ___!"
29 Had a cow
31 ___ salts
32 Luxury hotel accommodations
33 Safe
35 Mahler's "Das Lied von der ___"
38 Snowman of song
39 Villain
46 Can't stand
48 Amounts in red numbers
49 Notify
50 Ship's navigation system
51 Weird
53 Norse thunder god
54 Terse directive to a chauffeur
55 Panache
56 "___ of the D'Urbervilles"
57 Popular TV police drama
58 The WB competitor

by M. Francis Vuolo

ACROSS

1 Poi source
5 "The Thin Man" dog
9 Rum-soaked cakes
14 Stench
15 Where an honoree may sit
16 Friend, south of the border
17 Rocket scientist's employer
18 Prefix with potent
19 Alpine song
20 Not much
23 ___ glance (quickly)
24 Center of activity
25 Grammys, e.g.
29 Tip for a ballerina
31 Aide: Abbr.
35 Funnel-shaped
36 Craze
38 Hurry
39 Activities that generate no money
42 Surgery spots, for short
43 Indians of New York
44 Jack who ate no fat
45 Seeded loaves
47 Dog-tag wearers, briefly
48 Choirs may stand on them
49 Overly
51 Loser to D.D.E. twice
52 Boatswains, e.g.
59 R-rated, say
61 Poker payment
62 Confess
63 Tutu material
64 Rude look
65 Peru's capital
66 Back tooth
67 Slips
68 Fizzless, as a soft drink

DOWN

1 Cargo weights
2 Sandler of "Big Daddy"
3 Painter Bonheur
4 Face-to-face exam
5 Takes as one's own
6 Pago Pago's land
7 Salon application
8 Where Nepal is
9 Louisiana waterway
10 Microscopic organism
11 Bridge declarations
12 Questionnaire datum
13 Note after fa
21 Scottish beau
22 "A League of ___ Own" (1992 comedy)
25 Cast member
26 "What, me ___?"
27 Liqueur flavorer
28 Speed (up)
29 Blackmailer's evidence
30 Burden
32 English county
33 Ravi Shankar's instrument
34 Checkups
36 1052, in a proclamation
37 St. Francis' birthplace
40 Lingo
41 Raises
46 "A Streetcar Named Desire" woman
48 Directs (to)
50 Stream bank cavorter
51 "___ you" ("You go first")
52 Clout
53 Connecticut campus
54 Unique individual
55 Ranch newborn
56 Diabolical
57 Capital south of Venezia
58 Whack
59 Bank amenity, for short
60 Pair

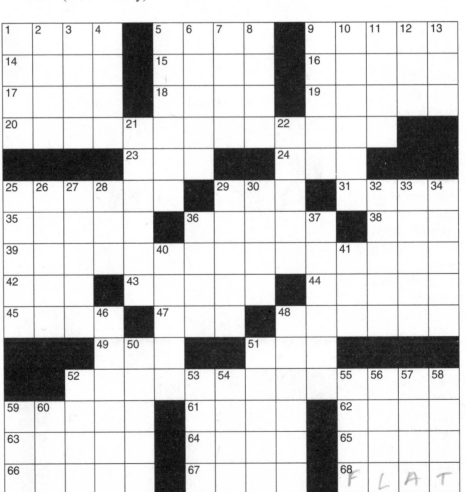

by Joy C. Frank

SHOES & SPORTS

Legit
Lagit
Ligit
Logit
Lugit

ACROSS

1 Be sweet on
6 "Quiet!" *Shh*
9 Boy Scout unit
14 The Bates ___, in "Psycho"
15 Soccer star Hamm
16 Baseball Hall-of-Famer Combs
17 Poolside wear
20 Flat formation
21 Harold Gray's Annie, for one
22 Louse-to-be
23 Mountain debris
25 Gate pivots *hinges?*
27 Bird of 29-Down
30 Smart-mouthed
32 Prefix with -asian
33 A, B, C, D or E
35 Marsh plant
39 Giveaway: Var.
41 Place for butts
43 Final authority
44 Copycat's words
46 Auction ending?
47 Race marker
49 Be a buttinsky
51 Disco flasher
54 Put a stop to
56 Jackie's second
57 Available, as a doctor
59 Org. for Annika Sorenstam
63 House wear
66 Kosher
67 Narc's grp.
68 Place for rouge
69 Idyllic places
70 Map rtes.
71 Acts the stool pigeon

DOWN

1 Radio letters
2 1996 Republican standard-bearer
3 Elevator maker
4 Meal
5 Polar helper
6 Campfire treat
7 Maximally cool
8 Truck stop fare
9 Court wear
10 "Awesome!"
11 Sumatra swinger
12 Pal of Kukla and Fran
13 Royal pains
18 Country singer Morgan
19 Contented sighs
24 Ranch wear
26 Russian's refusal
27 Gridiron "zebras"
28 Heavenly glow
29 Mouse, to a 27-Across
31 At the drop of ___
34 Audition tape
36 ___ Scott Decision
37 Celt or Highlander
38 Brontë's Jane
40 Hockey great Phil, familiarly
42 Mogadishu resident
45 Placed in a box, say
48 Late-night Jay
50 Oracle site
51 Fine fur
52 In a tough spot
53 Chain of hills
55 Fitzgerald and others
58 U.S.N. rank below Capt.
60 Hammer's end
61 Cyclist LeMond
62 Questions
64 ___ Tin Tin
65 I.B.M.-compatibles

Deup
repas
De_P

A	D	O	R	E		S	H	H		T	R	O	O	P
M	O	T	E	L		M	I	A		E	A	R	L	E
F	L	I	P	F	L	O	P	S	A	N	D	A	L	S
M	E	S	A			O	R	P	H	A	N		N	I	T
			S	C	R	E	E			H	I	N	G	E	S
R	A	P	T	O	R			S	A	S	S	Y			
E	U	R		W	I	D	T	H			S	E	D	G	E
F	R	E	E	B	E	E		A	S	H	T	R	A	Y	
S	A	Y	S	O		M	E	T	O	O		E	E	R	
			P	Y	L	O	N		M	E	D	D	L	E	
S	T	R	O	B	E		C	E	A	S	E				
A	R	I		O	N	C	A	L	L		L	P	G	A	
B	E	D	R	O	O	M	S	L	I	P	P	E	R	S
L	E	G	I	T		D	E	A		C	H	E	E	K
E	D	E	N	S		R	d	s		S	I	N	G	S

by Kent Lorentzen

ACROSS

1 Bongo or conga
5 Bellhop's burden
8 Integra maker
13 Diarist Frank
14 Concert halls
16 "Vacancy" sign site
17 Star of 59-Across
20 Got 100 on
21 Extinct bird
22 Brazilian hot spot
23 Director of
   59-Across
27 Pampering, briefly
28 Olive ___
29 Saragossa's river
30 Circusgoers' sounds
32 Understand
34 "___ Irish Rose"
38 Music featured in
   59-Across
42 English assignment
43 Slangy refusal
44 Classic soda brand
45 Tiff
48 PBS funder
50 III, to Jr.
51 Author of 59-Across
56 A.F.L. merger partner
57 Suffix with Peking
58 "___ #1!"
59 Theme of this puzzle,
   with "A"
65 Like bell-bottoms,
   nowadays
66 Claudius's successor
67 Highlander
68 Bus. aides
69 Little bit
70 Fair-hiring org.

DOWN

1 River regulator
2 Genetic stuff
3 Opens, as a gate
4 Hajji's destination
5 Proceed à la Captain
   Kirk?
6 Nimitz or Halsey:
   Abbr.
7 Glittering, like a
   diamond
8 Latin 101 verb
9 It's no bull
10 Wombs
11 Archaeologist's
   find
12 Free of problems
15 "Have ___ and a
   smile" (old slogan)
18 Wine: Prefix
19 Paint crudely
23 Plumlike fruits
24 Mtn. stat
25 Fiber source
26 Radio personality
   ___ Quivers
27 Repeated words in a
   famous soliloquy
31 Narc's discovery
33 Hamilton's bill
35 Fundamentally
36 Group values
37 Tibia's locale
39 Doc's needle
40 Half an Orkan
   farewell
41 Forest name
46 From the top
47 Ex-champ Mike
49 Antiquing agent
51 Capital of Ghana
52 Frasier's brother
53 Whistle blasts
54 Special Forces
   cap
55 Wipe clean
60 PC component
61 Ring victories, for
   short
62 Malay Peninsula's
   Isthmus of ___
63 Gloppy stuff
64 List ender

by M. Francis Vuolo

Note: The circled letters will show a "change in the weather."

ACROSS

1 Punching tool
4 Minus
8 Purity units
14 "Quiet down!"
15 Lie next to
16 Supreme Egyptian god
17 Summer weather phenomenon
19 Dreadlocks wearers
20 With little effort
21 Itinerary word
23 Nervous twitches
24 Like an old cigar
25 Repel, as an attack
27 25-Down, e.g.
29 Within view
30 Marina event
35 Drum majors' props
39 Basin accompanier
40 Coeur d'___, Idaho
42 Feminine suffix
43 Arnaz and Ball's studio
45 Eat quickly
47 Pick up
49 Bering, e.g.: Abbr.
50 Dark, heavy type
53 A black key
58 Colombian city
59 Bruised item, maybe
60 Automat, e.g.
61 Ersatz gold
63 Winter weather phenomenon
65 Launderer, at times
66 Sheriff Taylor's son
67 Former New York City mayor Beame
68 Admits, with "up"
69 Not very much
70 Part of CBS: Abbr.

DOWN

1 Hibachi residue
2 Toast choice
3 Tibet's capital
4 Like the Wild West
5 Popular site for collectors
6 Ford Explorer, e.g.: Abbr.
7 Martin of "Roxanne"
8 Martial arts wear
9 "I___ Rock" (1966 hit)
10 Went back to the top
11 Bit of silliness
12 CD segment
13 Get snippy with
18 Up to, briefly
22 Actor Holm
25 High school subj.
26 Ovine utterance
28 Some prom night drivers
30 Hospital unit
31 Have markers out
32 Loser to D.D.E.
33 Lots and lots and lots
34 A browser browses it, with "the"
36 Lennon's lady
37 Compass heading
38 Six-yr. term holder
41 It smells
44 Topper
46 Like most tires
48 Baseball put-out
50 Ballet rail
51 "Stand and Deliver" star
52 Après-ski drink
54 McHenry and Sumter: Abbr.
55 Olin and Horne
56 Sheikdom of song
57 Pounds on an Underwood
58 Salon creation
60 Director Kazan
62 Jackie Onassis' sister
64 Make a choice

by Eric Berlin

ACROSS

1 Cripple
5 Chorus member
9 Old adders
14 Alan of "The Seduction of Joe Tynan"
15 Ballet move
16 Early computer language
17 Light gas
18 Gawk at
19 Type of type
20 Examination, redundantly
23 Increase, with "up"
24 Quick on the uptake
25 Frisk, with "down"
28 "The Way We ___"
31 Perfectos, e.g.
36 Director Kazan
38 Colonel or captain
40 Gymnast Comaneci
41 Pestering, redundantly
44 Uniform shade
45 Student driver, usually
46 Slugger Sammy
47 Gets smart with
49 Try for a part
51 One of 100 in D.C.
52 Conquistador's prize
54 Whisper sweet nothings
56 Angry outburst, redundantly
63 Oscar winner Foster
64 Unable to decide
65 Took off
67 Maine college town
68 "Zounds!"
69 Jacob's twin
70 Von Münchhausen, e.g.
71 Lady of Lisbon
72 Medium-___

DOWN

1 "Hoo-ey!"
2 Baldwin of "Talk Radio"
3 Elvis or Madonna, e.g.
4 Lord's home
5 Skin cream ingredient
6 Longevity at the box office
7 Soft mineral
8 "Il Trovatore," e.g.
9 Driving the getaway car for
10 Island east of Java
11 Z ___ zebra
12 Like lowest-mileage driving
13 Diamonds, slangily
21 Stitch up
22 Bars at the checkout counter: Abbr.
25 Eats like a bird
26 Maui greeting
27 Louise and Turner
29 Carry on
30 Keyboard key
32 Comedian's stock
33 Sonora "so long"
34 Washer cycle
35 "Contact" author Carl
37 Invites
39 Patella's place
42 Get snockered
43 It puts the squeeze on
48 Hindu title
50 Singer McLean
53 Made a choice
55 Put forward
56 Mrs. Dithers
57 Dump problem
58 El ___ (weather factor)
59 Like some pizza orders
60 Gulf land
61 Rick's love in "Casablanca"
62 Something shed
63 Applicant's goal
66 Expected in

by Randall J. Hartman

ACROSS

1 Sagittarius, with "the"
7 "My gal" et al.
11 Any ship
14 Aplenty
15 Apple product
16 Wee one
17 Goddess of love's love
18 Washroom
20 "___ the season . . ."
21 Roof part
23 Certain refrigerators
24 Broke ground
26 Chicken order
28 Pub stock
29 Showy annual
31 This puzzle has a secret one, starting with the third letter of 4-Down
34 Prefix with classical
36 "___ we forget . . ."
37 Salon stiffener
38 "Unbelievable!"
42 Patient people
44 "Exodus" hero
45 Misses the mark
47 Govt. code crackers
48 What to do to read the secret message (going diagonally down, then diagonally back up the under side)
51 Inputs into a computer
55 Afternoon affairs
56 Say ___ (refuse)
58 Smarmy
59 Throat part
61 Scent
63 "If I Ruled the World" rapper
64 "Is everything all right?"
66 Manage, slangily
68 Dogfaces
69 Scruff
70 Regal fur
71 Plea at sea
72 Took action against
73 Cash in

DOWN

1 First name in mystery
2 Contacts from space
3 Skeleton site
4 Sweetie pie
5 Old railroad name
6 Cut again
7 Llama's head?
8 Docs' grp.
9 Hot issue
10 Con guy
11 "The Flintstones" setting
12 More than a pest
13 Popular ice cream
19 Locker room supply
22 Nobleman above a baron: Abbr.
25 Disavow
27 Greek Mother Earth
30 Booms' opposites
32 ID in a library
33 Overhead trains
35 ___ cloud (cosmic debris)
38 Monopoly token
39 Choral work
40 Portrait, e.g.
41 St. Paul's architect
43 Belafonte song opener
46 Scared a bit
49 "Calm down . . ."
50 Part of E.S.T.: Abbr.
52 Small digit
53 "Seinfeld" role
54 Modus operandi
57 Awed one
59 Marks
60 Island get-together
62 Hard to find
65 Reveal, poetically
67 Mil. authority

by Joe Bower and Nancy Salomon

ACROSS

1 Let out the waist of, e.g.
6 Ark or bark
10 Mexican Mlle.
14 Pet ___
15 Up to it
16 Rattler's posture
17 Supporter of the arts?
18 Title start of a 2003 Al Franken best seller
19 Still pink
20 Fool a onetime child actor?
23 Tiebreakers, briefly
25 Clean-air org.
26 Elite group
27 Cause a sleepy old man to stumble?
32 Car owner's document
33 With respect to
34 Toe the line
35 Black Russian ingredient
37 20's dispensers
41 "See ya!"
42 Orderly grouping
43 Express gratitude to a country singer?
47 Greasy ___
49 Rip-roaring time
50 Frisk, with "down"
51 Tie up a Midwest senator?
56 Wholly absorbed
57 Show opener
58 Like a luxury car
61 Suit to ___
62 Guitarist Atkins
63 Give a wide berth
64 Garden intruder
65 Unabridged dictionary, e.g.
66 The out crowd

DOWN

1 Mock, in a way
2 Grazing locale
3 Bikini atoll, once
4 At any time
5 Take over for, as a pitcher
6 Europe's ___ Peninsula
7 Eastern sashes
8 A Baldwin
9 New-Ager John
10 Dead Sea document
11 Band hand
12 Gets pooped
13 Heads-up
21 Number cruncher, for short
22 Croupier's tool
23 "Beetle Bailey" dog
24 Chicago paper, familiarly, with "the"
28 Panel layer
29 Lehár's "The Merry ___"
30 Publicity, slangily
31 Org. whose members are packing?
35 Chablis, for one
36 ___ Park, Ill.
37 "Exodus" hero
38 Secret exit, perhaps
39 Doll's cry
40 Part of CBS: Abbr.
41 Gives the boot
42 Election loser
43 Rug, so to speak
44 Emceed
45 Set off
46 Fall behind
47 Scarecrow stuffing
48 Chatter idly
52 It's true
53 Bounce back
54 Agenda unit
55 Zero, on a court
59 ___-Atlantic
60 QB's pickups

by Seth A. Abel

ACROSS

1 Like some appliances, electrically
5 Field of work
9 Daft
14 Bailiwick
15 Gossip tidbit
16 Wahine's welcome
17 Auto trailblazer
19 Eatery
20 Small sofa
21 "Drat!"
23 Wrap up
24 Ltr. holders
26 First course, often
28 Auto trailblazer
34 Kid-___ (Saturday a.m. fare)
35 "The Thin Man" canine
36 Operation at the Alamo
37 Yalies
39 Slangy denial
42 Protein bean
43 Freeze over
45 Self-identifying word
47 "All Things Considered" network
48 Auto trailblazer
52 Slip on the galley
53 Dead against
54 Little shaver
57 Suffragist Carrie
59 Plays the role of
63 Geologic period
65 What 17-, 28- and 48-Across were, so to speak
67 Alphabet set
68 Director Kazan
69 Equestrian's grip
70 Camera setting
71 Withhold from
72 Hot Springs and others

DOWN

1 Sounds of relief
2 Canadian native
3 Subject of an insurance appraisal
4 OPEC is one
5 Emergency need at sea
6 Skater Midori
7 Dork
8 Ellipsis alternative
9 Villains
10 Poetry-spouting pugilist
11 Muscle quality
12 Ergo
13 Prison exercise area
18 Gossipmonger
22 Here-there connector
25 Young lady of Sp.
27 Trident-shaped letters
28 Radioer's "Good as done!"
29 Toulouse "Toodle-oo"
30 "The Cider House Rules" co-star, 1999
31 Sierra ___
32 Land from which Moses came
33 Bring up
34 Bride hider
38 Spades or clubs
40 Explosive star
41 Refuse admission to
44 Prep mentally
46 Lumberjack's first cut
49 Reviewer of books, for short
50 Place of rapid growth
51 Soda bottle units
54 Fall faller
55 Gibbons and gorillas
56 "Go ahead!"
58 Scrabble piece
60 Trickle
61 Inter ___
62 Workers' ID's
64 Sound in a barn rafter
66 Martini ingredient

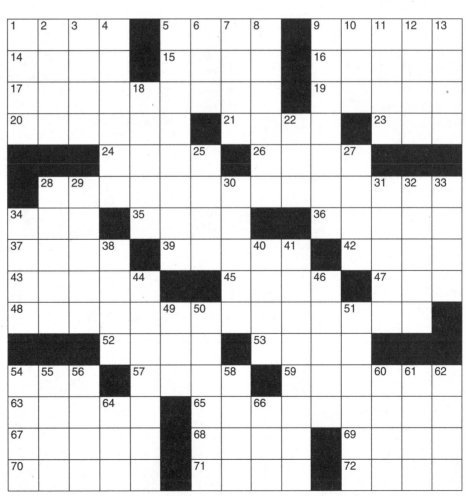

by Bob Frank and Nancy Salomon

ACROSS

1 Up to, in ads
4 Ozzy Osbourne's music, for short
9 Has a yen
14 Prefix with puncture
15 Big name in refrigerators
16 Good, in Guadalajara
17 Sound of hesitation
18 Desilu head
20 That is
22 Posted
23 Pan pal?
26 Ham, to Noah
29 One who knows all the secrets
30 Deep down
33 Educators' org.
35 Dickens's Heep
36 Jefferson's note
42 Yours, old-style
43 Suffix with expert
44 Spoiled
47 Austere
53 With 36-Down, "Next . . ."
54 Weevil's hatching place
56 Pennsylvania's __ Mountains
59 Usher's locale
60 Michael Jordan, for years
64 Rest and relaxation site
65 Egyptian Christians
66 Pi, e.g.
67 Often-hectic hosp. areas
68 Minute __
69 Old New Yorker cartoonist William
70 On the __

DOWN

1 Island where Gauguin painted
2 Harborbound, in winter
3 Light flux units
4 Fountain treat
5 Swift bird on foot
6 Center X or O
7 Japanese cartoon art
8 "Deck the Halls" syllables
9 Genesis brother
10 Rubik creation
11 Foremast attachment
12 Big picture?: Abbr.
13 Our sun
19 Cheery song
21 Move among the moguls
24 Former Attorney General
25 Composer Jacques
27 Test type
28 Utmost
31 Airline's home base
32 "__ tu" (Verdi aria)
34 Frazier foe
36 See 53-Across
37 Trachea
38 Que. neighbor
39 Cotillion girl
40 __ prof.
41 Bank take-back
42 Former flying inits.
45 Slip __ (blunder)
46 Bloodmobile visitors
48 Not digital
49 Sacrifice fly stat.
50 Ejected
51 Elite N.F.L.er
52 N.Y. Mets' div.
55 Go __ for (support)
57 Eight: Prefix
58 Wine holder
60 Syringe amts.
61 All the rage
62 Colorado native
63 XXVI doubled

by Alan Arbesfeld

ACROSS

1 One of five Norwegian kings
5 Times in history
9 Longed
14 Bit of mockery
15 Cancel
16 Spoils
17 Breezes through, as a test
18 Chanel competitor
19 Boxer Roberto
20 Story written by 38-Across
23 1960's radical grp.
24 Cities Service competitor
25 And
26 Quaker ___
28 1960's–70's baseball All-Star ___ Santo
30 It's sometimes hard to make them meet
33 Nicks
35 "___ does what Nintendon't" (old slogan)
37 ___ polloi
38 Writer born March 2, 1904
41 Gooey green substance in the title of a 38-Across story
43 Professional org.
44 It often thickens
46 Thief's "savings"
47 Goes on and on
49 Summer mo.
50 Dueler of 1804
51 Verve
53 Pitcher
55 Took a load off
58 Birthplace of 38-Across
62 Fleeced
63 ___ Minor
64 Service org. since the 1850's
65 Emerged
66 Verve

67 Hammer-wielding deity
68 Fellows
69 "Do it, or ___!"
70 Have the ___ for

DOWN

1 1973 "Love Train" singers, with "the"
2 Ripped (into)
3 Tautology spoken by the title character in 11-Down
4 Jacket accompanier
5 Overage
6 Cheers (for)
7 38-Across and others
8 Eye malady
9 Singer Paula
10 18 holes, say
11 Book written by 38-Across
12 And others, for short
13 Unit of force
21 Eases
22 Dance for two
27 Carbon dating determination
29 Fair-hiring agcy.
31 43-Across members
32 Religious person with a turban
33 Do-or-die time
34 Cookbook writer Rombauer
36 Crazy
39 70-Across, e.g.
40 Former franc part

42 P.O. delivery
45 38-Across's real name, in brief
48 Most clever
50 Miss the start
52 Aconcagua is their tallest peak
54 "Marat/Sade" playwright Peter
56 Fancy tie
57 Romanov V.I.P.'s
58 Kind of carpet
59 Site of a sweat bead
60 Disconcert
61 Fable

by Charles Barasch

ACROSS

1 Certain iron setting
6 Govt. bill
11 Mars or Milky Way
14 Really, really want
15 Toiled in the galley
16 "I love," to Livy
17 Old "Tonight Show" intro
19 Transcript fig.
20 CPR giver
21 Have a late meal
22 Unlit?
24 Scale of mineral hardness
26 Lions' lairs
29 Tee cry
30 Zeno of ___
31 Atmospheric region with a "hole"
34 Ladies of Spain
36 Word repeated after "Que," in song
37 Draft letters
38 Head honcho
42 Blood-typing letters
45 When repeated, a fish
46 Hose woes
50 Loofah, e.g.
54 Neighbor of Yemen
55 "___ girl!"
56 Hymn start
57 Fodder's place
58 Follower of Zeno
60 U-Haul rental
62 Make public
63 Haw's partner
64 Women's tennis immortal
69 Historic period
70 1940's–50's slugger Ralph
71 More despicable
72 Thesaurus entry: Abbr.

73 Big name in printers
74 Goes up and down and . . .

DOWN

1 Connived
2 Vibrating effect
3 Made of clay
4 "___ Maria"
5 Many a teen's room
6 Saint-___ (French resort)
7 Japanese drama
8 Hold title to
9 Half a score
10 Breyers competitor
11 Supermarket helpers
12 Current units
13 Lions, at times

18 Self-defense sport
23 Son-gun link
25 Swedish auto
27 Having a snack
28 Snick-a-___
32 Poet's preposition
33 Laddie's love
35 Jazzman Zoot
39 Letterman dental feature
40 Half a train?
41 Son of Seth
42 Makes ashamed
43 9-volt, e.g.
44 Cushioned footrest
47 In a friendly manner
48 1600's stargazer
49 "Z" makers, in comics
51 "Bali ___"

52 Wield authority
53 Dutch seaport
59 Word that can follow the ends of 17-, 31-, 38-, 50- and 64-Across
61 Blue shade
65 Place to put gloss
66 Elected officials
67 Corporate V.I.P.
68 "Flying Down to ___"

by Sarah Keller

BASEBALL

ACROSS

1 Talk like Jimmy Stewart
6 Minnelli of "Cabaret"
10 Frozen waffle brand
14 Noted Montague
15 First father
16 Potting need
17 Jellied garnish
18 Glazier's unit
19 Ditto, with "the"
20 Kingdom's dock?
23 Suffix with musket
24 Tic-tac-toe winner
25 Poet Elinor
27 Invent
30 Enzyme suffix
32 Baseball playoffs mo.
33 Mikhail of chess
34 Adage
35 Home of the Blue Devils
36 Municipality's dock?
40 Part of a financial portfolio
41 Yale, for one
42 Q-tip target
43 Put down, on the street
44 Place where you can get into hot water
45 No less than
49 Looks out for, at a heist
51 Commotion
52 Early Beatle Sutcliffe
53 Country's dock?
58 Diva Gluck
59 Breakfast food chain
60 Back, at the track
61 Depend (on)
62 Barrel of laughs
63 Hosiery hue
64 Breyers competitor
65 Adds (up)
66 Photographer Adams

DOWN

1 Hung loosely
2 More upbeat
3 Fuse unit
4 Small dam
5 Lead-in to motion
6 Traveler's work aid
7 Potato state
8 Billy of "Titanic"
9 From the U.S.
10 Composition with a viewpoint
11 Give 100%
12 Gadget-laden
13 Grand ___ Opry
21 Caught by the catcher
22 Meadow mother
26 Summer in Suisse
28 Just slightly
29 Indianapolis 500 time
30 Sound of relief
31 Fond of
34 Farm pen
35 Calamitous
36 Nitpicked
37 Socially improper
38 Future aves?
39 Record-setting Ripken
40 Pharmaceutical-safety org.
44 Retired flier
45 Changes to fit
46 "The way things are . . ."
47 One of a slapstick trio
48 Prison escape route, maybe
50 Cafeteria carriers
51 Underway
54 "Java" player Al
55 Home to Columbus
56 "Chiquitita" quartet
57 Freshman, usually
58 "You ___ here"

by Ron Sweet

ACROSS

1 Minty drink
6 Fallback strategy
11 Govt. property overseer
14 Loud, as the surf
15 Martini's partner
16 Mantra syllables
17 Author's sign-off?
19 College sweater letters
20 Add zest to
21 Like helium
23 Cold and wet
26 Ave. intersectors
27 Smells
28 One-named folk singer
30 A.D. part
32 "___ Bulba" (Brynner film)
33 Hardly tanned
34 Tiny fraction of a min.
37 Designer Cassini
38 One of the Osmonds
39 "Ignorance ___ excuse"
40 LP's and CD's: Abbr.
41 Microwave, e.g.
42 Yegg's job
43 Mary Hartman portrayer Louise
45 Is currently selling
46 Cellos' little cousins
48 Pricing word
49 PBS supporter
50 Keypad key
51 Compound of gold
54 Sort of: Suffix
55 Astronaut's sign-off?
60 Born, in bios
61 Mailing list items
62 Sole material
63 Norm: Abbr.
64 Search blindly
65 Mentholated cigarettes

DOWN

1 Start of a one-two
2 Suffix with strict
3 Part of PRNDL
4 Prominent donkey features
5 Unwed fathers
6 Use a button
7 Timber wolf
8 Simile center
9 Defense advisory org.
10 Two-piece wear
11 Nuclear physicist's sign-off?
12 Blue cartoon character
13 Bus. aides
18 "Later!"
22 Chuckleheads
23 Chopper part
24 Allan-___
25 Tailor's sign-off?
27 Captain Hook's henchman
29 Bargain hunter's stop
30 Risk taker
31 Lena of "Chocolat"
33 Do roadwork
35 Come after
36 Terra ___
38 Trunk growth
42 Five-time Kentucky Derby winner Bill
44 South Seas attire
45 Make well
46 Lines on leaves
47 Map enlargement
48 Plain writing
51 Spherical opening?
52 Lone Star State sch.
53 Money on the Continent
56 Former Mideast org.
57 Opposite of paleo-
58 An N.C.O.
59 Cocks and bulls

by Fred Piscop

ACROSS

1 Pleasant to look at
7 "Hold on a ___!"
10 Abba of Israel
14 Promgoer's rental
15 Airport monitor abbr.
16 Nathan of stage and screen
17 Colorful ring
18 Pal in the 'hood
19 Toggery, informally
20 Christmas tree
21 Grade booster
24 Big bash
26 Helps with the dishes
27 Make even smoother
30 The late Sen. Thurmond
34 "Folsom Prison Blues" singer
38 ___-Locka, Fla.
39 Oneness
40 Chews the scenery
43 Fr. holy woman
44 Luggage receipt
48 Synagogue scroll
51 Achieve
52 Snapple competitor
54 Galley gear
58 Sub sinker
63 It may be loaded at the casino
64 Word-of-mouth
65 Fam. member
66 Assail, as a reputation
68 Not prerecorded
69 ___ y Plata (Montana's motto)
70 Puts on a happy face
71 Sly glance
72 "Spring ahead" hrs.
73 Be a snitch

DOWN

1 Office crew
2 Radium discoverer
3 Put forth, as effort
4 Prefix with classical
5 Like some chatter
6 Sweet-talk
7 Audrey Hepburn title role
8 Gofers' tasks
9 Long reptiles, in short
10 First-born
11 Modem speed unit
12 "The King ___"
13 Egg holder
22 ___ II (razor brand)
23 Apt., e.g.
25 Seaside soarers
28 Brian of the early Roxy Music
29 Harmony
31 Classroom drudgery
32 Oil grp.
33 Mardi Gras wear
34 "___ do it"
35 Not fooled by
36 Yesterday: Fr.
37 Blood: Prefix
41 ___ WorldCom
42 "This can't be!"
45 Prepares to shave
46 Gorged oneself
47 ___-Tass (Russian news agency)
49 Branch in a trophy room
50 Snickering syllable
53 New England catch
55 Not for kids
56 Star in Orion
57 Taste or touch
58 "Mama" sayer
59 Canal of song
60 Finish a drive?
61 Main idea
62 Lazarus or Goldman
67 Orchestra area

by Sarah Keller

ACROSS

1 Big stinger
5 Org. whose approval is much sought
8 "Le __ Prince"
13 Opera solo
14 Costa __
16 The O in FeO
17 Call in a bakery
18 Tennis's Arthur
19 Slangy send-off
20 1986 Prince movie, after 29-Down
23 Calendar box
25 Opponent's vote
26 Cry from a butterfingers
27 Map miniatures
29 Letter carriers' org.
30 "No seats left" sign
33 Martin or McQueen
34 Initial stake
35 Not at home
36 By night, with 29-Down
39 Rightmost column
40 Suffix with young or old
41 Smallest
42 Thesaurus feature: Abbr.
43 Minnesota Twin, e.g., briefly
44 Dance at 23-Down
45 Set-to
46 Not dis, in Brooklyn
47 Sun. talk
48 Business sign, after 29-Down
53 Orangeish shade
54 Respite
55 Grub
58 Popular vodka, informally
59 Wash
60 Oscar winner Sorvino
61 Has, as a party

62 Place to hear a 13-Across, with "the"
63 Taking care of business

DOWN

1 Pallid
2 Exist
3 Year "The Graduate" came out, in short
4 Walkway
5 Set-to
6 Like good gossip columns
7 Overexerciser's woe
8 Growths that may be removed by surgery
9 Tests

10 __ Puente, the Mambo King
11 Prefix with logical
12 Beach bird
15 Former Ford minivan
21 Type in
22 Rodeo performer
23 Studio 54 and Xenon, famously
24 Cleopatra's paramour
28 Preceding nights
29 See 20-, 36- and 48-Across
30 Laundry challenge for a gymgoer
31 Fight down and dirty
32 Food in a shell
34 In the end

35 Hydrocarbon suffixes
37 Singer K. T. __
38 Movie for which Jane Fonda won an Oscar
43 Some old computers
44 Classic Olivier role
45 Silvery food fish
46 Dig (into)
48 Snack
49 Prefix with plasm
50 "Look __ Talking"
51 U.S. Pacific island
52 Captain of fiction
56 Prefix with color or cycle
57 Posed

by Tony Orbach

ACROSS

1 Play lookout for, for example
5 Praises
10 Vegetarian's no-no
14 Lollapalooza
15 Beginning
16 "Cogito, ___ sum"
17 V.I.P. #1
20 Blazing, as the eyes
21 Stirs up
22 Forest rangers' worries
25 U.F.O. fliers
26 Ammo holder
28 Fizzler
30 Like zoo animals
34 Very, in Versailles
35 Maze goal
37 "Where ___?"
38 V.I.P. #2
41 Dr. J's org., once
42 Unit
43 James who wrote "A Death in the Family"
44 Marooned, maybe
46 Chicago-to-Tampa dir.
47 Pants part
48 Barely lit
50 Blue eyes or curly hair
52 The "E" of PETA
56 Turn
60 V.I.P. #3
63 Group in a spies' network
64 Harden
65 Property right
66 London's ___ Park
67 Jargons
68 Actress Heche

DOWN

1 Aquatic plant
2 Small town
3 Carrier to Israel
4 Sushi staple
5 Running horse
6 Bibliographical suffix
7 Part of the Defense Dept.
8 ___ vu
9 Gaze intently
10 One of the Gorgons
11 Botches one
12 Chills and fever
13 Male turkeys
18 Mr. Unexciting
19 Cut irregularly
23 Decrees
24 Orange label
26 Corn holders
27 Over 18, say
29 One on the Atkins plan
31 Railroad measure
32 Roastmaster
33 It holds back the sea
34 Spicy cuisine
35 When said three times, a 1964 Beach Boys hit
36 Pigpen
39 Noble Italian family name
40 Spanish scarf
45 Fit to serve
47 Fuzzy fruit
49 Wizardry
51 "Angela's ___" (1996 best seller)
52 Inscribe permanently
53 "If ___ only knew!"
54 Grasped
55 Musical Horne
57 Conceited
58 1950's British P.M.
59 The Beatles' "Penny ___"
61 Sister
62 TV screen: Abbr.

by Bill Ballard

ACROSS

1 Tupperware sound
5 Viva ___ (by word of mouth)
9 Jazz genre
14 State firmly
15 Skeptic's scoff
16 Unescorted
17 Where to get hitched in a hurry
18 Brummell or Bridges
19 Laundry soap introduced in 1918
20 See 40-Across
23 Cozy room
24 Demagnetize, as a tape
25 "Heads up!" and others
27 Run-of-the-mill
30 Kingdom divisions, in biology
31 "What have we here?!"
32 Jill of "Diamonds Are Forever"
35 Stash
38 "Please," in Potsdam
40 Clue to 20- and 55-Across and 11- and 29-Down
41 Paris's river
42 Crude sort
43 Acela Express runner
45 17-Across's state: Abbr.
46 Breaks in relations
48 Hair snarl
50 Cloak's partner
52 Sudden outpouring
54 Make a miscue
55 See 40-Across
60 Regional flora and fauna
62 ___ Domini

63 General or major
64 Run-of-the-mill
65 Frees (of)
66 X-rated
67 Great Plains home
68 Ripken Sr. and Jr.
69 Thanksgiving dish

DOWN

1 Cutting remark
2 Iris's place
3 Patronize Hertz or Avis
4 Like some presidents
5 Pulsing with energy
6 Takes orders from
7 Stop
8 Needle case
9 Just
10 ___ Lilly and Co.
11 See 40-Across
12 Beginning
13 Lowly workers
21 Irregularly notched, as a leaf
22 Paula of CNN
26 Ultimatum ender
27 Ty of Cooperstown
28 Kent State state
29 See 40-Across
30 Rx dispenser: Abbr.
33 Photocopier problems
34 Cereal grain
36 Scott Turow title
37 "___ Only Just Begun"
39 H.S. math class

41 Do figure eights, say
43 Longfellow's bell town
44 Totally baffled
47 Like fillies but not billies
49 Close at hand
50 Coming-out
51 Get up
52 Braga of film
53 Gearshift sequence
56 Pusher's pursuer
57 Hearty party
58 E pluribus ___
59 Squeaks (out)
61 ___-Bo (exercise system)

by Allan E. Parrish

ACROSS

1 Job detail, briefly
5 24/7 auction site
9 Jazz group
14 Sledder's spot
15 Sub builder?
16 Burger layer
17 Pastel shade
18 Loafing
19 Pottery finish
20 Bad place for the modest
23 Tractor name
24 Many-headed serpent
25 ___ Lanka
28 Since 1/1, to a C.P.A.
29 It has 21 spots
31 Orchestra's percussion or strings, e.g.
33 Coniferous tree
35 Library ID
36 Band with the 1998 #1 hit "One Week"
42 Bard's river
43 Chief exec
44 Played a knight game?
48 ___ Amin
49 Chum
52 Leave speechless
53 "Peachy!"
55 Met offering
57 1997 steelworkers-turned-dancers film
59 Red River capital
62 Calvary letters
63 Pond gunk
64 Shady spot
65 Like eggs
66 Beget
67 Meager
68 Therefore
69 North Carolina university

DOWN

1 Sterne's "Tristram ___"
2 Card game for two
3 Gave the slip to
4 "___ de Lune"
5 Trim to fit, maybe
6 Nighttime inspection
7 Brass or pewter
8 Rates of return
9 French brandy
10 Just
11 Hamm of soccer
12 Dickens's pen name
13 "That's ___ for the books!"
21 Family auto
22 Smelter input
25 "Certainly!," south of the border
26 Boxer's wear
27 Vacationers' stops
30 Nest-egg letters
32 In good order
33 Fisheye ___
34 With it
36 Mexican peninsula
37 Declare openly
38 Philandering sort
39 Oil company structure
40 Played first
41 Self-evident truth
45 Casual top
46 Ram's mate
47 Desecrate
49 Tentatively schedule, with "in"
50 Conductor Toscanini
51 Nonprofessionals
54 Like some eclipses
56 Oater group
57 Animator's creation
58 Italian resort
59 Suffers from
60 Circle segment
61 Magic and Wizards org.

by Janet R. Bender

ACROSS

1 Spain and Portugal
7 ___ alai
10 Amtrak stop: Abbr.
13 Vietnamese port
14 End abruptly
16 Tense
17 Source of a cry at night
18 Wound
19 ___ Maria
20 Tree-lined road: Abbr.
21 Contribute
22 Uses the HOV lanes, perhaps
24 Butt of jokes
27 Blond shade
29 Krypton or radon
30 Security numbers
33 Groovy
36 ___ apso (dog)
37 It's south of Eur.
38 Sylvester's co-star in "Rocky"
40 Lay turf
41 "As luck would have it…"
44 Chemin de ___ (French railway)
45 Med. care provider
46 With a discount of
47 Victoria's Secret item
51 Hush-hush D.C. org.
53 Lena of "The Unbearable Lightness of Being"
54 Guitarist Nugent
55 Seasonal mall employees
59 "Praise be to God!"
61 After-class aides
62 Inclination
63 Even (with)
64 Seattle-to-Las Vegas dir.
65 Rhoda's TV mom
66 Talk show groups

DOWN

1 Person on a poster
2 Undoing
3 Chemical endings
4 Gives off, as heat
5 ___ We Trust
6 Slates
7 Louis-Dreyfus of "Seinfeld"
8 Not yet apprehended
9 Suffix with expert
10 Simply smashing
11 Shrimper's net
12 Courtroom figs.
14 Shore dinner special
15 Some needles
23 Trattoria course
24 Women, casually
25 Dos cubed
26 Military sch.
28 Leave a permanent mark on
31 Bank features
32 Large barrel
33 Run away
34 Is unwell
35 Howls like a dog
39 Brave, for instance
42 Rich, as a voice
43 24-hour
44 Penalized, as a speeder
47 Paint layers
48 "Deutschland über ___"
49 Creator of Pooh and Piglet
50 Nikon rival
52 Place for sweaters?
56 Hit the bottle
57 ___ Sea, east of the Caspian
58 Lith. and Lat., once
60 Wreath

by Eric Berlin

ACROSS

1 Trunk item
6 Job seeker's success
11 Gridlock
14 Poe's middle name
15 Bisect
16 Mentalist Geller
17 All-freshman team?
19 Zero
20 Ugly Duckling, in reality
21 Reflect (on)
22 Arcade coin
24 So-so
26 Bridle's partner
27 Peter Cottontail?
32 Tonsil neighbor
33 Smallish field
34 Put on TV
37 Boone, to rustics
38 Have a ball?
40 Blue Triangle org.
41 Inventor Whitney
42 Fill-in
43 Heart of France
44 Answer to "Who wrote 'The Highwayman'?"
48 Historical Scottish county
50 Summoned Jeeves
51 M-1, for one
52 Tokyo ties
54 Charlie Chaplin's widow
58 '60s muscle car
59 Milliner on the move?
62 Poet's preposition
63 Zoo critter
64 Campfire treat
65 "Shame on you"
66 Supersized
67 Tournament favorites

DOWN

1 ___-serif
2 Furrow former
3 Thomas ___ Edison
4 Drops from on high
5 Letter accompanier: Abbr.
6 "Yeah, right"
7 Web site sect. for newbies
8 Chimney channel
9 Zsa Zsa's sister
10 Bureaucratic tangle
11 Place for miscellaneous stuff
12 Sharon of Israel
13 Eeyore's creator
18 Oscar winner Jannings
23 Lyrical lines
25 Dr. J's old league: Abbr.
26 Nimble
27 Au naturel
28 Horse course
29 Item in a musician's pocket
30 Arthur Marx, familiarly
31 Columbus Day mo.
35 Hosp. areas
36 Like a compliant cat
38 Banana waste
39 Early hrs.
40 "Dunno"
42 Aspirin alternative
43 Bamboozle
45 Olive in the comics
46 Milk container?
47 Redeem, with "in"
48 Insider's vocabulary
49 Priests' administrations
52 "Rubáiyát" poet
53 Screen door sound
55 Oklahoma Indian
56 One who's unhip
57 Aphrodite's lover
60 ___ pro nobis
61 Big jerk

by Lee Glickstein and Nancy Salomon

ACROSS

1 Wise competitor
5 Quack
10 On vacation
14 Snack sold in a stack
15 Crystal set
16 Lens holders
17 Soccer commentator's cry
18 Shelley's "Adonais" is one
19 List-ending abbr.
20 "Aha!"
23 Caper
24 Little one
25 Four-bagger
27 Hosp. workers
28 Top worn with shorts
30 "All in the Family" network
32 Arctic bird
33 Soccer star Hamm
34 ___ correspondent
35 Singer/songwriter Laura
36 Honky-tonk instruments
40 Mountaintop
41 Aurora's counterpart
42 Wonderment
43 Deli sandwich, for short
44 Corots, Monets and such
45 Sp. Mrs.
46 Qualifiers
49 Red Sea peninsula
51 Cartoon collectible
53 Spokes, e.g.
55 Passable
58 Some drive-thru features, briefly
59 Not as friendly
60 Tennis score after deuce
61 Old-fashioned dance
62 "___ luck!"
63 Evening, in ads
64 Retailer's gds.
65 "Mmm, mmm!"
66 Leave in, to an editor

DOWN

1 River blockage
2 In the vicinity
3 Bakery supplies
4 Longtime Chicago Symphony maestro
5 Air Force One passenger: Abbr.
6 Soft, white mineral
7 Keats's "___ a Nightingale"
8 Bedtime drink
9 Ma with a bow
10 "All systems ___!"
11 How a 43-Across is usually prepared
12 All Olympians, once
13 Designer monogram
21 Play segment
22 Sounds of doubt
26 "King Kong" studio
29 Raring to go
31 Hare's habitat
33 Mystery man
34 Scale amts.
35 Del.-to-Vt. direction
36 Elated
37 Spot and Felix, e.g.
38 Après-ski treat
39 Tony, Oscar or Hugo
40 Middle manager's focus?
44 Balloon filler
45 Most guileful
46 "Hurray for me!"
47 Limited
48 Major paperback publisher
50 Bridal path
52 Gives off
54 Bates and King
56 Pinball stopper
57 Horse-drawn vehicle
58 Pitching ___

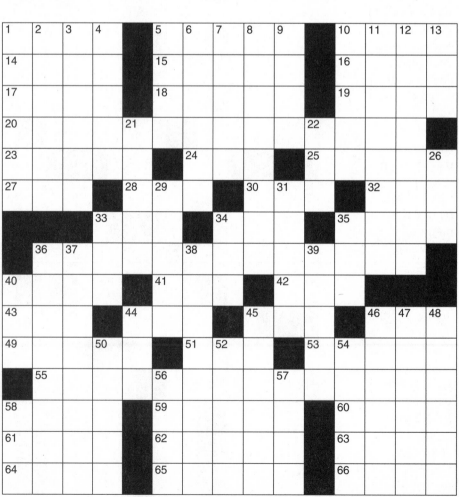

by Elizabeth C. Gorski

ACROSS

1 Doze (off)
4 Following
9 Infield fly
14 Pub offering
15 "Death, Be Not Proud" poet
16 "Maria ___," 1940s hit
17 At leisure: Abbr.
18 Pact made at The Hague?
20 Legacy sharer
22 Directors Spike and Ang
23 Co., in France
24 Talks wildly
26 One more
28 Emulated O. Henry?
31 Many eras
32 Distress signal
33 ___ to go
37 Six-time U.S. Open tennis champ
40 Fool
42 Dweeb
43 Longing
45 Onetime neighbor of Israel: Abbr.
47 Neckline style
48 Where chocolate candy is made?
52 Procession
55 Sensation
56 Mancinelli opera "___ e Leandro"
57 They're welcome on the back
59 Epoch of 50 million years ago
62 Part of a shirtmaker's education?
65 Female rabbit
66 Place to moor
67 Stan's foil, in old films
68 Not well
69 Reluctant
70 Interminably
71 Taboos

DOWN

1 D.E.A. agent
2 Butter alternative
3 Removes from power
4 Summing
5 Quarters
6 Explosive
7 Abbr. at the bottom of a business letter
8 Consider again
9 Kind of ad
10 Corrida cry
11 Miss ___ of the comics
12 Loosen
13 Reimburser
19 Pavarotti, notably
21 ___ de Cologne
25 Portico in Athens
27 Beginner
28 Work in the garden
29 Wander
30 Promulgate
34 Gets elected
35 ___-do-well
36 Joel of "Cabaret"
38 Estrangement
39 God's way, in religion
41 Umpire's call
44 Mystery writer's award
46 Arrived quickly
49 Mounts
50 Was too sweet
51 Middle X or O
52 Rhodes of Rhodesia
53 College town on the Penobscot River
54 University of Missouri locale
58 W.W. II battle town
60 ___ contendere
61 Fish caught in pots
63 Tennis call
64 Suffix with mod-

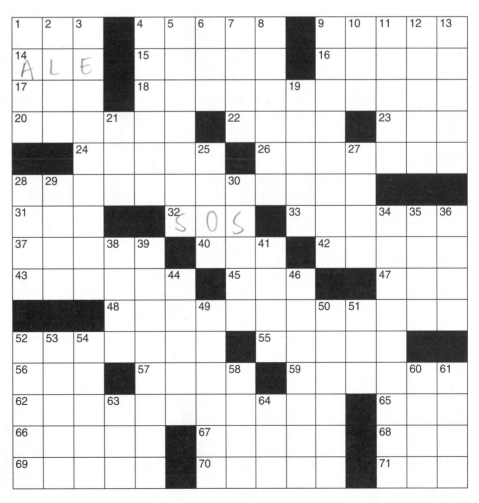

by Richard Chisholm

ACROSS

1 Verboten: Var.
5 Boats' backbones
10 "The Nazarene" writer Sholem
14 Park and Lexington, e.g., in N.Y.C.
15 Decorated Murphy
16 Starlet's goal
17 Ceremony for inventors
19 In alignment
20 Off the track
21 Rankled
23 Lager holder
24 Burlesque star Lili St. ___
25 One of Alcott's "Little Women"
26 Jean Arp's art
28 Stair part
31 Greeting for a villain
34 Holy Iraqi
37 In reserve
38 Bat material
39 Is headed for a fall
41 Baseball rarity
42 Ill will
44 Lantern-jawed celeb
45 Hide's partner
46 High-strung
47 Shiites or Amish
49 Easy card game
50 Place to relax
52 Sophisticates they're not
56 Soak through
59 Coin flipper's phrase
60 "How sweet ___!"
61 Low-cal beer in reserve?
63 Ides of March rebuke
64 Actor Delon
65 In perpetuity
66 Leak slowly
67 Jack who was famously frugal
68 Laura of "I Am Sam"

DOWN

1 Spanish appetizers
2 Sailor's "Stop!"
3 Midler of stage and screen
4 Cyber-handles
5 Name in a stuttered 1918 song title
6 Where Lux. is
7 Uplift spiritually
8 Pepsi bottle amount
9 Meets, as a bet
10 Sister of Apollo
11 Bad place to build?
12 Whodunit board game
13 Pay mind to
18 "Peter Pan" dog
22 Gogol's "___ Bulba"
24 Caravan beast
27 Conk out
29 Falco of "The Sopranos"
30 Need a bath badly
31 Dish that's "slung"
32 Culp/Cosby TV series
33 Word processor for sailors?
35 Munched on
36 Brainy group
39 ___ Haute, Ind.
40 Sturgeon delicacy
43 Joins forces (with)
45 Silenced
48 Crack from the cold
50 Played out
51 Praline nut
53 Critic Barnes
54 Check falsifier
55 Howard of morning radio
56 They're cut into wedges
57 Sermon ending?
58 Simple rhyme scheme
59 Big Apple college inits.
62 They're related

by Fred Piscop

ACROSS

1 10K, e.g.
5 Wheedler's tactic
10 Jungle crushers
14 ___ Bator
15 Land of a billion
16 Basilica area
17 Start of an Oscar Wilde quote
20 Revolutionary Allen
21 Comics shriek
22 Out of bed
23 Bakers' wares
25 Strange sightings
27 Quote, part 2
31 Cost-controlling W.W. II agcy.
34 Jacob's twin
35 Et ___ (and the following)
36 Cozy spots
38 "I cannot ___ lie"
40 Make a knight, e.g.
42 Utter disorder
43 See 61-Down
45 Dr. Seuss's Sam ___
47 "Rule Britannia" composer
48 Spain's Juan Carlos, for one
49 Quote, part 3
52 ___ En-lai
53 Slinky's shape
54 Bawdyhouse manager
57 Bleachers cry
59 ___ Jean Baker (Marilyn Monroe)
63 End of the quote
66 Excursion
67 Met offering
68 Civil wrong
69 Coin flip
70 Theroux's "endless night"
71 Summers in Québec

DOWN

1 Deserving a slap, maybe
2 Touched down
3 Country singer Johnny
4 Summarize
5 Tonic's partner
6 Brand-new
7 ___ fixe (obsession)
8 Meeting of spacecraft
9 "Mangia!"
10 Groundwork
11 Chooses, with "for"
12 1975 Wimbledon winner
13 Perceived
18 "Sleep ___"
19 Like many an O. Henry story
24 Pothook shape
26 Half a sawbuck
27 Awful smell
28 Grenoble's river
29 Come from behind
30 Furnish with gear
31 Midwest air hub
32 Hacienda drudges
33 Pack animals
37 A Brontë sister
39 Cause of wheezing
41 Graph with rectangular areas
44 "___ 'nuff!"
46 Meadow call
50 The Continent
51 Actress Lollobrigida
52 Roughs it
54 Feminist Lucretia
55 Michael Jackson's old do
56 Honored guest's spot
58 Neighborhood
60 Knee-slapper
61 With 43-Across, approximately
62 Little scurriers
64 Auction assent
65 "Uh-uh!"

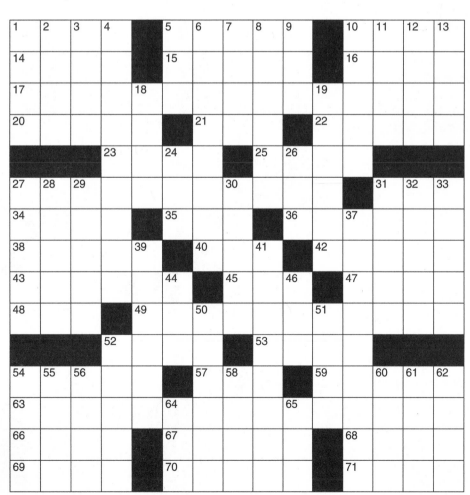

by Ed Early

ACROSS

1 Rugged rock
5 Incite
9 Unlike a dirt road
14 Whopper
15 White-tailed eagle
16 Spry
17 Fusses
18 Makes lace
19 Like maples but not firs
20 Area between two scrimmage lines
23 Jul. follower
24 Largest of the British Virgin Islands
29 Chemical process also called hyperfiltration
33 Attention-getter
34 Radio feature
35 Successful
36 Flared-spout pitcher
38 Military newbie
41 Heredity unit
42 Grief
44 Rotators under the hood
46 ___ Lingus
47 Make crazy
51 Increased
52 Took off
53 Yellowstone employees
59 Video game pioneer
63 Bluish green
64 "The Grapes of Wrath" figure
65 Get ready for Web-surfing
66 Northern Oklahoma city
67 Take a break
68 Hard stuff
69 Lightning catchers
70 Inquires

DOWN

1 Family group
2 Obnoxious
3 Baseball brothers' name
4 Holst who composed "The Planets"
5 "Stop living in your fantasy world!"
6 Kind of hygiene
7 1998 animated film with the voice of Woody Allen
8 Spanish explorer who discovered the Mississippi
9 Capital of Sicily
10 Get on in years
11 By way of
12 Keebler worker?
13 Susan of "L.A. Law"
21 Regretted
22 Rejections
25 Chinese mafia
26 Bony
27 Toy train maker
28 "___ your instructions . . ."
29 Express differently
30 Lash site
31 Mineo of "Exodus"
32 Vote in
33 Gossipy Hopper
37 Gad about
39 Relative of "Phooey!"
40 Green gems
43 Timber from Maine
45 Long-necked bird
48 Hagen of Broadway
49 Luggage carrier
50 Some wool
54 Gambler's game
55 Police cry
56 Stretches (out)
57 Hazard
58 Nears the western horizon
59 Vestment for a priest
60 As well
61 Back then
62 Role on "Frasier"

by Nancy Kavanaugh

ACROSS

1 Luau instruments, for short
5 Noted plus-size model
9 Nice to wear
14 Like Playboy models
15 "Hud" Oscar winner Patricia
16 Be nuts about
17 Qatari V.I.P.
18 Turns abruptly
19 Novelist Ephron
20 Old telephone feature
23 Proofreader's mark
24 G.P.A., slangily
25 Put a value on
27 When summer starts
30 Cry over
32 Geographical septet
33 Kabob holder
35 Pitcher part
38 See 41-Across
40 Historic time
41 With 38-Across, what the four key parts of this puzzle are
43 Uno + due
44 Conductor Toscanini
47 State openly
48 Brawl site in a western
50 Horrifies
52 Yalta's peninsula
54 Stowe equipment
55 Hearty party
56 Gymgoer's goal
62 Earth's ___ layer
64 19-Across's sister
65 Medieval chest
66 Wades across, say
67 "The heat ___!"
68 Bring up
69 Rendezvous
70 Rock's Rundgren
71 The end of each of 20- and 56-Across and 11- and 29-Down is a popular one

DOWN

1 Addict
2 ___ sabe
3 Turnpike toll-paying locale
4 Big Orange of college sports
5 Pepsin and rennin, for two
6 Gettysburg victor
7 Yule trio
8 Adamson's lioness
9 Crude dude
10 Ukrainian port
11 Fuji flow
12 Part of a Happy Meal
13 "The Second Coming" poet
21 Seek a seat
22 Poor, as excuses go
26 Put into slots
27 "___ that special?!"
28 Within earshot
29 "Howards End" director
30 Kicked off
31 Fancy pitcher
34 Green Hornet's sidekick
36 Hit Fox show, in headlines
37 Mass seating
39 Mall attraction
42 Eminem and Dr. Dre, for two
45 Gad about
46 Bay Area city
49 Makes right
51 Pizza order
52 Video game heroine Lara ___
53 Stubble remover
54 New England catch
57 Complex dwelling
58 "Eh"
59 Black-and-white treat
60 Final Four org.
61 Tombstone lawman
63 Ballpark fig.

by Allan E. Parrish

ACROSS

1 Opportunity to hit
6 Shoots 18, say
11 Rocks in a bar
14 Long green
15 The Beatles' "Eight Days ___"
16 Turf
17 Result of eating ice cream too fast, possibly
19 Moth-eaten
20 Best guess: Abbr.
21 Fastens with a band
22 "That is ___ . . ." (in other words)
24 Town next to Elizabeth, N.J.
26 Flexible, electrically
27 Fondue dip
32 Bops hard
35 Light as a feather
36 Pot's top
37 Spa wear
38 En ___ (all together)
40 Place for a ham
41 Where Schwarzenegger was born: Abbr.
42 "Lost our lease" event
43 Airplane seating option
44 Entreater's words
48 Asta's mistress
49 The whole ___ (everything)
53 Must, slangily
55 Debaters debate it
57 Shaq's alma mater: Abbr.
58 Copy
59 Sunshine State vacation area
62 Snore letter
63 3 on a par-5 hole, e.g.
64 Largish combo
65 Golfer Ernie
66 Collar inserts
67 Quaint footwear

DOWN

1 Color of waves of grain, in song
2 Sculpted figure
3 Bath toys
4 2001 role for Will Smith
5 Comb stoppers
6 Attic
7 Was in the red
8 Dregs
9 Shriner's topper
10 Missing many details
11 Kind of triangle
12 RC, for one
13 Whirling water
18 "___ 'er up!"
23 Pindar work
25 One-named supermodel
26 Plot unit
28 Studio prop
29 Insult, slangily
30 Spot for a warm pie
31 Falco of "The Sopranos"
32 Shawl or stole
33 Billing unit
34 Some voters
38 Yucatán native
39 Gran Paradiso, for one
40 Per ___
42 Attacks from the air
43 Sub sinkers, in slang
45 Young 'un
46 Catches sight of
47 Like gastric juice
50 Dementieva of tennis
51 So far
52 Corrodes
53 Stare intently
54 Kadett automaker
55 Fraternity party attire
56 Paris airport
60 Long. crosser
61 Keystone lawman

by Jim Hyres

ACROSS

1 "___ as I can tell . . ."
6 Hurdles for future attorneys: Abbr.
11 Pudding fruit
14 Florida's Key ___
15 Florida's ___ Center
16 Form 1040 datum: Abbr.
17 Danish theologian (speller's nightmare #1)
19 Swe. neighbor
20 "As I Lay Dying" character
21 Afternoon: Sp.
22 What "nobody can" do, in song
23 Musical for which Liza Minnelli won a 1978 Tony
25 "___ it a shame"
27 German philosopher (speller's nightmare #2)
32 Walloped, old-style
35 Learning style
36 Cpl., for one
37 Astronomical ring
38 Pipe cleaner
40 '20s touring cars
41 First daughter in the Carter White House
42 Certain Scandinavian
43 With regrets
44 Swedish statesman (speller's nightmare #3)
48 Locked (up)
49 Printing goofs
52 Romulus or Remus
54 City maps
57 Seldom seen
59 Colonial ___
60 Russian composer (speller's nightmare #4)
62 "Out of sight!"

63 Freak out
64 Navel variety
65 Brit. lawmakers
66 Reliance
67 Ceaselessly

DOWN

1 ___-Seltzer
2 Francis or Patrick, e.g.
3 Sassy
4 Accepts, as terms
5 Seoul soldier
6 Smooth, in music
7 Trade jabs
8 Military sch.
9 Railed against
10 The "S" in E.S.T.: Abbr.
11 Tweaked
12 Fe, to a chemist
13 Politico Hart
18 Design on metal
22 Cloning need
24 One-spot
26 "___-Devil"
28 Fraternity fun
29 Almost forever
30 Earth Day subj.
31 Pinkish
32 Head of old Iran
33 Papa's partner
34 Quadrennial events
38 Impoverished
39 T.L.C. givers
40 Speed reader?
42 Cheer leader?
43 Camera type, briefly

45 Game pieces
46 On-the-go group
47 Roughly
50 Spoonful, say
51 Alan of "The In-Laws"
52 Time in office
53 Trendy sandwich
55 Island party
56 Dangerous slitherers
58 Ogled
60 Nonunion workers: Abbr.
61 Pooh's pal

by Matt Skoczen

ACROSS

1 Military bigwigs
6 Pad user
11 Gullible one
14 Consume
15 Luau serving
17 Wine bouquet
18 Consider, as a thought
19 Periodic arrival that causes much angst
21 Big times
22 Hardly a he-man
23 Member of a board of dirs.
24 Flower part
28 ___ Paulo
29 ___-all (score)
30 Really good joke
34 Seat at a wedding
37 What a 52-Across on a group of 19-Acrosses is
40 Whitney and others: Abbr.
41 Aim
42 Roman writer
43 Some Harvard grads: Abbr.
44 Certain Wall Street activities
46 Some are pale
48 La ___
51 Money guarantor, for short
52 Student's dream
57 "Hail, Stanford, Hail!," for one
59 Swashbuckling Flynn
60 Song from "No, No, Nanette"
61 Aptly named English novelist
62 Yearbook sect.
63 Kind of code at some schools
64 "The Sixth ___"

DOWN

1 Symbol on California's flag
2 Like a 52-Across
3 On
4 Clash of heavyweights
5 Spread out
6 Writer's guidelines
7 Turner and Louise
8 Diary bit
9 Penury
10 Sculler
11 Flat replacement
12 TV spy series starring Jennifer Garner
13 What stylophiles collect
16 Wing: Prefix
20 Equipment in kids' toy "telephones"
23 Prefix with legal
24 Dis
25 Perfectly
26 Gardner and others
27 ___ culpa
28 "Frasier" setting
31 Cereal grain
32 Actress Charlotte
33 Dodge City's home: Abbr.
34 Invoice stamp
35 House shader
36 Methods
38 Broadcasts
39 Like
43 Coffee for late at night
45 Go-carts
46 Grace ___ of "Will & Grace"
47 Certain beans
48 Tre + quattro
49 Ships' workers
50 Big dos
51 Saturated substances
52 Henry VIII's sixth
53 Place for a knot
54 Mother's mother, informally
55 Miniature sci-fi vehicles
56 Sheltered, at sea
58 Stylish, in the '60s

by Kevan Choset

ACROSS

1 "60 Minutes" airer
4 Gator relative
8 Nyasaland, now
14 Stephen of "The Crying Game"
15 Quad building
16 Readied for print
17 Post-O.R. stop
18 Meat marking
19 Brings disgrace to
20 Knowing no more than before
23 Part of a Vandyke
24 Mangy mutt
25 Stitch up
28 Lanchester of film
29 Words after a rude encounter, maybe
33 "___ extra cost!"
34 Devious sorts
35 One pointing, as a gun
39 Feel awful
41 Secret meeting
42 Mazola competitor
44 Gets a gander of
46 F.B.I.'s prime quarries
48 Twofold
52 Dr. who handles otitis cases: Abbr.
53 Neolithic ___
54 Where Idi Amin ruled
56 Buffet deal
59 Positive aspect
62 Swarming pest
63 Bio stat
64 Gawks
65 Low-cal
66 D.C. V.I.P.
67 Lecherous goatmen
68 Divorcés
69 Sink trap's shape

DOWN

1 Shrink in fear
2 Act nonchalant
3 Steamy spots
4 Water park slide
5 Most reckless
6 Shoppe sign word
7 Lobster portion
8 Snafus
9 Followers
10 Pants-on-fire guy
11 20's dispenser, for short
12 Teeny
13 Driver's lic. and others
21 Airport info: Abbr.
22 Convenience store bagful
25 Neuter
26 Part of B.P.O.E.
27 All-star game team, maybe
30 ___ roll (winning)
31 Like tasty cake
32 Anthem contraction
33 Metal joiner
35 Very top
36 Mineral in spinach
37 Atomizer's release
38 N.Y. winter setting
40 General in gray
43 Like a rowboat that's adrift
45 Teach
47 Dissenting vote
48 Vice president Quayle
49 Apprehension
50 Almanac sayings
51 Nears midnight
55 Billionaire Bill
56 Open-roofed
57 Leer at
58 Operating system on many Internet servers
59 ___ Constitution
60 Sch. group
61 Warmed the bench

by Nancy Kavanaugh

ACROSS

1 "If it ___ broke . . ."
5 "Guilty," e.g.
9 Clio winner
14 Most stuck-up
16 Poker ploy
17 "M.T.A." singers, 1959
19 Makes merry
20 Chart shape
21 "Bearded" flower
22 Mall binge
25 Murals and such
28 Dover's state: Abbr.
29 Rang out
31 Like gastric juice
32 40 winks
33 Group values
34 Paul Scott chronicles set in India
37 Weather map area
38 Have more troops than
39 Right on the map
40 Response to someone pointing
41 Actress Peeples
44 Take a gander at
45 Make ___ of (botch)
46 U.S.M.C. V.I.P.'s
47 German article
48 Is fearful of
50 Schubert chamber work
56 Fritter away
57 Unusual sort
58 Place for a kiss
59 Hatchling's home
60 Wagnerian earth goddess

DOWN

1 ___ Lindgren, Pippi Longstocking's creator
2 Naturally belong
3 It may be seen, heard or spoken, in a saying
4 Quick puffs
5 A.T.M. necessities
6 Trouser part
7 Pothook shape
8 J.D. holder: Abbr.
9 Golfer Palmer, to pals
10 See socially
11 Former Russian orbiter
12 "___ was saying . . ."
13 Prefix with natal
15 Up to, for short
18 Newspaper page
22 Home of the N.H.L.'s Sharks
23 Awards to be hung
24 Positions of esteem
25 Need liniment
26 Knee-slapper
27 Six-pointers, in brief
29 Hair-splitter?
30 LAX abbr.
31 Envelope abbr.
32 Gumball cost, once
33 The "E" in Q.E.D.
34 Cafeteria carrier
35 Vacuum feature
36 Buddy in Bordeaux
37 Lab charge
40 Mae West's "___ Angel"
41 Less cluttered
42 "You're so right!"
43 Courtroom fig.
45 Broadcaster
46 Sci-fi, for one
47 James of blues
48 The Everly Brothers, e.g.
49 Josh
50 Onetime Pan Am rival
51 Linden of "Barney Miller"
52 Body shop fig.
53 Java container
54 ___ kwon do
55 Football game divs.

by Len Elliott

ACROSS

1 Sir, in India
6 Gounod production
11 Word with toll or roll
14 ___ acid
15 Cartoonist Kelly and others
16 Singer on half the 1984 album "Milk and Honey"
17 Hard-to-please labor protester?
19 Bird's beak
20 ¢¢
21 Unc's wife
23 Busta Rhymes rhymes
27 Like some of the Sahara
28 Flies off the handle
29 West Indian native
30 Mar. 17 figure, from 58-Across
31 Hooch
33 Punch in the stomach response
36 Shirts and blouses
37 Beetle Bailey's commander
38 ___'acte (intermission)
39 With 4-Down, modern printing fluid
40 Farm fence features
41 Prefix with -gon
42 A paramedic may look for one
44 Employ
45 Popular Ford
47 Skilled in reasoning
49 Eve's downfall
50 Lose at the bank?
51 Race unit
52 Cheap promotional trip?
58 See 30-Across
59 1973 #1 Rolling Stones hit
60 Bench site
61 Long-distance letters
62 Sailors' stories
63 Like a beach

DOWN

1 Doofus
2 Parisian pal
3 Drunk's utterance
4 See 39-Across
5 Political protest of sorts
6 Because of, with "to"
7 Successful negotiation results
8 The "E" of B.P.O.E.
9 Way to go: Abbr.
10 "Steps in Time" autobiographer
11 Pretty woman's hat?
12 Singer Bryant
13 ___ Smith, first female jockey to win a major race
18 Cross and Parker products
22 Where: Lat.
23 Musical breaks
24 ___-Detoo ("Star Wars" droid)
25 Plaything that yips?
26 Vacation spots
27 Loll
29 Gear teeth
31 Au naturel
32 Globe
34 Holy Roman emperor, 962–73
35 Swiss money
37 Talk back
38 Creepy: Var.
40 Toronto ballplayer
41 Multicar accidents
43 www.yahoo.com, e.g.
44 Pilgrimage to Mecca
45 Actress Shire
46 Besides, with "from"
47 Actor Alan
48 "The Highwayman" poet Alfred
50 Bridge builder, e.g.: Abbr.
53 Italian article
54 Actress Vardalos
55 "The Wizard of Oz" locale: Abbr.
56 Bitter ___
57 Slinky or boomerang

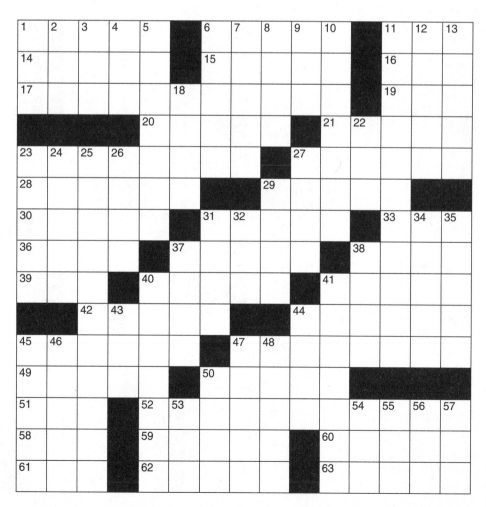

by Roy Leban

ACROSS

1 Home to Honolulu
5 Sticky stuff
9 Mends, as socks
14 "The Good Earth" mother
15 Good lot size
16 "The Waste Land" poet
17 Where to find a hammer, anvil and stirrup
19 Oro y ___ (Montana's motto)
20 Charlie Rose's network
21 An Arkin
22 Ease up
23 It may be found in front of a saloon
26 Tone-___ (rapper)
27 Strong hand cleaner
31 "Doe, ___ . . ." ("The Sound of Music" lyric)
34 Former Queens stadium
36 6 on a phone
37 Picture-filled item often seen in a living room
41 "C'___ la vie"
42 Missing the deadline
43 Bonkers
44 Hopelessness
47 What 20-Across lacks
48 Foyer
54 Former White House pooch
57 Private eyes
58 Romance
59 Seed coverings
60 International business mantra
62 Carnival show
63 Lends a hand
64 Valuable rocks
65 Odist to a nightingale
66 McCartney played it in the Beatles
67 Top ratings

DOWN

1 That certain "something"
2 It may be airtight
3 Verb with thou
4 Sturm ___ Drang
5 Irish dialect
6 Continental divide?
7 Big ape
8 ___ capita
9 Unseat
10 Apportions
11 Inlets
12 Post-it
13 Ollie's partner in old comedy
18 Capital of Punjab province
22 Faithful
24 Staff leader?
25 First-year West Pointer
28 Melville romance
29 Before long
30 Snaillike
31 Passed with flying colors
32 Teaspoonful, maybe
33 Young newts
34 Football legend Bart
35 Where a rabbit may be hidden
38 10-point type
39 First-born
40 Twaddle
45 Small shot
46 Liqueur flavorers
47 Admission
49 Courtyards
50 Must-haves
51 Vigilant
52 Waterproof wool used for coats
53 Silt deposit
54 Word that can follow the end of 17-, 23-, 37-, 48- or 60-Across
55 "Dies ___" (liturgical poem)
56 Old Italian coin
60 Groovy
61 Twaddle

by Sarah Keller

ACROSS

1 ___ the Red
5 Fragrant blossom
10 "Right on!"
14 Woodworking groove
15 Excitedly
16 Stack
17 He wrote "Utopia" in an ancient language
19 Yard sale tag
20 Partner of "ifs" and "ands"
21 Arterial trunks
23 Do a favor
26 Be charitable
28 Tilted
29 Oxidize
30 A.A.A. suggestion: Abbr.
33 Office stamp
34 Better halves
35 Disney Store item
36 "How Sweet ___"
37 Mocks
38 Something that shouldn't be left hanging
39 Twilight time to a poet
40 More immense
41 Rear
42 TV prog. with a different host each week
43 Cupid's counterpart
44 Author Lee
45 Inner circle member
47 Keats and others
48 Hogan dweller
50 Seed cover
51 Oscar winner Guinness
52 Blind poet who often wrote in an ancient language
58 Desertlike
59 Gladden
60 Dust Bowl refugee
61 Pianist Dame Myra
62 Dravidian language
63 ___ contendere

DOWN

1 Summer hrs. in N.J.
2 Cheer
3 Life-changing statement
4 Farm vehicles
5 Endured
6 Many PC's
7 London lav
8 Vacuum's lack
9 Purifies
10 Not close
11 He taught an ancient language in film
12 Old London Magazine essayist
13 Celebrated Prohibition-era lawman
18 Tool with a cross handle
22 Feedbag feed
23 "Golden" things
24 Vanquished
25 What 17- and 52-Across and 11-Down all were
26 Curtain
27 North Carolina's ___ Banks
31 Some china
32 Church V.I.P.'s
34 Myopic cartoon character
37 Certain Boeing
38 Church music maker
40 Muslim pilgrimage
41 Arm bones
44 Spam producer
46 Adds punch to, as punch
48 Bygone auto
49 Toward shelter
50 Not pro
53 Commercial suffix with Motor
54 Biblical ark passenger
55 Ref's decision
56 3-in-One product
57 "The Matrix" role

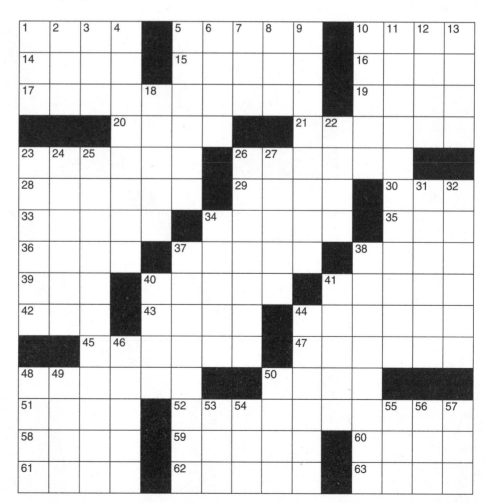

by Gene Newman

ACROSS

1 Eyes
6 Marx brother's instrument
10 Says further
14 An element, to the ancients
15 Turkish official
16 Dinette spot
17 The plain in Spain
18 Turn
19 One of TV's Sopranos
20 Fixes a flat, like a supermodel?
23 Outlaw
24 Bulletin board item
25 Sporty imports
29 Trim to fit, maybe
31 D.C. setting
34 Management course subject?
35 Oral, e.g.
36 Literally, "I forbid"
37 Cleans a windshield, like a snake?
40 Baseball rarities
41 Betting group
42 Ward off
43 Zeta follower
44 Whoop
45 Plays loudly
46 Cel character
48 ___ de vie
49 Eliminates a blind spot, like a cosmonaut?
55 'Hood
56 It may get plastered
57 Roberts of "Everybody Loves Raymond"
59 Do in
60 Double Stuf, for one
61 Poor Richard's Almanack item
62 Folks in smoke-filled rooms
63 Blouses and sweaters
64 Lacking slack

DOWN

1 Wise one
2 Math class, for short
3 Jazz home
4 "Beany & Cecil" boat Leakin' ___
5 Jail fixtures
6 Safe place
7 Census data
8 Mother of Zeus
9 Ineligible for benefits, say
10 Bit of slapstick
11 Guard
12 Ready to serve
13 Blue shade
21 Driver's need
22 Tit for ___
25 Photo finish
26 Arctic native
27 Lots and lots
28 Super scores
29 Laud
30 Willy Wonka's creator
32 Metric volume
33 Law school subject
35 Organic compound
36 Cheer starter
38 Hirer's posting
39 Worth on the open market
44 Cry before "Over here!"
45 Dickensian outburst
47 "Love Train" singers, with "the"
48 Cultural values
49 Singer Guthrie
50 Poi source
51 Going together, after "in"
52 Fashion
53 Shah's land, once
54 Teamsters' vehicles
55 Egyptian cobra
58 "Savvy?"

by Mike Torch

ACROSS

1 Like a Thanksgiving turkey
6 Some of this and some of that
10 Met star
14 Boarding areas
15 Commotion
16 Lena of "Chocolat"
17 Friendship
18 Descartes's "therefore"
19 Hurl an insult at
20 Truce after a fistfight?
23 Short flight
24 Smoothing tool
25 Court cutup
29 Terrier type
31 Site for cyberbidders
32 Point after deuce
34 Intensified, as sound
39 On the outs with a relative?
42 ___ tube
43 Tallow source
44 Nut job
45 Cool treats
47 Leaving no remainder
49 Caterer's heater
53 Dundee denial
54 Genetic engineer's observation about his pet?
60 Designer Gucci
61 Villain's work
62 Islamic holy war
64 Pull (in)
65 Boring way to learn
66 Come to mind
67 Arboretum sight
68 Ornamental vessel
69 Title role for Streisand

DOWN

1 Links org.
2 Souvlaki meat
3 Gas, e.g.: Abbr.
4 Intro to physics?
5 It contains the id
6 Tough to climb, perhaps
7 Whig's rival
8 Add a fringe to
9 Suggestive of a forest
10 Egg purchase
11 Tale of Troy
12 Coach Lombardi
13 Rile up
21 Imam's book
22 Song of praise
25 "Star Wars" warrior
26 Black, poetically
27 Cut, as a log
28 Newcastle's river
29 Skull cavity
30 Where pants may be worn
33 Two caplets, say
35 Distance not run in the Olympics
36 Working stiff
37 Tree hugger's subj.
38 Declare untrue
40 Circular gasket
41 Super bargain
46 Stick together
48 MTV figure
49 Like some bombs
50 Tippecanoe's mate
51 Vaudeville's ___ Foy and the Seven Little Foys
52 TV exec Arledge
53 N.Y. Jet or Phila. Eagle
55 Admit openly
56 Place to build
57 Home for the Murphys and O'Connors
58 Gossip
59 Biblical star locale, with "the"
63 Actor Benicio ___ Toro

by Fred Piscop

ACROSS

1 Nerd
6 "When it's ___" (old riddle answer)
10 Corp. money managers
14 Midway alternative
15 Fix up
16 In ecstasy
17 See 36-Across
20 Modem termini?
21 Icky stuff
22 No-goodnik
23 Smoked delicacies
24 One of the Gulf States
25 See 36-Across
29 Inventor Swift
32 Feet, of sorts
33 Take in
34 Helen, to Menelaus
35 Ancestry record
36 Clue for 17-, 25-, 43- and 55-Across
38 Weight
39 Impart
40 Shine, in ad-speak
41 Jack ___ ("24" agent)
42 Relative of -trix
43 See 36-Across
46 Starlet's dream
47 Winner of a posthumous Pulitzer
48 Sydney señorita
51 Son of Seth
52 Jazz grp.
55 See 36-Across
58 Is addicted to, maybe
59 Actress Skye
60 Steve of country music
61 Swiss chard, e.g.
62 Did a sendup of
63 Golden Hind captain

DOWN

1 Former North Carolina senator
2 "Kapow!"
3 Canal sites
4 Fraction of a joule
5 "Night Fever" group
6 Melodic passage
7 Yo-yo
8 Put on
9 Utility bill sharer
10 Debate airer
11 Spore producer
12 "That's ___ haven't heard"
13 Sebaceous gland woe
18 Flax pod
19 Cause of cold sweat
23 Fell away
24 Shimmering stone
25 Dame, e.g.
26 Things to hawk
27 Signs to heed
28 "___ the Beat" (1982 Go-Gos hit)
29 Highway headache
30 Have for sale
31 Big-city newspaper department
34 One known for spouting off
36 Many a dictator's problem
37 Balm ingredient
41 Like holy water
43 Onetime White House pooch
44 Prohibited
45 Wide-eyed
46 Mark McGwire's position
48 Much-used pencil
49 Engine attachment
50 Abbé de l'___ (pioneer in sign language)
51 German article
52 Writer Ephron
53 Like some mail
54 To ___ (exactly)
56 Keystone ___
57 DeSoto, e.g.

by Barry Silk

ACROSS

1 Ford or Chevrolet
5 Far from cordial
10 Waffle House alternative
14 Tel ___
15 Kind of toast
16 In the altogether
17 Event advertised in the classifieds
19 Clean Air Act target
20 Constriction of the pupil
21 Stumpers?
23 One of the Chipmunks
24 Spark plug, e.g.
26 Electrical glitch
30 Basilica part
33 Slippery ___
34 Time piece?
35 Jungfrau is one
36 Fighters at Lexington
39 One past due?
40 Actress Witherspoon
42 Enjoy, with "up"
43 Part of Air France's fleet until 2003
44 Place to buy wine
48 Boarders
49 Crop up
53 Sportscasting position
55 Web mags
56 It has a pocket
57 Time appropriate for 17-, 26- and 44-Across?
60 Nebraska tribe
61 Robin player of 1938
62 Rich source
63 "The King and I" co-star
64 Fits together
65 Charon crossed it

DOWN

1 Source of igneous rock
2 Benefit
3 Bolshoi rival
4 Hard to pin down
5 Skunk River city
6 Guitar great Paul
7 Commercial suffix with Rock
8 Shaped like a fish stick
9 Spenser's "The ___ Queene"
10 Parts of feet
11 Will Rogers and others
12 A hound may pick it up
13 Tent holders
18 1992 Heisman winner ___ Torretta
22 Cruising
24 "___ never work!"
25 Most off-tasting
27 Gift that's hung around the neck
28 Go-___
29 Peepers
30 50+ org.
31 "Nolo," for instance
32 Eventgoer
36 First A.F.L.-C.I.O. president
37 Makes lace
38 1995 trial name
41 Helter-___
43 Soaps, e.g.
45 Some meter readers
46 Unbroken
47 Bulldoze
50 Bullion unit
51 Like a fleabag
52 Reo contemporary
53 Out of control
54 Marquee time
55 Conduit bends
58 E.R. workers
59 Ellipsis part

by Jim Hyres

ACROSS

1 Country's McEntire
5 Professional pitcher
10 Atomic groups: Abbr.
14 Trash can, e.g., on a computer
15 Lollapalooza
16 What Hamlet called Polonius
17 Late beloved entertainer
19 Steak order
20 Some diner orders
21 Prince ___ Khan
22 Suffix with prank
23 Up to now
25 Be in the red
26 Home, sweet or not
27 17-Across's alias
30 California's San ___ Dam
31 Like some phone nos.
32 Flight board abbr.
33 Part of a hookah
34 Least amount of caring
35 Longtime record label
36 Dandy
39 "My country" follower
40 "Nice!"
41 Wine: Prefix
42 Where 17-Across was inducted in 1990
47 3-D graph line
48 Last: Abbr.
49 Violinist Zimbalist
50 Declines
51 ___-Magnon
52 Like community property
53 Lit ___ (college course, slangily)
54 17-Across's first national TV show
58 Repeated call to a dog
59 Crop up
60 Biblical shepherd-turned-prophet
61 Former Iranian president Bani-___
62 Sportscaster Jim
63 Handshake's meaning, maybe

DOWN

1 Tease
2 Author Umberto
3 Hair holder
4 Low socks
5 Juice drinks
6 Haircuts
7 Nontraditional haircuts
8 Pretty shrub
9 Part of a Mad. Ave. address
10 Chocolate and almond treat
11 One with a silver tongue
12 1960's TV western
13 Dorm room staple
18 James of jazz
23 Scopes trial grp.
24 Suffix with ptero-
25 Normal force felt on earth
26 Taj Mahal city
28 Like the "Too-ra-loo-ra-loo-ral" lullaby
29 Cheesy snack
34 Five-spots
35 Ale ingredient
36 Dreaded
37 Treater's phrase
38 Pound piece
39 Popular party game
40 Permit to enter
41 Like some vehicles
42 Moravians, e.g.
43 California fossil site
44 Variety of sandpiper
45 Light show
46 Family problem
51 Actor Jackie
52 Court cry
55 Summer clock setting: Abbr.
56 ___ favor
57 Designer inits.

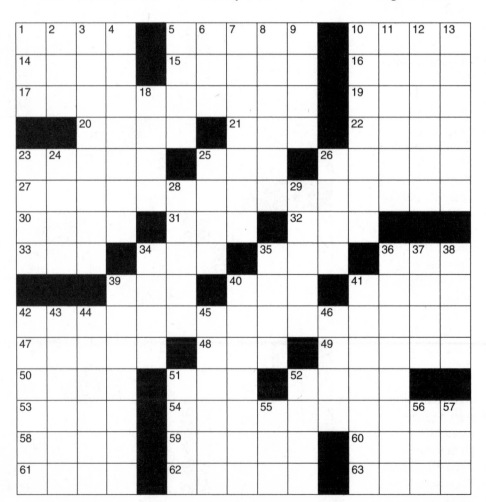

by Roy Leban

ACROSS

1 Lagoon locale
6 Triumphed
9 Former Montreal N.L.'er
13 Amos of "Amos 'n' Andy"
14 Cow chow
15 Terrify
16 Start of a quote by Anton Chekhov
19 Friend of Fido
20 "Go, team!"
21 Stopped
22 Idle fancy
24 Slugger Gonzalez
25 Quote, part 2
31 Phantasm
32 Hypnotist's imperative
33 ___-friendly
34 Boot
35 Windows preceder
36 Smile
37 It's an honour: Abbr.
38 Horse's motion
40 South Seas attire
42 Quote, part 3
45 6:1 or 3:2, say
46 Canned
47 Educate
50 Appropriate
51 Blowtorch fuel
54 End of the quote
58 Composer Copland
59 Like Burns's "tim'rous beastie"
60 Penned
61 Verve
62 Young 'un
63 Furnish with a fund

DOWN

1 Open a bit
2 Strengthen, with "up"
3 Cameo stone
4 Flower wreath
5 Something that's illegal to drop
6 End of many a riddle
7 Courtroom affirmation
8 Home of the IRT and BMT
9 ___ terrible
10 Yule
11 Horse's motion
12 Flat
15 Restless
17 Kind of whiskey
18 Obtuse's opposite
22 Habeas corpus or mandamus
23 Event on "The Sopranos"
24 Some sails
25 Island in a Beach Boys lyric
26 "___ at the Bat"
27 Like a chimney sweep
28 Graceful bird
29 Medium for writing "Happy Anniversary"
30 Dance partner?
31 Grove
35 Los ___ de los Muertos (Mexican holiday)
36 Electrical network
38 Descend
39 Discombobulate
40 A mile a minute
41 "Hail!," to Horace
43 Overly
44 Ended, as a subscription
47 Attempt
48 Scorch
49 Spy Mata ___
50 Zone
51 Saintly
52 A factory worker might make a dash for it
53 Dish cooked in a pot
55 Hole maker
56 Be in the hole
57 Ashes holder

by Ethan Friedman

ACROSS

1 Shout from the sidelines on TV
6 "Monty Python" airer
9 "Concentration" puzzle
14 Expo '70 site
15 "Seinfeld" uncle
16 Visibly shocked
17 Casino slickster
19 Caddie, basically
20 Dangerous cargo, in modern lingo
22 Humble reply
23 "Charlotte's Web" author
27 Sheriff's party?
29 Snickers
30 Like some eels or catfish
33 Genesis firstborn
34 Sleek, in car talk
35 "I'm so glad!"
36 Elevs.
37 Toaster treat
40 State Dept. figure
41 Comics shriek
42 Met number
43 Opposite of endo-
44 Shows contempt for
46 Potential retiree
48 Gold rush territory
49 Shamefaced
50 W.W. II ally
52 Major fiction
54 "Go ahead, ask!"
56 What 17- and 37-Across and 11- and 25-Down each comes to?
61 Two-door conveyance
62 Aladdin's sidekick
63 Instant message recipient, maybe
64 Like unlucky toreadors
65 Iron-pumper's unit
66 Writer who's in the minority

DOWN

1 Ad __
2 "Love __ Sickness" (Daniel poem)
3 Deface
4 Gave the go-ahead
5 Five iron
6 Mark, as a trail
7 Road shoulder
8 Accede to the district attorney, perhaps
9 Blow the whistle (on)
10 Self-server
11 Bad coffee, informally
12 Manipulator
13 Light-footed
18 Panama and porkpie
21 "__ is human . . ."
23 Makes aquatints
24 Much traveled
25 Sugary cocktail
26 Clucker
28 Nae sayer
30 Trouble constantly
31 "You are not!" retort
32 RoboCop, e.g.
37 Bench locale
38 Mork's leader on "Mork & Mindy"
39 Place for cocktails
43 Chang's twin
45 Low Countries locale
46 Margarita feature
47 Ratify by stamping
49 In a lather
50 Maritime grp.
51 "Buzz off!"
53 Sensation, slangily
55 Sitcom newsman Baxter
57 Lobster eggs
58 Brownie
59 Take captive
60 Like some wells and lectures

by Mitch Komro

ACROSS

1 5-Across handle
5 Sharp weapon, slangily
9 Rope fiber
14 Mozart composition
15 Animal with a scut
16 Shiraz native
17 Start of a message on a Lincoln Center T-shirt
19 Honor, in academe
20 See 13-Down
21 Wedding reception ritual
23 Clan emblems
24 T-men, e.g.
25 Cathedral city
28 Great balls of fire
29 "The Immoralist" author
30 Liberate
31 Walked over
33 Butchers' offerings
35 Message, part 2
39 Doings of Hercules
40 Table section
41 Cross to bear
42 Mother of Horus
44 1938 Physics Nobelist
49 Sword conqueror
50 Aware of
51 Word processing command
52 ___ Lama
54 Babar's queen
55 Spiral-horned antelope
57 End of the message
59 Tubular pasta
60 Jam-pack
61 Morlocks' victims in "The Time Machine"
62 Fragrant oil
63 Does some tailoring
64 Can blemish

DOWN

1 Things to kick
2 "Am too!" rejoinder
3 Cinco de Mayo event
4 Tear to shreds
5 Round at a bar, maybe
6 Keep
7 Tick off
8 Discharged, as gases
9 Eliot's Marner
10 S. & L. offerings
11 Sweet wine
12 What's more
13 With 20-Across, receive a posthumous honor
18 Cage-wheel runner
22 One-named singer
24 Opera that inspired the T-shirt slogan
26 Popular jeans
27 Sycophant's word
29 Statehouse V.I.P.
30 Pro
32 Soprano in "The Barber of Seville"
34 Stymie
35 What a groom may groom
36 Plentiful
37 John ___ Passos
38 Realtor's abbr.
39 Prune
43 Zigzag, e.g.
45 Smoothed out
46 Fix, as a pump
47 Women's prison figure
48 "Looky there!"
50 Grayer, maybe
51 Appears to be
53 "___ Karenina"
54 Secretive sort
55 Rater of m.p.g.
56 Court cry
58 Bonanza find

by Nancy S. Ross

ACROSS

1 Check, as the horizon
5 Pick out
9 Home feature
14 Lotion additive
15 Walk in water
16 They may be spent in France
17 Restaurant lines?
18 Atlas section
19 Some transportation stocks
20 End of a line
23 Swamp goo
24 Charged particle
25 Move with stealth
28 The Merry Men, e.g.
30 Like a wallflower
33 "___ as good as another"
34 Symbol of stubbornness
35 Race in an H. G. Wells story
36 Ending for a line
39 Curved lines
40 2%, maybe
41 Tolerate
42 #26 of 26
43 Up for something
44 Film components
45 Quadrennial conventiongoer
46 Sci-fi writer Frederik
47 Ending line
53 Bond before Dalton
54 Joint problem
55 Creep (along)
57 Oktoberfest air
58 "When in ___ . . ."
59 Clothing line
60 Hint of light
61 Parishioner's line
62 One getting a decoration

DOWN

1 1950's–60's singer Cooke
2 Staff symbol
3 Top-of-the-line
4 Ones getting "worry lines"?
5 "Dirty Dancing" costar
6 Stickum
7 Garfield's pal
8 Go lickety-split
9 Certain 36-Across
10 Greg Evans comic strip
11 Diva's lines
12 Car payment
13 Curved line

21 Settle down for the night
22 Sal of "Exodus"
25 Shade of yellow
26 Harden
27 London coppers
28 Montana city
29 "It's a Sin to Tell ___" (1936 hit)
30 Done in
31 Bunch of people
32 "Omigosh!"
34 What to call a lady
35 Add frills to
37 Russian range
38 Snack chip
43 Stadium cheer
44 Tone down
45 Winter wear

46 Feather in one's cap
47 Hammer or tongs
48 Doughnut's center
49 Taj Mahal city
50 Weaving machine
51 Kind of pad
52 Operation memento
53 Auto ad stat.
56 Med. care plan

by Mark Diehl

ACROSS

1 Crash site
4 Babe in the woods
8 Black rock
14 Language suffix
15 "Would __ to you?"
16 Alchemist's concoction
17 Apiece, at Wimbledon
18 Jungle woman
19 With subtlety
20 Wedding man lookin' at the newspaper?
23 Late-night host
24 Tripe
29 Surgeon's request
32 Spill material
33 Man, for one
34 Gasket
36 Sacred spot
37 Durable piece of boxin' equipment?
42 Rubbernecked
43 Russian alternative
44 Largest of seven
45 Commencement wear
46 Mix movies
51 Name trump, in bridge
53 Jai __
54 Result of a silo tippin' over?
59 Nimble
63 Fit for service
64 Newspaper supply
65 Batten down
66 The gamut
67 Genealogy word
68 Warming device
69 Not a lick
70 Muff

DOWN

1 Choker components
2 Slumbering
3 Presidential middle name
4 Where Suva is
5 Presidential middle name
6 White House section
7 Poetic adverb
8 Soil
9 Out on __
10 Mortal thing
11 What Carry Nation carried
12 Diamond __
13 Take a shot at
21 Slip on
22 Ancestry
25 Check
26 Analogy phrase
27 Montenegro native
28 "Take this!"
30 Olympian's quest
31 Years of note
32 Ready for use
35 David, "the sweet psalmist of __"
36 Turkish title
37 Old oath
38 Carnation container
39 Grist for DeMille?
40 MTV's "__ World"
41 Lt. saluter
45 Copernicus, for one
47 Pit contents
48 Marilu Henner's "Taxi" role
49 Best Actress of 1936 and 1937
50 Tackle box item
52 All lit up
55 Help for some students
56 Concerned with
57 Light stuff
58 Use a crystal ball
59 Camel's end?
60 River to Solway Firth
61 Company with a dog logo
62 Call at first

by Richard Silvestri

ACROSS

1 Leaves may be put in it
7 Prohibits
11 Sass
14 Like most plumbing nowadays
15 Mount SW of Messina
16 Suffix with Canton
17 Candice Bergen role
19 Our sun
20 Before
21 Kitchen wrap
22 Fisticuffs
24 Boxing locale
26 Bye-byes
28 Cheer (for)
29 Ginger cookies
31 Morning TV co-host
33 Felt smug
35 Supermarket divisions
36 ___ Zeppelin
37 First mate
38 Flourish
42 Deceive
46 "Paper Moon" actor
48 Laundromat appliance
50 Not fer
51 Rowdy ___, Clint Eastwood's role in "Rawhide"
53 Ocean predator
54 Ripple lovers
56 Bedding item
58 Brooch
59 Moon-landing vehicle, for short
60 Stephen Sondheim title character
63 Former Spanish queen
64 It may be grand
65 More loved
66 Hideout
67 Soaks (up)
68 One who might issue a challenge

DOWN

1 Track officials
2 Accustoming (to)
3 Kind of gland
4 Champagne-opening sound
5 Wonderment cries
6 Have a ___ (attempt)
7 Dressed down
8 Lacking a musical key
9 Hurricane dir.
10 Without
11 Clorox company household cleaner
12 Chemical relative
13 Jai alai balls
18 Put one's foot down?
23 Muffs one
25 Address abbr.
27 Poles and Czechs
30 Discharge from the military
32 Triangular road sign
34 Wee
37 Ford of the Ford Models agency
38 Fished with a net
39 Cleanliness
40 Dustin Hoffman film
41 ___ time flat
42 Marshall ___ (Eminem's real name)
43 Mancinelli's "___ e Leandro"
44 Many a taxi's destination
45 Judge
47 Not be so hard
49 Stopped flowing, as a stream
52 Burpee's packetful
55 Concordes
57 Chinook salmon
61 Go a-courting
62 Light brown

by A. J. Santora

ACROSS

1 Cybertrash
5 Snooker shot
10 Caffeine source
14 Diamond
   Head site
15 Seller, usually
16 Son of Seth
17 Dense one
18 They're trimmed
19 Free gym
   membership, e.g.
20 [   ] bar
23 Bear
24 Bounded along
25 Rasputin, for one
28 Dieter's dread
30 "@#$%!," e.g.
31 Down East
33 George's musical
   brother
36 [   ] saver
40 Clinch, with "up"
41 Ways off
42 ___ the wiser
43 Infatuated
44 Best
46 Put forward
49 "Zip it!"
51 [   ] shuttle
57 Big batch
58 Dope in a den?
59 Bean concoction?
60 Towering
61 Part of MGM
62 Yachter's woe
63 ___ Stanley
   Gardner
64 Idyllic spots
65 Trauma team:
   Abbr.

DOWN

1 Something odd
   about the wash?
2 Whiten
3 Salty greeting?
4 Soaks at spas
5 Composite picture
6 Edgar or Hugo

7 Like a snicker
8 Employer,
   to many
9 Gaelic tongue
10 Continued
11 Slightly ahead
12 "M" star, 1931
13 Set, as a price
21 Kimono closer
22 Roswell crash
   victim, supposedly
25 Soft shoes
26 Lock name
27 Pack away
28 Musicians' jobs
29 Santa ___
31 Where to see some
   of 32-Down's work
32 See 31-Down

33 Shirt name
34 France's ___ Coty
35 Part or parcel
37 Millay's Muse
38 Chase game
39 Very quickly
43 Fat container?
44 Thingamabobs
45 Fun and games,
   for short
46 Collagist's need
47 Prize that,
   surprisingly,
   contains a large
   amount of tin
48 Stable spot
49 To a degree
50 Reversal
52 Iditarod terminus

53 Took off on
54 Grandfather
   of 16-Across
55 Like some markers
56 Flat hats

by Norma Johnson

ACROSS

1 Tiny bit
5 Counting everything
10 Matinee ___
14 Like some bait
15 Loggers' contest
16 Compete in a 15-Across
17 Nondrinker
19 "Ignorance ___ excuse"
20 It'll tell you where to go
21 Bomb squad's compensation, say
23 Retina feature
25 Mandlikova of tennis
26 J.F.K. posting: Abbr.
27 ___ Canals
29 Reuters competitor
31 Liner stopovers
33 Vow of silence taker
38 Townshend of the Who
39 Way up?
40 Old Culp/Cosby series
44 TV bigot
47 Winter wear
50 Family nickname
51 Frozen Wasser
52 Tailless simian
53 Kemo ___
57 Game piece
59 Rowdy sort
62 "Baloney!"
65 It's off the NE coast of Corsica
66 Endive, e.g.
68 Cub or Card, e.g.
69 Fill with joy
70 Western Canada native
71 Theater award
72 Reveal
73 Calls for

DOWN

1 Claudia ___ Taylor (Mrs. Lyndon Johnson)
2 Ticket info
3 Winter wear
4 Tagalong's cry
5 N.Y.C. subway line
6 Biblical boatwright
7 He's prayed to five times a day
8 Gibbons of TV
9 Navigation acronym
10 Footnote abbr.
11 Rid one's mind of
12 Hardly spare
13 Big name in insurance
18 Admit (to)
22 Desert rarity
24 Protestant denom.
27 "The racer's edge"
28 Metallurgist's material
30 Canal locale: Abbr.
32 Bones' partner
34 Reach a high
35 Skater Babilonia
36 Architect Ludwig ___ van der Rohe
37 Round trip?
41 Pesky insects, colloquially
42 Province east of N.B.
43 Abbr. in old letter sign-offs
45 Too hasty
46 Manipulating
47 Orphan's need
48 Rocky dethroned him in "Rocky II"
49 Sandwich with sauerkraut
54 Photographer Adams
55 ___ Street, Home of the Blues
56 Great brilliance
58 Poet Federico García ___
60 Hoosier industrial center
61 Green Hornet's valet
63 Hunt for
64 Till stack
67 Thieves' place

by Randy Sowell

ACROSS

1 Cornhusker State city
6 Moronic
10 Tacks on
14 Emmy-winning role for Sally Field
15 Kazan who won a 1-Down for Lifetime Achievement
16 Rock's Mötley ___
17 Transcript?
19 Camel feature
20 Santa ___ winds
21 Dawn, to Donne
22 Cue
24 Stress hard
26 Witch's conveyance
27 On the sly
29 $$$ dispenser
32 Put down
35 Source of easy money
37 The Bruins of the Pac-10
38 Hits repeatedly
40 Geraldine Chaplin's mother
41 Run wild
43 Towns, informally
44 Floors, briefly
45 One showing signs of a cold
48 Sudden inundation
50 Payment procrastinator's penalty
54 Peloponnesian War victor
56 It may be strong or long
57 Lacking a mate
58 ___ Bell
59 Driver ed?
62 Airing
63 Patron saint of Norway
64 Japanese noodle dish
65 Coin in Cancún
66 The latest
67 Good Housekeeping approvals

DOWN

1 See 15-Across
2 Loy of "The Thin Man"
3 Crosswise, on deck
4 Holed up
5 Ex payments
6 Formal order
7 ___ Bator, Mongolia
8 Former Russian orbiter
9 Unwelcome ink
10 Sound from a 45-Across
11 Certain college music student?
12 Eyesore
13 9: Abbr.
18 Male turkeys
23 "Portnoy's Complaint" author
25 Distiller Walker
26 Fabergé cologne
28 Staff symbol
30 Chinese secret society
31 New corp. hires
32 The edge of night
33 Outer: Prefix
34 Taking notes and writing essays?
36 "___ fired!" (Trump catchphrase)
38 Large container of brass?
39 Falco of "The Sopranos"
42 H.S. junior's test
43 They lay it on the line
46 Plumps up
47 Not of the cloth
49 Utah city
51 Pro ___ (perfunctorily)
52 50's Ford flop
53 Idyllic spots
54 Obey a red light
55 Piece of glass
56 Deli side dish
60 Ring "Rah!"
61 Dubai is part of it: Abbr.

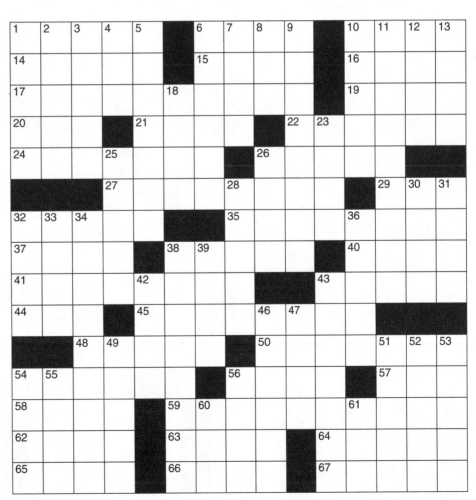

by Nancy Salomon

ACROSS

1 Sugar source
5 Work on in a sound studio
10 Not assigned, after "on"
14 Gray's subj.
15 Turk's neighbor
16 Weightlifter's action
17 Hurl tableware?
19 Indian tourist city
20 Big bird
21 Fashion maven Klensch
22 Arm bones
23 Miss of mystery
25 Hurl cookware?
28 Couldn't get enough of
29 Prefix with verse
30 Take action against
31 Tomorrow's opposite: Abbr.
32 Unit of light intensity
35 River to the North Sea
36 Hurl toupees?
39 ATM card necessity
42 Small diving bird of the North Pacific
43 Olympian Lipinski
47 Lennon's lady
48 Three after B
49 Overdone
50 Hurl parts of a typewriter?
53 Safe places
54 Sends
55 Jetty
57 Govt. collectors
58 Whizzed (through)
59 Hurl an entree?
62 "Hard ___!" (nautical cry)
63 ___ Selassie
64 Clive Cussler thriller "___ Gold"
65 Hollow plant
66 Classic Icelandic works
67 Arm of the British military?

DOWN

1 Southern tip of New Jersey
2 Turn into cartoon form
3 ___ way
4 "Yadda, yadda, yadda"
5 Biathlete's need
6 Piccadilly Circus statue
7 Assassinated Jacobin
8 Well contents
9 Fraternity letters
10 It's overhead
11 Certain dog feature
12 Slip on paper
13 Teaching load
18 Butlers and maids
22 Putting to work
24 Short shot
26 Bizarre
27 Sty sniffer
32 Stuffy sort
33 Cornball
34 Hooter
37 Cabbies
38 "The Man" of Cardinals history
39 Britney Spears, e.g.
40 Having debt
41 Emphatic denial
44 Of interest to archaeologists
45 Daily grind
46 Like king crab
49 Cargo areas
51 Radar reading
52 Calamari
53 "___ alive!"
56 Longtime John Wooden team
59 Hero to Fidel
60 Scammed
61 "___ the Last Rose of Summer" (old song standard)

by Randolph Ross

ACROSS

1 Grub
5 Word to Cratchit
8 E-business
14 Fax, say
15 Outer: Prefix
16 Sesame paste
17 64-Across's option for a 38-Across or a 13-, 18-, 28- or 42-Down
19 Blotto
20 Mouths, anatomically
21 Acquired relative
23 In order
24 Advil alternative
26 Barely manage, with "out"
29 Pitching star
30 "Later!"
31 Where to find Washington or Lincoln
33 Orch. section
34 Shady street's name
36 Nile slitherers
37 Pro ___
38 Student's worry
42 Part of w.p.m.
43 Pope John ___ (1316–34)
44 Roll-call call
45 Beatle spouse
46 "We ___ please"
48 One of two "certainties" in life
52 Beer belly
53 Title for Tussaud
54 Shoe lift
56 Witticism
58 Grows light
60 "___ Beso" (1962 hit)
61 Opens, in a way
64 See 17-Across
66 Summer cooler
67 The works
68 Sand
69 Spiced up
70 Literary inits.
71 One of the Katzenjammer Kids

DOWN

1 $100 bills, slangily
2 Town crier's cry
3 Marked down
4 Part of w.p.m.: Abbr.
5 Bingo relative
6 Armpit, anatomically
7 Granada greeting
8 Sot's woe, for short
9 Stable morsel
10 Fund-raising suffix
11 Film buff
12 Intermissionless play
13 Student's worry
18 Student's worry
22 From Cardiff, say
25 Watchful pair
27 Phi Beta ___
28 Student's worry
32 Unspoken
35 Writer Gorky
38 Give up
39 Makes steamy
40 Frost-covered
41 Thunder sound
42 Student's worry
47 "Them's the breaks!"
49 Nissan S.U.V.
50 Enter gradually
51 Curling and hurling
55 Ltr. accompaniers
57 Brad of film
59 Fruit spray
62 ___ Dee River
63 Blue
65 "Bleah!"

by Michael Shteyman

ACROSS

1 Mandrake's field
6 It may be painted red
10 Nailed obliquely
14 Human rights activist Bonner
15 Gazetteer figure
16 ___ dixit
17 A de Mille
18 Petits ___ (French peas)
19 Naldi of old films
20 Hamlet's slayer
22 Milk-related
24 "Tsk!"
25 Metallurgist's creation
26 Walks about
30 Four-star
34 Small bit
35 Pack away
36 Kind of colony or code
37 Mid 11th-century date
38 Words with 1-, 6-, 10-, 67-, 68- and 69-Across, and 1-, 13-, 26-, 33-, 53- and 59-Down
41 Egg: Prefix
42 Mystery writer Stanley
44 11-Down's player
45 A util.
46 Smashed
48 Shore line
50 Schusser's locale
52 Sport ___ (car category)
53 Worse, as excuses go
56 Place to play
60 Dix + un
61 Diamond call
63 Yogi's language
64 Commandos' arms
65 Night fliers
66 Internet marketing
67 Tooth part
68 Stomach tightness
69 Macarena, e.g.

DOWN

1 Prix fixe offering
2 Pond floater
3 Spliced item
4 Resistance to change
5 Eject
6 It's played at night
7 ___ y plata (Montana's motto)
8 Brecht collaborator Kurt
9 Some French consonants
10 Old photo
11 Bee's nephew, in old TV
12 Are, in Aragón
13 Do business
21 Footnote abbr.
23 Overthrows
25 Fertility goddess
26 x
27 Rich kid in "Nancy"
28 At an incline
29 ___ minérale
31 ___ Gay
32 Frenzied sort
33 Lego unit
38 Fishhook line
39 "Vive le ___!"
40 Provide, as with a quality
43 "Smart decision"
45 Retiree's title
47 Makes a small profit
49 Designed like Dürer
51 Seafood mouthful
53 Count in a march
54 Singer Stuarti
55 Basso Pinza
56 Take a load off
57 Son of Judah
58 Keatsian or Pindaric
59 Horse-race distance
62 "Alice" waitress

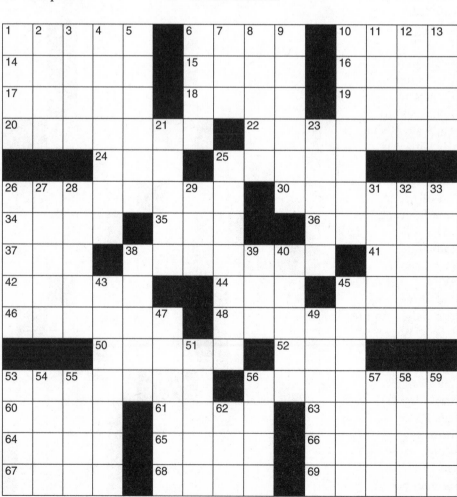

by John Underwood

ACROSS

1 Set of principles
6 Young 'uns
10 Hospital units
14 Former Big Apple mayor Abe
15 Wise one
16 Skater's leap
17 1937 Triple Crown winner
19 Lothario
20 Abracadabra stuff
21 1978 Triple Crown winner
23 Dutch disease victims
25 Tropical tuber
26 1941 Triple Crown winner
30 Mell Lazarus comic strip
34 Tony winner McKellen
35 Ishmael's skipper
36 Like a Triple Crown winner
37 Reply to the Little Red Hen
39 1935 Triple Crown winner
41 Dirty dishes locale
42 Number of Triple Crown winners through 2003
44 Small change
46 Hindu honorific
47 Removed from copy
48 1919 Triple Crown winner
50 "Java" trumpeter Al
52 Designed to minimize wind resistance
53 1948 Triple Crown winner
57 Rhythmic numbers
60 "Metamorphoses" poet
61 1943 Triple Crown winner
64 Sitarist Shankar
65 Eye up and down

66 Duffers' warning cries
67 Shoelace problem
68 In custody
69 Said with a sneer

DOWN

1 "Charlotte's Web" author's monogram
2 Bulls or Bears
3 ___-kiri
4 Graphics machine
5 Façade part
6 ___ Friday's (restaurant chain)
7 That certain something
8 Having open windows, maybe
9 Infection fighter

10 Sots' sites
11 Midterm, for one
12 Apollo astronaut Slayton
13 Musher's transport
18 "Heeere's Johnny!" announcer
22 "___ la Douce"
24 Dog-paddled
26 Plied with Bordeaux or Burgundy
27 Outsider, in Hawaii
28 Big name in chips
29 Primitive counters
31 A wee bit wet
32 The writer Saki's real name
33 Welcome to one's home

36 Radiator adjunct
38 "Enough, already!"
40 Wife of Zeus
43 Revision, informally
45 Importers' duties
48 Flunky
49 Deodorant type
51 Copier company
53 Party popper?
54 Novelist Turgenev
55 Modern recorder
56 No longer legal
58 Hollywood's Hatcher
59 Give a special berth
62 Homer's TV neighbor
63 Mao ___-tung

by Nancy Salomon

Note: Arrange the four circled letters in the grid to get a word that defines the four unclued answers.

ACROSS

1 "___ Network" (1980's comedy series)
5 Old U.S. gas brand
9 Tear carriers
14 Celebratory dance
15 Canal section
16 Match
17 Stratford's stream
18 Ice cream thickener
19 Be a kvetch
20 See note
23 Item in a bucket
24 Mason or McBeal: Abbr.
25 Birch family trees
27 "Journey Into Fear" novelist
30 "Saint Joan" star Jean
32 Head boss, initially
33 Women's titles
35 Kind of dealer
38 Schoolbooks
40 Slippery ___
41 Hawk's descent
42 Cookbook direction
43 Up-to-the-minute
45 Swiss canton
46 "___ done!"
48 Knife or club
50 Water surrounded by sand dunes
52 Soccer star Mia
53 "___ Too Late" (Carole King hit)
54 See note
60 Pat-down
62 Actor's goal
63 Like a churl
64 Parishioner's donation
65 "Gee whiz!"
66 Commotions
67 Floor it
68 Pale
69 Piper's wear

DOWN

1 Clarinetist Artie
2 Sheltered bay
3 Walked on
4 Home wrecker
5 Hyundai model
6 Waterlogged
7 Object of a union's anger
8 Gumbo vegetable
9 Dilly-dally
10 "Not my thing at all!"
11 See note
12 Andrea Bocelli, for one
13 Oozes
21 Tabloid duos
22 Slaps the cuffs on
26 Chess result, sometimes
27 Does something
28 Run into
29 See note
30 Like ocean air
31 Noted plus-size model
34 Start a hand
36 1960's–70's Italian P.M.
37 Wash or dry cycle
39 Peter, Paul and Mary, e.g.
41 Morel morsels
43 Late-night funnyman
44 Dark-complexioned
47 Ready to fire
49 Metroliner company
50 Hitchers' hopes
51 Take ___ down memory lane
52 Like Siberian winters
55 Annika Sorenstam grp.
56 Vientiane's land
57 Quattro maker
58 Temple figure
59 Hatchling's home
61 Cow or sow

by Allan E. Parrish

ACROSS

1 Reunion group
5 Cheese from Europe
9 Capital of Bolivia
14 Altar happening
15 Investigatory aid
16 Rare eye color
17 Controversial apple spray
18 "Whatcha ___?"
19 Increased
20 Dealer in ointments?
23 Model information: Abbr.
24 Eye cover
25 "Star Wars" creature
27 None-too-bright Broadway backer?
33 Wrestling throw
37 Don ___ de la Vega, a k a Zorro
38 Zhivago's love
39 Swelling
42 British weapon
43 Time and ___
45 African desert
47 Some dairy records?
50 Aleutian island
51 Pageboy, for one
56 Modifying wd.
59 Kangaroos at the South Pole?
62 "___ the Raven, 'Nevermore'"
64 Place
65 One way to run
66 Loosen
67 Currier's partner
68 Zola novel
69 Syrian leader
70 Shoulder adjoiner
71 Impressionist

DOWN

1 Uncouth
2 Purple shade
3 In any way
4 Chutzpah
5 Lamp support, perhaps
6 Word with chain or prize
7 ___ Minor
8 Director Sam of "American Beauty"
9 Mean way to go
10 Like
11 Sprite
12 State confidently
13 Last section of a London telephone directory
21 Cupid's counterpart
22 Milk source
26 Purchase at a Jewish deli
28 Small amount
29 1957 Best Supporting Actress Miyoshi ___
30 "___ life!"
31 City ENE of Budapest
32 Actress Anderson
33 Spill the beans
34 Island with Kaala Peak
35 "Shoot!"
36 1945 conference site
40 ___ de tête (French headache)
41 Draft locale
44 Sold for
46 "Pronto!"
48 "Citizen Kane" studio
49 Sergeant's order
52 Toothpaste once advertised by Bucky Beaver
53 Chart anew
54 Dull speaker
55 Schindler of "Schindler's List"
56 Shade by the beach?
57 Demands for payment
58 Scribbles (down)
60 Egoistical, demanding sort
61 Dickens's villainous clerk
63 Aunt, in Aragón

by Alan Arbesfeld

ACROSS

1 ___ law (early Germanic legal code)
6 N.B.A. nickname
10 Aid by being a lookout, e.g.
14 Verdi aria
15 Former World Cup star
16 Tropical tuber
17 Noted arrival of 2004
19 1917 revolution casualty
20 R-V connection?
21 Berne's river
22 Flippant
23 Grate on
24 "Well, ___ here!"
27 Monroe, for one
30 Monopoly avenue
33 Salt ___
34 Take care of
36 Farm female
37 A in Paris
38 Adjective for 17-Across
39 Bled
40 Nutritionist's abbr.
41 Declare
42 Parched
43 Extras in "The Mexican"
45 Small hooters
47 Hidden
48 Goose egg
49 Sea
51 See 52-Across
52 With 51-Across, get mad
55 Foreman's locale?
56 17-Across, for one
60 Astra maker
61 They're sometimes put on
62 Dock site
63 Lived
64 ___ poem
65 Plain place to live?

DOWN

1 Some movies: Abbr.
2 In ___ (stuck)
3 Place
4 Mineral suffix
5 "Parent" of 17-Across
6 Box
7 17-Across, e.g.
8 ___ Khan
9 "Sister" of 17-Across, familiarly
10 Reach
11 Capital of St. Kitts, visited regularly by 17-Across
12 Important times
13 Conservative Brit
18 Hurry
22 Shooting sport
23 Sign
24 Adjective for 17-Across
25 Law partner?
26 Tool sharpeners
27 Book jacket writing
28 Hunt in Hollywood
29 17-Across, for one
31 Be ready for
32 Imparts
35 Match play?
38 Congregation members
42 Part of ATV
44 Be suspended
46 Adjective for 17-Across
49 Forehead
50 Seasoned
51 Lift off
52 Kind of steward
53 Hibernian's land
54 Olympics event
56 Jazzman
57 City in a Peter Allen song title
58 Coffee server
59 17-Across, e.g.

by David J. Kahn

ACROSS

1 "Star Wars" gangster ___ the Hutt
6 Basilica center
10 Police dept. alerts
14 Bubbling on the burner
15 Part of 5-Down: Abbr.
16 "Star Trek" speed
17 Belt tightenings
19 Director Kazan
20 Hearty hello
21 Draft dispenser
23 Play one's part
24 Directed skyward
27 Silly 70's fad
29 Pitcher's tour de force
31 Factor in shipping costs
32 Sling mud at, say
33 Composer Satie
35 Bother persistently
38 Nightmarish street
39 Trite truth
41 Tony-winning Hagen
42 Big name in polls
44 Fill till full
45 Nest builder in the eaves
46 Thunderous sound
48 Motorist's stop
50 Reddish-brown
53 Endangered bamboo eaters
54 Nabokov title heroine
55 Sign of a full house
56 Dessert wine
57 Course listing
59 Title of this puzzle, in reference to 17- and 39-Across and 11- and 26-Down
64 Program problems
65 Finishes (up)
66 Love a lot
67 X and Y, on a graph
68 Could cuts, e.g.
69 Hill broadcaster

DOWN

1 Pugilist's poke
2 ___ Dhabi
3 Physique, so to speak
4 Result of teasing?
5 Yankees' div.
6 Table salt, to a chemist
7 ___ Darya (Asian river)
8 Sporty Chevy, briefly
9 Fake
10 Leave dumbstruck
11 Protection for the royal family
12 Building block
13 Small rows
18 Nervous laugh
22 Facedown
24 Family name at Indy
25 Chihuahua chicken
26 Not much moolah
27 Early political race
28 "Not ___ bet!"
30 Love personified
34 Flying toy
36 Clueless
37 Spanish snacks
39 Toots one's own horn
40 Tyrant
43 "Telephone Line" grp.
45 Job-seekers' reading
47 French fragrance
49 Runway surface
50 Deadly snake
51 For two, in music
52 Hubbub
56 "Hey, over here!"
58 Naval inits.
60 Stephen of "Still Crazy"
61 Go one better than
62 All competitor
63 One with a six-yr. term

by Nancy Salomon

ACROSS

1 Nonplussed
6 Winter hookup
10 Nudges
14 15-Across's instrument
15 ___ Shankar
16 View from Toledo
17 Show of smugness
18 Thunderclouds, perhaps
19 Put away
20 Astounded by how much weight you've gained?
23 Beach lotion letters
25 Born in France
26 Dirty looks
27 "Really!"
29 Little swabs
32 Actress Verdugo
33 "___ giorno!"
34 From ___ Z
37 Deprived of fast food chains?
41 "Help!"
42 Just-for-fun activity
43 Even if, briefly
44 Source
46 One offering securities
47 Pageant wear
50 Geologist's time
51 ___ Plaines, Ill.
52 Tireless in pursuit of weight control?
57 Hardly chivalrous
58 Pedestrian sign
59 Em and Polly
62 Son of Aphrodite
63 Lui's opposite
64 "Ciao!"
65 Bad impression?
66 Practically devoid of customers
67 Cravings of a sort

DOWN

1 Nincompoop
2 Tiny ___
3 Stretching may relieve it
4 Sandwich man?
5 Bill Clinton, e.g.
6 Exploratory spacecraft
7 Poor, as excuses go
8 Kaput
9 Birds take this
10 James and Jackson
11 Use a soapbox
12 Unselfish sort
13 Garden bagful
21 Get into a pool
22 High peak
23 Peels off
24 Salk's conquest
28 Compass heading
29 Berries buy, at a supermarket
30 Honky-___
31 Ltd., in the U.S.
33 Food for regular folks?
34 4.0 earners
35 [titter]
36 Signs of spoilage
38 Kind of shot
39 Lives it up
40 They, in Marseille
44 Most liberal
45 Loutish sort
46 Roth ___
47 Wiped out
48 Accustom
49 Building wing
50 Urged, with "on"
53 Sent packing
54 Mosaic piece
55 "To Live and Die ___"
56 Island feast
60 ___ Offensive
61 Sophs. in two years

by Seth A. Abel

ULYSSES

ACROSS

1 Lowlife snitch
4 Woman of distinction
8 With 67-Across, author of "Ulysses"
13 Catherine who was the last wife of Henry VIII
14 Sacked out
15 The chosen, socially
16 Tinted windows locale
17 Tax-exempt bond, briefly
18 Wife of 56-Across who said 69-Across
19 Setting for "Ulysses"
22 Aussie outlaw Kelly
23 Industrial pollutant
24 Ancestry
28 Journalist/author Rick
30 Egyptian sun god
32 Roman sun god
33 Resort island near Venezuela
35 Nice, as clothes
38 1904 date in "Ulysses"
41 Cord that you hope doesn't break
42 Bert who hosted "Tattletales"
43 "___ Over but the Shoutin'" (book by 28-Across)
44 Go south, as a market
46 Stand for a portrait
50 Not stick to the path
53 Part of r.p.m.
55 Some germ cells
56 Hero in "Ulysses"
59 Three-toed animal
62 Others, to Cicero
63 Aleutian island
64 Dwight's two-time challenger
65 In the mail
66 Dear, in a billet-doux
67 See 8-Across
68 Outfits
69 Last word of "Ulysses"

DOWN

1 Oakland athlete
2 Force mounted by Philip II
3 Setting for a Homeric epic
4 Curses
5 Gulf emirate
6 Carte du jour
7 Fit for the dinner table
8 Pack tightly
9 Single-handedly
10 Measure of thickness
11 Night school course: Abbr.
12 Oink pad?
13 Secondary strategy
20 "Same here"
21 Flowering shade tree
25 Kind of prof.
26 "Oh my ___!"
27 English cathedral city
29 Tattoo identification, maybe
31 Mexican silver mining center
34 Comfortable with
36 Reflected sound effect
37 "Orinoco Flow" singer
38 Composer Styne
39 The Runnin' Rebels of coll. sports
40 Overthrowing
41 Lousy
45 What's for dinner
47 Alleviate
48 Brings to mind
49 Politico Alexander from Tennessee
51 ___ artery
52 Hawk's home
54 Prunes, say
57 Food item sold in bars
58 Like some lingerie
59 ___ Mahal
60 Furor
61 Thickness

by Paula Gamache

ACROSS

1 Lobbying grps.
5 Bigot's comment
9 Skim, as soup
14 "___ Rhythm"
15 The Old Sod
16 Fred's dancing partner
17 Bass brass
18 It lacks roots
19 Baseball squads
20 Karl's confused query in Córdoba?
23 Masseur's target
24 "Washboard" body parts
25 Etna spew
28 Without proper planning
31 Jurist Fortas
34 Treat unfairly, slangily
36 Wish undone
37 Q.E.D. part
38 Colin's confused query in Como?
42 May event, for short
43 Now published
44 Actor Davis
45 Low isle
46 Pedal-to-the-metal sort
49 Suffix with racket
50 Place to sweat
51 Laudatory lyrics
53 Knut's confused query in Cannes?
61 Roswell crash victim, supposedly
62 Highlands tongue
63 Dizzy of the Gas House Gang
64 Bounded along
65 Walk like a sot
66 Hostile one
67 Chances upon
68 Order (around)
69 Marginal mark

DOWN

1 Nitty-gritty
2 Lago filler
3 Baseball's Georgia Peach
4 Bean's support
5 Add zing to
6 Demon of Semitic lore
7 Push
8 Scan
9 Waltzer's river
10 Touches up
11 Boggy places
12 Smart ___
13 Radio host John
21 Writer Loos
22 Packed away
25 Tasty jelly
26 Journalist Alexander
27 One in "another fine mess"
29 Sharp ridge
30 Boy in a Johnny Cash song
31 Pop up
32 Count in music
33 It'll knock you out
35 Succeed, as a proposal
37 Some rails
39 November stone
40 Cry's partner
41 Bridge authority
46 Shells out
47 Puts out
48 Rangers and Corsairs
50 Unwelcome forecast
52 They're jerked
53 Conceal, in a way
54 Relative of the yucca
55 Ready
56 Hop, skip or jump
57 Food item whose name appears on its side
58 Not own
59 Fill to surfeit
60 Contract into folds

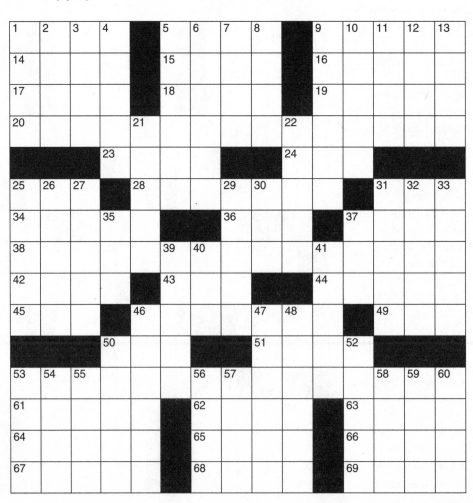

by Jim Goodsell

ACROSS

1 "Hardball" channel
6 Tim of "WKRP"
10 Actor McGregor
14 Car hitch-up
15 Best of theater
16 Put on a scale
17 Mic check #1
20 Coverage co.
21 Gets across?
22 Like a sad sack
23 Long, long time
24 Within: Prefix
26 Mic check #2
31 Like hawks and auks
32 Words to an
   "old chap"
33 Genetic letters
36 Fix up
37 One of the Jacksons
39 Utah national park
40 A no. that's good
   when under 3.00
41 Laundromat loss,
   maybe
42 A beatnik may
   beat it
43 Mic check #3
47 Minister to
48 Carry on
49 Burger King
   or The Gap
52 Call after a toss
54 Toward the rear
57 Mic check #4
60 ___ Sea, east of the
   Ustyurt Plateau
61 Italian wine town
62 Latish bedtime
63 Puts on
64 40-Across, e.g.
65 Campus buys

DOWN

1 "How ___?"
2 Impostor
3 Prefix with second
4 Bull's urging
5 Draw near
6 Move, as a picture
7 Shangri-la
8 Sort of
9 Patriotic org.
10 Heretofore
11 Diminish
12 Straddling
13 Eye of ___ (witches'
   brew need)
18 Straddling
19 Thurber's
   fantasizer
23 Slightly
25 Straight, at the bar
26 Broken, in a way
27 Constantly
28 1967 war locale
29 Sounds from pens
30 Certain gasket
34 Scrapped, at NASA
35 Before long
37 Sportscaster
   Madden
38 Conclusive trial
39 Type of court
   defense
41 Court reporter
42 One in charge
44 Photos
45 Like dusk
46 Something
   seen with the
   Virgin Mary
49 Election hanger-on?
50 Sub
51 Actor Rickman
53 Prov. bordering Mont.
54 Michael J. Fox's role
   on "Family Ties"
55 Cyclist's problem
56 Some gobblers
58 Suffers from
59 Vane dir.

by Brendan Emmett Quigley

ACROSS

1 High-testing group
6 Drill locale: Abbr.
10 Frisbee, e.g.
14 Huffs and puffs
15 High-priced ticket request
16 ___ family, including bassoons and English horns
17 Very inclined
18 Director Kazan
19 Claimant's claim
20 Flirt's Valentine's gift?
23 Cry after a thoughtful silence
26 ___ the day
27 Enter cautiously
28 One illegally using a handicapped space?
32 Times Sq., e.g., in N.Y.C.
33 Beach Boy Wilson
34 Prospecting bonanzas
36 A dispiritingly large amount of e-mail
37 Extended families
39 ___ West of "Batman"
43 Pale with fright
45 Sticker figure
46 Massage locale
49 www.eyeglasses.com?
52 Crafty
54 Madeira Mrs.
55 "Get the picture?"
56 1960 Terry-Thomas movie (and title of this puzzle)
60 Embroidered ltr., often
61 "Whip It" rock group
62 Grayish
66 Stridex target
67 Sign
68 Wax removers
69 Clutter
70 Rumpelstiltskin's output
71 Flower part

DOWN

1 Mil. go-getters?
2 Proceed after grace
3 Wichita-to-Omaha dir.
4 Potpourri
5 Headache helper
6 Pub container
7 Cherry ___
8 Not fer
9 Maze features
10 Dim bulbs, so to speak
11 Graceful birds
12 "Amen!"
13 Small-plane maker
21 Sister
22 Croupier's tool
23 Getaway stoppers, briefly
24 Heavenly strings
25 "Dite alla giovine," e.g.
29 ___ sutra
30 Steak cut
31 Saturn model
35 Hindu wrap
37 Messy dish to eat
38 Spy novelist Deighton
40 Lodgings, informally
41 Tummy trouble
42 Parcel (out)
44 Neglected neighborhood
45 Things to mind
46 Dr. Seuss character
47 Frolic
48 Diet doctor
50 Donny or Marie
51 "Rin Tin Tin" TV night: Abbr.
53 Honors grandly
57 Verne captain
58 First name in daredevils
59 Toy with a tail
63 Chill
64 Univ. figure
65 Designer monogram

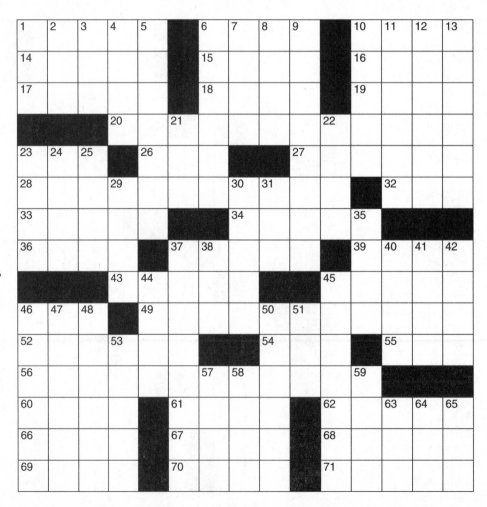

by Lee Glickstein and Nancy Salomon

ACROSS

1 "Poppycock!"
5 Iraqi port
10 Thompson of "Family"
14 Big name in oil
15 In-box contents
16 Wife, in legalese
17 Line to Penn Station
18 Sweater for the cold-blooded?
20 Cold-blooded idler?
22 TV extraterrestrial
23 Corrida cries
24 1983 Keaton title role
28 Microwave setting
30 Property receiver, in law
32 Latin 101 verb
33 Soaps, to soap operas, once
34 Cold-blooded dice roll?
38 Pit crew member
41 Salinger lass
45 Testified
46 English port
49 Tapir feature
50 Long, long time
51 Fictitious Richard
52 Cold-blooded children's play activity?
56 Cold-blooded fungi?
59 Samoan capital
60 Last of the Stuarts
61 Reason for a raise
62 Shape with a hammer
63 Stuff
64 Straws in the wind
65 Once, once

DOWN

1 Chaucerian verse form
2 1969 Mets victims
3 Napes
4 Gunpowder holder
5 Narcotic-yielding palms
6 Talisman
7 Calcutta wraps
8 Classic hotel name
9 ___ breve
10 Summer attire
11 Send packing
12 One of a Disney septet
13 Pairs holder?
19 Regal fur
21 Sticky stuff
25 Phone trigram
26 Key contraction?
27 ___ amis
29 Assume anew, as burdens
30 Barbary beast
31 Powell co-star in 1930's films
33 Jiffy
35 1598 edict city
36 "Wheel of Fortune" buy
37 A little butter?
38 Hosp. staffers
39 Velvet finish?
40 Navy noncom
42 Bass variety
43 Professors World Peace Academy group, informally
44 White-tie, say
46 Once-divided place
47 Homing pigeons' homes
48 Having one sharp
50 Prior to, in dialect
53 Air: Prefix
54 Feature of many a sympathy card
55 Get an eyeful
56 Put out
57 No longer divided
58 Collection suffix

by A. J. Santora

ACROSS

1 When doubled, a seafood entree
5 Is visibly frightened
10 Off one's trolley
14 "Yeah, right!"
15 Work ___
16 Pop's Brickell
17 Gigantic instrument?
19 "Take ___!" (track coach's order)
20 Holed up
21 First name in horror
22 Actress Sorvino
23 Instrument made in the lab?
27 Straits of ___
28 Tee follower?
29 Crew need
30 Set alight
33 Quattros, e.g.
37 Greet the day
39 Take your pick?
41 Federico of the Clinton cabinet
42 Touch up
44 Up
46 Early fifth-century year
47 Ridge of Homeland Security
49 Like some burgers
51 Instrument found at the Super Bowl?
56 Donald, to Dewey
57 Opposite of paleo-
58 Order of corn
59 "I'll be ___ of a gun!"
60 Missing instrument?
65 Ste. Jeanne ___
66 King of Thebes slain by Theseus
67 Inner: Prefix
68 January 1 song word
69 Surfer wannabe
70 Mail: Abbr.

DOWN

1 Shelley queen
2 "___ recall . . ."
3 Arrogant one's place
4 More uncertain
5 Chips' place
6 1955 merger grp.
7 Eric Clapton hit with a never-ending chorus
8 Flynn of "Captain Blood"
9 Dumpster emanation
10 Request to the Enterprise
11 Seat-of-the-pants performance
12 Papal wear
13 Calyx part
18 ___ one
23 Miner's filing
24 Binding exchanges
25 Magna ___
26 Roll-call call
27 "Watch out!"
31 P.C. part
32 When repeated, a cry of approval
34 U.S. citizen-to-be
35 The Dow, e.g.
36 Port ___ (Suez Canal city)
38 Door
40 1991 Grammy winner Cohn
43 Point
45 Keepsake
48 Good guy
50 Sanford of "The Jeffersons"
51 Thigh muscles
52 Take back
53 Squirrel's find
54 Old, but new again
55 Like unpopular umps
61 Mauna ___
62 Omega
63 Orch. section
64 Brillo rival

by Eric and Janinne Berlin

ACROSS

1 White House affair, maybe
5 Beyond's partner
10 Part of Latin 101 conjugation
14 ___ Bator
15 Measure from the elbow to the end of the middle finger
16 Results may do this
17 With 33-, 36- and 40-Across, American born 7/28/1929
19 Press
20 Hip bone
21 Vital
22 Actress Hayek
23 Boating mishap
24 Neighbor of a Vietnamese
26 Period of time
28 Gary's home: Abbr.
31 Periods of time
32 Off
33 See 17-Across
35 Hall of Fame QB Dawson
36 See 17-Across
37 Name that's an alphabet trio
40 See 17-Across
41 Modern medical grps.
42 Composer/writer Ned
44 Cable inits.
45 Ages and ages
46 Most blue
48 ___-mo
49 Right hands
50 New Deal inits.
53 Celebrity photographer Herb
56 Where D.D.E. went to sch.
57 Topper made popular by 17- and 36-Across
59 Retro phone feature
60 Laughing gas, for one
61 "Born Free" lioness
62 Lodges
63 Baseball datum
64 Part of CBS: Abbr.

DOWN

1 Kodak competitor
2 Mideast carrier
3 Reserved
4 Commission's task
5 Top-notch
6 Mail may be sent in this
7 Award for Tony Kushner
8 Like old records
9 Summer on the Seine
10 Wilbur or Orville Wright
11 Florida player
12 Bouquets
13 "Seduced" senator of film
18 Man in black?
22 Cry on a hog farm
25 During
26 "2001" mainframe
27 See red?
28 Structural members
29 Votes in Versailles
30 Kirsten of "Spider-Man"
34 Marble feature
36 Genuflection points
37 Without a hitch
38 Proverbial brickload
39 Seagoing letters
40 Trials
41 DNA structures
42 Granola ingredient
43 One who's "out"
46 Any of the Fahd ruling family
47 ___ 12 and 20
48 Angel's favorite letters
51 Dancer's exercise
52 13-Down player
54 Itar-___ news agency
55 E.R. order
57 Med. test result
58 ___ canto

by Mark Elliot Skolsky

ACROSS

1 Variety of guitar
6 Walked (on)
10 Touches with a live wire
14 Volcanic creation
15 Part to play
16 Jacques's steady
17 Make smooth
18 Crude org.
19 Mushroom cap part
20 Hand raiser's declaration
23 ___ de guerre
24 Far from haute cuisine
25 1945 John Wayne western
27 Hand raiser's shout
32 The Louisville Lip
33 Freedom from hardship
37 "Tell Laura ___ Her" (1960 hit)
40 Burrowing insect
41 "I mean it!"
42 Leeway
44 Not healthy
45 Hand raiser's cry
50 Fountain basin feature
53 Violinist Leopold
54 Yes, to 16-Across
55 Hand raiser's request
61 Girl in Lou Bega's "Mambo No. 5"
63 "Dies ___"
64 Confident way to solve crosswords
65 Not completely closed
66 "Don't look at me!"
67 Griffin of the N.B.A.
68 Bird that "at heaven's gate sings," in Shakespeare
69 Within the hour
70 Rough tools

DOWN

1 Stock market turns
2 Parliament city
3 Not piquant
4 Take back
5 Opera with "Ave Maria"
6 ___ l'oeil
7 Part of a climber's gear
8 Couturier Cassini
9 Figures out
10 Quick sidestep
11 Protein acid
12 Person who sits in front of a cabin
13 City famously visited by Martin Luther King Jr. in 1965
21 Motion picture angle: Abbr.
22 "Beyond the Sea" singer, 1960
26 Numbers game
27 Banshee's cry
28 "___ Enchanted" (2004 film)
29 Gasser
30 Ask for more issues
31 Beaver, e.g.
34 "Dream Children" essayist
35 Threshold
36 Peddle
38 Short biography
39 Body of good conduct
40 Hurry-scurry
43 Waifs
46 Adopt, as a pet
47 March sound
48 Harder to grasp
49 "Beverly Hills 90210" girl
50 Fable conclusion
51 Board used in "The Exorcist"
52 It was played by George Harrison
56 Suffix with sock
57 Denouncer of Caesar, 63 B.C.
58 Supports
59 Use scissors
60 Squeezes (out)
62 Torah holder

by Raymond Hamel

ACROSS

1 Govt. agency since 1949
4 They may be sordid
9 Early associate of Freud
14 Popular Quaker cereal
15 Eight-ish?
16 Sporty Japanese car
17 Marceau character
18 See 33-Across
19 Intimidate, with "out"
20 Lovable curmudgeon of 1970's TV
23 Excitement
24 Treetop nibbler
28 Brownstone front
32 Play the peeping Tom
33 With 18-Across, capital of the United Arab Emirates
36 Mustang site
38 A Turner
39 Noted rehab facility
43 End in ___
44 Bucks
45 Winter Chi. clock setting
46 Lassie, for one
49 Close-knit group
51 Patella
53 Majestic
57 "The Blue Dahlia" star
61 Wing it
64 Lose one's mind
65 Loire valley product
66 Something thrown for a loop?
67 Atlantic Ten school home
68 Ike's command, once: Abbr.
69 The Dow, e.g.
70 More sound
71 Easygoing

DOWN

1 Spoil
2 Prepare eggs in a way
3 Stray place: Abbr.
4 Sole-searching, maybe?
5 Suffer
6 Shot
7 No-no: Var.
8 Armrest?
9 Current measure
10 British P.M. before Gladstone
11 Put in position
12 List ender
13 Fan noise
21 Pinafore letters
22 Laotian money
25 Swiss capital
26 Conclusion
27 Formally approve
29 Gut reaction?
30 Blue Moon of baseball
31 Contender of 1992 and 1996
33 One way to be taken
34 Be assured of
35 Handy
37 Scent
40 Air
41 Mid second-century year
42 Home of Goose Bay
47 Solitary confinement cell, in slang
48 Ring locale
50 Slithery swimmer
52 Bounces on a stick
54 Court instrument
55 Japanese dog
56 Tanglewood site, in Massachusetts
58 One of Asta's owners
59 "___ the case"
60 Nursing home staff?
61 Clay, now
62 Rather in the news
63 Cause of many trips, once

by Alan Arbesfeld

ACROSS

1 Drug buster
5 Eight furlongs
9 Fishermen's pailfuls
14 1998 Sarah McLachlan hit
15 Double agent Aldrich
16 Sleep disorder
17 Fake cover stories
19 "Bad" for "good," e.g.
20 Dress with a flare
21 Stephen Foster classic
23 Back of the boat
25 Key of Beethoven's Symphony No. 7: Abbr.
27 Attacked with zeal
28 Not nerdy
30 Bikini blast, briefly
32 Stumblers' sounds
33 Get a program on the radio
35 Mars explorer
37 Homeric epic
38 Familiar Olympics chant
39 King protectors
43 Watch
45 Catch between bases, say
46 K.C.-to-Little Rock direction
48 Surveyors' calculations
50 ___ Stanley Gardner
51 Grand
53 Equine quipster
55 Airline to Amsterdam
56 Hermit
58 Omnium-gatherums
60 Running wild
61 Shocked response in conversation
65 Reaches over
66 Move, in Realtor-speak
67 Easy gait
68 "Roots" writer
69 Once, once upon a time
70 Hightailed it

DOWN

1 Get the drop on
2 Stir
3 Tubes on the table
4 Being the reason for
5 Best bro
6 Pooped person's plaint
7 Pacific ring
8 "Happy Motoring" company
9 Méphistophélès player in "Faust"
10 Valedictorian's feat, perhaps
11 Comparatively cockamamie
12 Court contest
13 "Contact" astronomer
18 ___ Fail (Irish coronation stone)
22 Modern viewer's option, briefly
23 When Hamlet sees his father's ghost
24 Cager's offense
26 Destination for many pilgrims
29 "Three's a crowd"
31 March master
34 Exiled Amin
36 Org. concerned with PCB's
38 Onetime TWA rival
40 Place with sawdust
41 Zero
42 Leaf holder
44 Gallivants
45 J. Alfred Prufrock poet
46 Himalayan guide
47 Mixer
49 Wakeup calls
51 Riffraff
52 Cracked
54 Performed
57 Fictional Jane
59 Barn birds
62 Donne's "done"
63 Big brute
64 Koppel of ABC

by Nancy Salomon and Levi Denham

Note: Each of the three theme answers below (20-, 36- and 54-Across) can be clued with the same three letters.

ACROSS

1 Chick on the piano
6 P.D.Q. in the I.C.U.
10 Casing
14 Ph.D. hurdle
15 Part of S.N.L.
16 Narrow way
17 Try to bite
18 Mental flash
19 Aboard
20 [See instructions]
23 Flamenco shout
24 Sushi selection
25 Comb stopper
27 Harangues
30 Toward the tail
32 Copacabana site
33 Youth
34 Dedicated lines?
35 Kennel sound
36 [See instructions]
41 Leave the scene
42 Satisfy the munchies
43 50-50, e.g.
44 Old discs
45 Orthodontist, for one: Abbr.
46 Calls the shots
50 Words of assistance
52 Sidekick
53 Cry of insight
54 [See instructions]
59 Cork's country
60 Confess
61 Camel caravan's stop-off
62 Tend the sauce
63 Victory goddess
64 Advil alternative
65 Caribbean and others
66 Rock radio pioneer Freed
67 Administered medicine

DOWN

1 Swindle
2 Yankee opponent
3 Cousin of an épée
4 Zing
5 Vino region
6 Covers with gunk
7 Kind of basin
8 State firmly
9 Sign of sorrow
10 "Wake of the Ferry" painter
11 Pocket protector?
12 Cabinet post since 1849
13 Opposite of paleo-
21 Ribbed
22 Follower's suffix
26 Barn section
28 Heaps
29 Letter from Greece
30 Flap
31 Productive
34 Frequently, in verse
35 "Whoopee!"
36 Healthy
37 Speed up
38 Ornamental vine: Var.
39 "___ Kapital"
40 What a person may become when kneeling
45 Society newbie
46 Obscure
47 Political movements
48 Prosper
49 Got fresh with
51 Mike who played Austin Powers
52 Lawrence Welk specialty
55 Sicilian hothead?
56 Come up short
57 Loathsome person
58 Sign of sanctity
59 Double curve

by Richard Silvestri

ACROSS

1 Holiday visitor, maybe
6 Sporty car, for short
10 Plum Nascar position
14 Western necktie?
15 Crashing sort
16 Hera's mother
17 Knew
20 Dish cooked in a pot
21 Trim, in a way
22 Key material
23 Ludwig Mies van der ___
25 Gospel writer
27 New
33 Prefix with arthritis
34 Forum greeting
35 Brought up
37 Mao's successor
38 Alistair who wrote "Ice Station Zebra"
42 Put away
43 Ex-D.C. baseballers
45 See 27-Down
46 Derby place
48 Nu
52 Rough tool
53 Kitchen flooring, for short
54 Scarecrow's composition
57 Viking's deity
59 Bubble wrap sounds
63 Gnu
66 Feels punk
67 Peace Nobelist Ducommun
68 2000 N.B.A. M.V.P.
69 Spymaster's worry
70 Rx amts.
71 Famous "hostess with the mostest"

DOWN

1 Poop
2 Seasonal air
3 Veg out
4 Fertility goddess
5 Chinese dynasty name
6 Homes
7 Like a Hail Mary pass
8 Woodstock phenomenon
9 1950's political initials
10 Poor Richard's Almanack item
11 "You gotta be kidding!"
12 Wolf's look
13 "Duck soup!"
18 Classic soft drink
19 Triathlete's need
24 Baseball's Blue Moon
26 Iris's place
27 With 45-Across, noted Arctic explorer
28 Bar order, with "the"
29 ___ Department
30 Novelist Carr
31 Wipe out
32 Dry out, informally
36 Prefix with god
39 Bellicose god
40 HOV lane users
41 It's inert
44 Berlin boulevard
47 Barbecuer's buy
49 Fancy marbles
50 Skips over
51 50's car features
54 Ponzi scheme, e.g.
55 Cream was one
56 Frank holder
58 Socially challenged sort
60 Reveals, in verse
61 Survey map
62 Ward of the screen
64 Rainy
65 Author Clancy

by Jim Conklin

ACROSS

1 Second in a series
5 Ship to remember
10 Saudi citizen
14 Singular person
15 Spirit
16 Showroom sample
17 S
20 Squab alternative
21 Shortstop of fame
22 Significant period
23 Started moving
27 Sea or way ending
29 Screenwriter James
30 Sister of Thalia
31 Sexy person
37 Scream or be rowdy, as a child
38 Strapped
39 Signature tune
44 Spill consequence
45 Solo for Renata Scotto
46 Sort of cuisine
47 Snaps again
52 Select
53 Skirt style
54 Schaffhausen's river
57 's
63 Sporting blade
64 Stockpile
65 Scoreboard postings
66 Series of legis. meetings
67 See eye to eye
68 Sour fruit

DOWN

1 Seckel's cousin
2 Single-named singer
3 Soothing, weatherwise
4 Site where trees are displayed
5 Start to function?
6 Sandy's sound
7 Swearing-in words
8 Scand. land
9 Sounds of hesitation
10 Stella who founded an acting conservatory
11 Send for information
12 Slay, in a way
13 Sick and tired
18 Soap may be found like this
19 Spoon-bender Geller
23 Scrooge's cry
24 Sense of self
25 Salon offering
26 Scale's top, sometimes
27 Skillful act
28 St. Louis sight
32 Still woolly
33 Similes' relatives
34 Stunning
35 Shorten, in a way
36 Sandberg of baseball
40 Stood no more
41 Smeltery input
42 "Seduction of the Minotaur" author
43 Station ration
47 Sprints
48 Split to unite
49 Speeders' penalties
50 Stud fees
51 Sun. talk
55 Spanish boy
56 Seneca's being
58 "So that's it!"
59 Slot filler in a gearwheel
60 Seaman
61 Spleen
62 Shelley work

by Richard Silvestri

ACROSS

1 European capital of 2½ million
5 Part of N.A.A.C.P.: Abbr.
9 Business school subj.
13 Mouth site?
15 Endangered goose
16 Prefix with magnetic
17 Love
18 Nursery offering
19 Certain rug worker
20 Like LP's
22 Latin 101 verb
23 Appropriate
26 Comic strip set in Coconino County
28 Messes up
29 Article in Die Zeit
30 Around
33 Hosp. picture
34 Not worth debating
35 Birthplace of Hans Christian Anderson
36 Pioneer in vaccination
38 Rampaging
39 Watching
40 Copycat
41 Computer units: Abbr.
42 Commercial prefix with foam
43 Careered
44 U.S.S. ___, ship in 2000 news
45 1933 RKO hit
47 0 letters
48 Plant with pods
50 Doesn't ignore
52 Crawl (with)
53 "Beetle Bailey" dog
54 "Me, too"
58 San ___, Italy
59 Mouselike animal
60 Order beside a car door
61 About half of binary code
62 Milk dispensers
63 Certain race . . . or a cryptic title to this puzzle

DOWN

1 Spectra maker
2 Polit. designation
3 "Xanadu" rock group
4 Greeting card features
5 Frontal, to an anatomist
6 Reynaldo, to Polonius
7 Blessed act?
8 Not self-sufficient
9 Wagered
10 Classic comedy figure
11 "___ bien!"
12 Reason for an R rating
14 Business card abbr.
21 Barely make
23 Presto and others
24 Out-and-out
25 It opened its first store in Winston-Salem, N.C., in 1937
27 1950's–60's Hungarian premier János
31 In working order
32 Less wordy
34 Physics particle
35 Tense
37 "1000 Oceans" singer, 1999
38 Some women's shoe features
40 Peter or Paul, but not Mary
43 One way to the top?
44 Baby
46 Boxing need
48 Other: Sp.
49 Neato
51 Bother
55 Downed
56 Bit of time: Abbr.
57 Publicity

by Michael Shteyman

ACROSS

1 Often-told truths
5 ___ facto
9 Tricky shot
14 Racer Luyendyk
15 Gardener's purchase
16 Some saxes
17 Lava geese
18 It's passed on
19 Contents of some John Cage compositions
20 Start of a question
23 Adjusts
24 Big ___
25 Whomps, briefly
28 Old Mideast combine: Abbr.
29 John Dean, to Nixon
32 Sure way to lose money
34 "Gosh!"
35 Ruined
37 A star may have one
38 Middle of the question
41 Place
43 Discernment
44 Common ratio
46 Sample
50 Chamber piece?
49 Dispatched
51 Monk's title
52 Driver's aid: Abbr.
54 Track racer
56 End of the question
60 Like workhorses
62 Arcade name
63 V.I.P.'s opposite
64 It's passed on
65 Compelled
66 Wading bird
67 Ottawa-born singer/songwriter
68 Turned up
69 Cry that might be appropriate at this point in the puzzle

DOWN

1 Retreat
2 Passage between buildings
3 Bingo announcement
4 "Toodles!"
5 Mirage
6 Magician's sound effect
7 Draped dress
8 Things to be read
9 Om, e.g.
10 Cream ingredient
11 Malodorous pest
12 Coded message
13 Language suffix often seen in crosswords
13 Compass dir. often seen in crosswords
21 African grazer
22 Put words in someone's mouth?
26 Anthem contraction
27 Platform place: Abbr.
30 Is hip to
31 1995 country hit "Someone ___ Star"
33 "Dagnabbit!"
35 Latched
36 Affectedly dainty, in England
37 Extinct Namibian shrub genus: Var.
38 Coordinated effort
39 Like some seats
40 First
41 Trip producer
42 W.W. II Pacific battle site, for short
44 Appropriate
45 Blazing
47 Cat
48 Desired response to "Take my wife . . . please!"
50 Open-sided shelter
53 Perfume source
55 Noted archer
57 What a germ may become
58 Good sign
59 Ticks off
60 Hearst kidnapping grp.
61 Dear

by Patrick Merrell

ACROSS

1 Séance happening
4 Wows, in comedy
9 Pub decoration
14 Put one past
15 Out of port
16 Home without a refrigerator
17 Post office delivery: Abbr.
18 Represent
19 Israeli party
20 "Whatever!"
23 Chores
24 Active sorts
25 King's home
28 Roman emperor after Galba
29 Cook, as beans
30 Premier under Mao
31 Union with 2.7 mil. members
32 Out of shape
33 "Look, ma, no cavities!," e.g.
34 Padlocks, say
38 Finnish architect Alvar ___
40 Irish girl's name
41 "The Paper Chase" topic
44 Capital south of Chernobyl
45 Sleep: Prefix
47 Memorable kicker
48 MGM motto word
49 "Ditto"
50 Name that means "beloved"
51 Sales rep's need
53 Company famous for Centipede and Battlezone
56 Tangle
57 Muscle car
58 "Eat!"
59 "Don't ___ soul!"
60 Modern: Ger.
61 Astronauts experience it
62 Computer bulletin board administrator
63 Most Mets games are on it: Abbr.

DOWN

1 Pet food brand name
2 Get going
3 Grocery items
4 Doesn't run
5 Bananas
6 Top of the class
7 2004 . . . with a hint to the starts of 20-, 34- and 51-Across
8 Back-talker
9 Red-haired soprano
10 Weekend-starting cry
11 Member of an order
12 Slip in a pot
13 Go-ahead
21 Bout stopper, briefly
22 Trick ending
25 Eighth-century king
26 Tel. book contents
27 Plumber's piece
29 Hi-___ monitor
30 It's chaos
32 Pal
33 Encouraging French word
35 Off-road transport, briefly
36 Golfer from South Africa
37 Sixth-century year
38 Alias
39 One mode of travel
42 On one's toes
43 Eliminate
45 Certain smoke signal
46 Keats and others
47 Kodak print
49 Seeking damages
50 "It's ___!" ("Simple!")
51 Vivacity
52 Prairie building
53 Wood shaper
54 20-20, e.g.
55 Cabinet dept.

by Roy Leban

ACROSS

1 Ready to work
8 "Now where ___?"
12 Kennedy adviser
13 End ___ era
14 Start of a definition of "elbonics" (a word that doesn't exist but should)
16 Greek god sometimes pictured as blindfolded
17 Novelist Seton
18 Each
20 Delighted reaction
21 Gathering place: Abbr.
23 Delilah player in "Samson and Delilah"
25 Definition, part 2
29 Israel-based bank
30 Kind
31 Kind of history
33 Actor Herbert
34 Definition, part 3
39 1961 Literature Nobelist ___ Andric
40 Drill
41 "___ fallen . . ."
42 "Siddhartha" author
44 Definition, part 4
49 Oil worker?
51 Alway
52 Cry of dismay, in poetry
53 Roll maker?
54 Came down
57 Token look-alike
58 End of the definition
62 Some bills
63 Do some stock speculating
64 Station name in England
65 How "Waltzing Matilda" is to be played

DOWN

1 Holiday cheer?
2 Cholers
3 Confederate
4 "Wheel of Fortune" request
5 C, alternatively
6 Not very profitable
7 "A kind of praise": John Gay
8 Try to win a hand
9 House with a steep roof
10 Caesar Park International Airport site
11 Sell out, in a way
12 Kind of vote
15 Proverb ending?
16 Have something
19 Choice
21 Former name of Sulawesi
22 Ginza locale
24 Everywhere
26 Teledyne Water ___
27 One keeping one's own company
28 Work unit
32 Blazing
34 Holy war
35 Make too much of
36 Hollywood studio department
37 Something that may be rolled over: Abbr.
38 Court matter
43 Paul and Carly
45 CH₃
46 The Rockets of the Mid-American Conference
47 Accustom
48 Holiday quaff
50 ___ chi ch'uan
55 Castor's mother
56 Big World Cup power: Abbr.
57 Diva, e.g.
59 Letters on a brandy bottle
60 Season in Haiti
61 Big World Cup power: Abbr.

by David J. Kahn

ACROSS

1 Six-time Best
   Actress nominee
5 Score
10 Move slowly
14 Onetime newsman ___
   Abel
15 Flip over
16 Air-cooled
   machine gun
17 Cave explorer's need
18 Where explorer John
   Cabot was born
19 Take to mean
20 Road repair tools
23 Barbecue items
24 Test for some srs.
25 Program begun
   under Kennedy
28 "Thou pleasing,
   dreadful thought,"
   to Addison
33 Western hoopster,
   for short
34 Gillette product
35 Norma Webster's
   middle name
36 Shrink
40 Ike's command
   in W.W. II
41 "Armageddon"
   author
42 Film producer
   credited with
   discovering Sophia
   Loren
43 Woody Allen–like
46 Snags
47 Two-time U.S. Open
   winner
48 "No problem!"
49 Classic geocentric
   theory
57 Certain sitar piece
58 Cant
59 "___ Road" (1999
   Oprah's Book Club
   selection)
60 ___ house (down-home
   music site)

61 TV exec Arledge
62 Tennis score
63 Silent parts of
   20-, 36- and 49-Across
64 Schlepper
65 R-rated, maybe

DOWN

1 Sustenance for
   a sea urchin
2 Joie de vivre
3 White coat
4 Plato's ideal
5 Where Jonny
   Moseley won a
   skiing gold medal
6 "Golden Boy"
   playwright
7 N.B.A.'s Kukoc

8 Bigmouthed critter
9 Helmets and such
10 Rockne player
11 Former Dodger
   Hershiser
12 Enthusiasm
13 Periods
21 Nursery buy
22 Elementary letters?
25 Town near Snowmass
26 Mail, in Marseille
27 "Shame ___!"
28 Reason to be good
29 ___ chic
30 Figure skater
   Slutskaya
31 Toothsome
32 Himalayan sightings
34 Longfellow's bell town

37 Fool
38 Silly trick
39 Guiding light
44 Circuit breakers
45 Adjective
   sometimes used
   with 60-Across
46 1970's Plymouth
48 Bakery treat
49 Brace
50 Mending stuff
51 Blackguard
52 Buck chaser?
53 Jerome Kern's "___
   Love"
54 Cry before
   applause
55 Pop singer Carmen
56 Countless

by Alan Arbesfeld

ACROSS

1 Sidepiece
5 Sockeroo
10 Some noncoms: Abbr.
14 "Gewehr ___!" (German military order)
15 Befuddled
16 "American Pie" actress Reid
17 Michael Jordan or Dr. J
19 "Ohhhh . . ."
20 Big Twelve powerhouse
21 Former beau or belle
23 Type spec: Abbr.
25 Opera ___
26 Workshop fixture
30 Opposite of whole
33 Film director Resnais
34 Dial-up ___
36 10¢ picture
37 Actress Sorvino
38 Title character of TV's "The Pretender"
39 Female singer who was Grammy's 1985 Best New Artist
40 Wash out to sea
41 Clubs, say
42 Steps over a fence
43 Tiara
45 Metric measures of area
47 Dance from Cuba
49 "Phooey!"
50 Person with a figure like Olive Oyl
53 "Uh-uh"
57 Apple variety
58 Interactive part of some Web pages
60 Have some fancy provisions?
61 Edit
62 Cousin of an org.
63 Stops: Abbr.
64 Opera that climaxes with a firing squad
65 "Toodles!"

DOWN

1 Attic buildup
2 "Take a Chance on Me" group
3 Lowdown
4 Capital on the Paraná
5 Dances to "Cali Pachanguero," e.g.
6 Parts of a range: Abbr.
7 Regarding
8 Barkers
9 Set
10 Leader born in Georgia
11 Soiree
12 Disneyland sight
13 Convenience for an ed.
18 Grow dark
22 Born in
24 Truman's Missouri birthplace
26 Docile, now
27 Suspect eliminator
28 Title girl of a 1966 pop hit
29 Goodness
31 Confuse
32 Ashes, e.g.
35 Administered, as medicine
38 Big flier
39 Not change
41 Burlap material
42 Barber's accessory
44 Knuckleheads
46 Home of six N.H.L. teams
48 Memorable mission
50 Sellers' solicitations
51 Send out
52 Abbr. after some telephone numbers
54 "Casablanca" role
55 "___ la vie"
56 Peak near the Gulf of Catania
59 Mandela's onetime org.

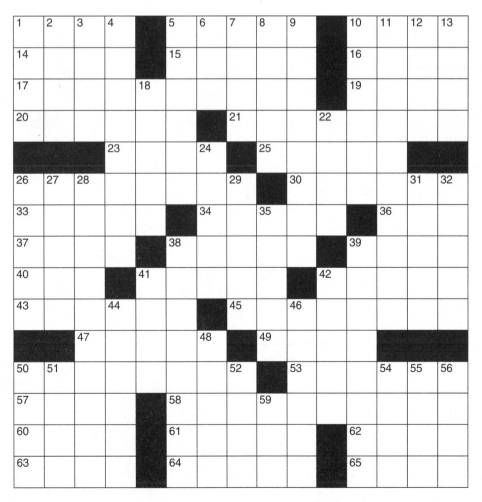

by Craig Kasper

ACROSS

1 Film, in Variety
4 Pant
8 Neighbor of Orlando
14 Call ___ day
15 What un lago holds
16 Card game for two
17 Like some memoirs
19 Bad news from a credit card company
20 Patron saint of goldsmiths
21 Have the lead
23 Outdated
24 Wind-borne deposits
26 Hindu incarnation
28 Pressured
30 Musical aptitude
33 High nests
36 Insult, slangily
37 Goya's "Duchess of ___"
38 Porter classic
40 Close cousins
42 "Come here often?," e.g.
43 Queue after Q
45 Certain foundation
46 "Evil Woman" band, for short
47 Humors
49 Chicago university
50 Like some physical tests
54 Creepy one?
57 Caged
59 Beak
60 Playoffs
62 Abandon
64 Handsome youth
65 Architect Saarinen
66 Used
67 1973 Peace Nobelist
68 Lozenge
69 ___ in Thomas

DOWN

1 Computer bit
2 ___-Greek
3 Birchbark
4 Hood's gun
5 Wrinkles, say
6 Harem keeper
7 Chitchat
8 Checked, as a box
9 Bygone deliverer
10 Estate
11 Hosp. testing techniques
12 Announcements from the cockpit, briefly
13 Hard to hold
18 Can't stand
22 Plant root
25 "Did You Ever ___ Dream Walking?" (1933 hit)
27 Themes
29 Off the mark
30 Lodge group
31 Rose's love, on Broadway
32 Carry on
33 Mandrel
34 Pianist Gilels
35 Splitsville
37 Dragging on the shore
39 Bar at the bar
41 Part of N.B.
44 Sent before e-mail
47 Sheep gatherer
48 Person with binoculars
49 Chinese weight unit
51 Unpaid servant
52 Refuges
53 Yorkshire city
54 Tunisian port once a stronghold for Barbary pirates
55 Spiders' nests
56 Soon
58 Corrida beast
61 Lith., once
63 "Alley ___"

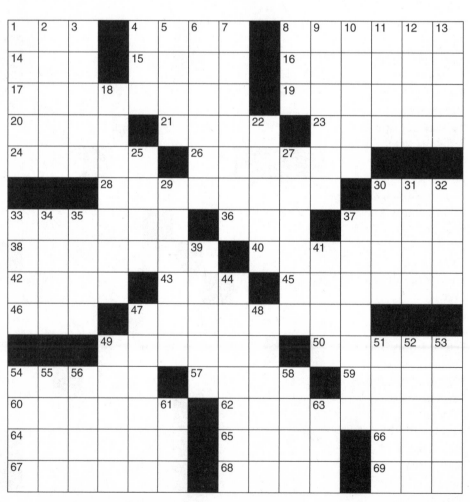

by Alfio Micci (1918–2004)

ACROSS

1 Musically detached: Abbr.
5 Capital examiners, briefly
9 Fairy tale brother
14 Bleeper's target
15 See 32-Across
16 Asian currency
17 Psychic's furniture?
20 Beast of burden
21 Gets a move on
22 Something big in front of the sofa?
26 Bowls
27 Laugh sound
28 Barrett, formerly of Pink Floyd
31 Madrid mousers
32 With 15-Across, a noted London theater
34 Chiang ___-shek
35 Vamooses
36 Plus ___ (theme of this puzzle)
37 Big name in sneakers
38 Richmond-to-Virginia Beach dir.
39 Breakfast item
40 "Left ___ own devices . . ."
41 Like a lobster
42 Ingredient of black bottom pie
43 One way to sort a list
44 Savings of a German opera star?
47 Disinclined
50 Auxiliaries
51 Two features of a hurried golf game?
56 The least bit
57 Helen's mother
58 180° turns, slangily
59 Virile
60 Helen's land
61 See 47-Down

DOWN

1 Covering for a bald spot
2 ___ chi (martial art)
3 Off-road goer, for short
4 Mexican-Americans
5 Shinnies
6 Cartoonist's drawing
7 White, informally
8 Sabbath msg.
9 Freezer locale
10 Buzz
11 ___ facto
12 Come across
13 1986 World Series champs
18 Grannies
19 Herr Schindler and others
22 Blade
23 Poker phrase
24 Checked for accuracy
25 One without manners
28 Top of the Alps?
29 Washington city
30 Gas station choice
32 Believer's belief
33 Way in Québec
36 Some early 20th-century French artists
37 Matter of little importance
39 Irascible
40 Supercompetitive
43 Down time
44 Dryly amusing
45 Having more reason
46 Friendly term of address
47 First resident of 61-Across
48 Ars longa, ___ brevis
49 Hunter of fiction
52 PC key
53 "If only ___ listened . . ."
54 View finder?
55 Fig. in identity theft

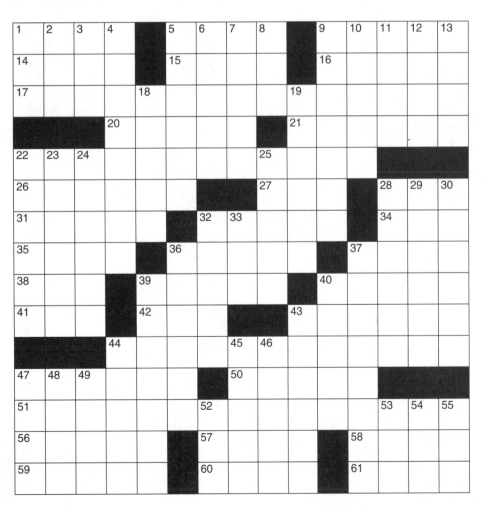

by Manny Nosowsky

Note: The circled square has two answers.

ACROSS

1 Mandlikova of tennis
5 Narrow
9 Cold response?
14 Any of the Beatles, once
15 Rolling rock
16 Language akin to Tahitian
17 Kind of system
19 Ones quick with a line?
20 Washington V.I.P.'s
22 Secretary, e.g.
23 Sci. facilities
24 Antiknock fluid
26 Obsolescent suffix
27 Mr. Bumble's position in "Oliver Twist"
30 Verb with thou
33 Cronus or Oceanus
35 Salad option
37 Cause for swearing
42 Band
43 "The Brady Bunch" girl
44 Milk source
45 Danger signal on the prairie
48 "Caught ya!"
51 Paper towel hawker, in old TV ads
53 Mitchum competitor
55 Ragamuffin
57 Prior to the 20th Amendment, what 20-Across would do on 37-Across, or when they would do it
61 Of an old empire
63 Like Congress
64 Limelight milieu
65 Turkish chiefs
66 In any case
67 Sighed (for)
68 Hand-over-mouth reaction
69 Dry

DOWN

1 One with a pad, maybe
2 Trims
3 At least
4 Party desirables
5 Declined
6 Mennonite decoration
7 Former Wall Street insider Boesky
8 Fountain order
9 Org. for an OB/GYN
10 One who's left holding the bag
11 Old country, maybe
12 Meteor materials
13 Pen sound
18 "___ Autumn" (Woody Herman hit)
21 N.L. Central team: Abbr.
25 Biblical king
27 A.C. letters
28 Stalk outgrowth
29 Put on ___
31 VCR maker
32 Lord's Prayer pronoun
33 Primitive percussion instrument
34 Roles in "Frankenstein" movies
36 Even one
37 Harbor problem
38 When, for an eager beaver
39 Cheese type
40 Dusk-___-dawn
41 Chemical suffix
46 "Fire" preceder
47 It gets in hot water
48 Achieve success
49 One trying to run from home
50 Cling
52 Adult
53 A continent: Abbr.
54 37-Across oaths, e.g., or 37-Across parades follow them
55 Trace
56 Oppositionist
58 Capital occupied by the Germans in 1941
59 Figureheads?
60 Lock securer
62 "The Simpsons" neighbor

by Patrick Merrell

ACROSS

1 Marking on an old MIG
5 Some degs.
8 Item thrown on a barbecue
13 Part
14 ___ Vista
16 Team subset
17 Certain Protestant
19 They get into jams
20 Santa's wife?
22 Lots
23 Once popular street liners
24 Marina sight
26 Architecture critic Huxtable and others
27 I.C.U. test
30 Library holding
31 Inlets
32 "The Egg ___"
33 Utility's advice to an excavator?
36 Yank, e.g.
37 It comes from une tête
38 Knife brand
39 Bowl features, for short
40 Kind of mark
41 Western Australia's capital
42 Round part
43 Host
44 Make attractive requests?
50 Region famous for the blues
51 Infinite
52 Oil holder
53 Miss. neighbor
54 Writer Murdoch
55 Dentist's advice
56 Understand
57 Word in many business names

DOWN

1 "Phooey!"
2 Scoop holder
3 Cut short
4 Director of exercises, in brief
5 ". . . And God Created Woman" star, 1956
6 Unfamiliar
7 Cartoonist Drake
8 Whence the line "Thy word is a lamp unto my feet"
9 Blues
10 1984 Peace Nobelist
11 ___ Ski Valley (western resort)
12 QB's gains
15 Precede
18 Pregame ritual
21 Conflict
24 Produce
25 High points
26 Broadcast
27 Opposite of vote down
28 Head of Hollywood
29 1970's–80's singer Vannelli
30 Group known for pranks, in short
31 Steer elsewhere
32 Showy bloom
34 Cyclist
35 Give a waiver
40 Floral envelope parts
41 "The Scarlet Letter" woman
42 Digital data
43 Carry ___ (sing on pitch)
44 Stamp
45 Additionally
46 Low digits
47 Architect Saarinen
48 A ___ apple
49 Flat tire indicator
50 Telephone trio

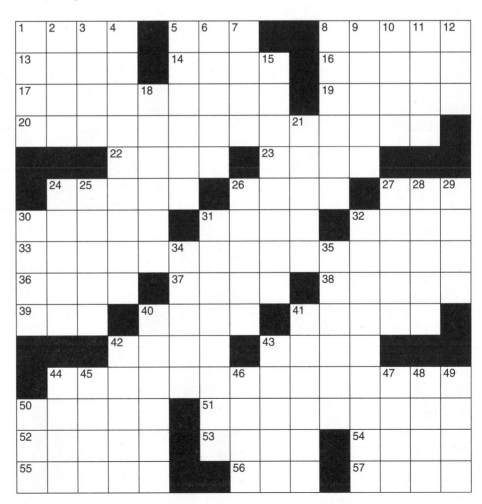

by Jeremy Thomas Paine

ACROSS

1 Run up
6 Building block
11 It's a mess
14 Range orphan
15 Oscar winner Zellweger
16 "This ___ shall pass"
17 Hippo tail?
18 Zoo for newborns?
20 Ceremonial drumstick?
22 Suffix with sermon
23 Stretch out
24 "A Taste for Death" author
26 Fall behind in a race
31 Police blotter abbr.
32 Best friend's dinner, maybe
33 Musical selection
36 Racing initials
39 Liquid ___ (refrigerant)
40 By hook or by crook, e.g.
41 Plains tribe
42 Camera ___ (film festival prize)
43 Pounding tool
44 Folk singer Seeger
45 Cable giant
47 Wizard
49 1950's Firedomes
53 "Charge" missing from 18-, 20-, 55- and 61-Across, and 11- and 28-Down
54 "Wishing won't make ___"
55 Plum permit?
61 Popular pen pitcher?
63 Scamp
64 Quirk
65 Soccer great Maradona
66 Oil holder
67 When Can. celebrates Thanksgiving
68 Sound some strings
69 Nations Unies members

DOWN

1 Extra: Abbr.
2 Extra
3 Like a kid at the circus
4 Buck
5 Deem appropriate
6 Florence's river
7 Unsuccessful candidate in the 2004 primaries
8 Ahead of the pack
9 Amish growth
10 Sushi stock
11 Actuary?
12 Nutty cake
13 Couples
19 Point on a line graph
21 Bottom, slangily
25 Cookie holder
26 Domain
27 Blue Bonnet, e.g.
28 Athlete worshipers?
29 Some spa mixtures
30 Issues
34 Single-edged knife
35 First name in cooking
37 Lug
38 Equal
41 International trade place
43 S.F. hours
46 Nitwit
48 Make do
49 Mark of conformity?
50 Work ___
51 Footnote abbr.
52 So-called "cradle of civilization"
56 Sauce brand
57 ___-Penh
58 The rain in Spain
59 Tallow source
60 Some volleyball hits
62 Bar-goers' needs

by Lee Glickstein and Nancy Salomon

ACROSS

1 "Come to ___"
5 Second-highest peak in the Cascades
11 Brown, for one
14 Big production
15 Lethargy
16 J.F.K. overseer
17 Lean and tough
18 Poke holes in
19 Army fig.
20 One who went to school in Middletown, Conn.
23 Blue part of a map
24 "Sure!"
25 WB show named for its star
28 Unite
29 It's stranded
32 First name in Communism
33 Actress Milano of "Charmed"
36 Kitchen supervisor, sometimes
37 Like the 1995 film "Sense and Sensibility"
40 Quarterback Phil
41 Dressed like Cinderella
42 "The Magic Flute" parts
43 Go on and on
44 Sei halved
47 ___ Station
48 Jennifer Lopez album "J to ___ LO!"
51 Whitish
53 It's based in Tripoli
57 Ruckus
59 Slight, in a way
60 Miles off
61 Remembrance Day mo.
62 Activity in which nothing is going on?
63 Drew (near)
64 Anger, with "off"
65 Hits the 5 and 10, say
66 Place for a pad

DOWN

1 Huddle
2 For one
3 Puckered
4 Refuges
5 Not leave home
6 Many a gardener
7 Set forth
8 Garden tool
9 Add
10 Province
11 In case it's called for
12 Hoover, e.g., informally
13 N.B.A.'s ___ Ming
21 Like a Möbius strip
22 Timed sporting events
26 Spanish newborn
27 Tatyana of "Fresh Prince of Bel Air"
30 Big Apple inits.
31 ___ Spumante
32 Its home is on the range
33 Stylish suit
34 D.C. V.I.P.
35 "Not ___ eye . . ."
37 Desperate
38 Romantic Sammy Cahn/Jule Styne song
39 Sheep's cry
40 Easy mark
44 1981 thriller about a stalker
45 Call again?
46 Big part of an order
48 Binding
49 Odyssey or Passport
50 To have, in Paris
52 Kiss
54 Trash sites
55 Language of the British Isles
56 Radiation units
57 Fire ___
58 Forest female

by David Liben-Nowell and Ryan O'Donnell

ACROSS

1 One of a migrating herd
4 Dance related to the cha-cha
9 Area of South Africa
14 Not be alert
15 Simmering, perhaps
16 Wear
17 Exerciser's target
18 *Apollo 17 was the last one
20 *Let me make one thing perfectly clear," e.g.
22 Means of detection
23 ___ al-Fayed, friend of Princess Diana
24 U.S.P.S. cargo: Abbr.
25 Weak
27 *Buckeye beauty
31 Was artificially cooled, for short
32 Improvise
33 College sweater letter
34 Black, in poetry
35 *"If only!"
37 Pitch
38 Set-to
39 Bender
40 C.I.A. director under Clinton and Bush
41 *Get a closeup of
43 Units of capacitance
44 Roy portrayed in "Angels in America"
45 Portia to Brutus, e.g.
46 Cause for a blessing
48 *Lottery player's happy shout
52 *Meat loaf recipe instruction
54 Keats subject
55 Make up (for)
56 ___ can of worms
57 Blood-typing abbr.
58 Some KFC orders
59 Having a little kick
60 Old White House inits.

DOWN

1 Chew on
2 Collars
3 How the answers to this puzzle's starred clues all appear
4 Like a song of lament
5 Oxygen-deprived
6 14 years before the Battle of Hastings
7 One in charge of a ship's rigging
8 Cries of pain
9 This year's recruits, figuratively
10 "Gunsmoke" star
11 Animation figure
12 Just ___ on the map
13 Wallace who wrote "Ben-Hur"
19 Thin strips
21 Subject of a Donne quote
24 Neeson of "Nell"
25 Irish P.M. Bertie
26 Queen Amidala's home in "Star Wars" films
27 Hollywood bigwig Michael
28 Like the answers to this puzzle's starred clues
29 Looks embarrassed
30 Doesn't handle pressure well
35 Boo follower
36 In a bit
37 Shore bird
39 Change for a Jefferson
40 Airport route
42 Book of hexagrams
43 Irate
46 Against
47 Certain cap source
48 Palm for thatching
49 Yokemates
50 TV neigh-sayer?
51 "Picnic" playwright
52 Dated
53 Word with waste and want

by Byron Walden

ACROSS

1 Alphabetical trio
4 Advance, slangily
8 Bush and others
14 Warranty regis. info
16 Full-scale
17 Start of a resolution by comedian Steven Wright
18 "___ never deceives us; it is always we who deceive ourselves": Rousseau
19 Unmoved
20 Cleaning agent
21 Respond to
22 507, on a slab
24 Little more than
25 Uncle Jorge, e.g.
26 Comment by the work-weary
27 Law office employees, informally
28 More quaggy
31 2000 Richard Gere title role
32 Middle of the resolution
35 Joule fraction
36 Piece maker
39 Pasty-faced
42 ___ River, N.J.
43 Traffic-stopping org.?
44 Plenty mad, with "off"
45 Speaker's name?
46 Hex
48 Losing it?
50 Esteem
52 ___ income
53 End of the resolution
55 The big chill
56 Al Franken, for one
57 Grammy winner Santana
58 River of Flanders
59 Good things to rack up: Abbr.

DOWN

1 Uncanny ability
2 Woman's name from Latin for "happiness"
3 Benefactors
4 Ballet slipper material
5 Novel idea
6 Spending according to plan
7 Big digit
8 Polynesian porch
9 The first "A" of A. A. Milne
10 Action just before a war
11 Carpenter's tool
12 Show of lights
13 Cordwood measures
15 Not ___ many words
20 Sandwich maker's brand
21 Impersonal banker
23 Shrews
26 Wind chimes sound
27 Old hands
29 Call in a hurry
30 Honker
31 Retreats
33 Umpteen
34 Off-itinerary jaunt
37 Bony fish
38 "2001" processor
39 Like the modern age
40 New York's ___ Lake
41 Tumble
42 One in a stroller
45 Elaine of "Seinfeld"
46 Trail left by an animal
47 Sound from a Burmese
49 Othello foe
51 One-named supermodel
53 Prayer possessive
54 Scale amts.

by Elizabeth C. Gorski

ACROSS

1 Pinafore letters
4 Loony
8 ___ valve
14 Wine cask wood
15 Repeat after me?
16 Intoxicated
17 Kids' "communication" toys
20 Is repentant
21 "What a shame"
22 Chop (off)
23 Sierra ___
24 Makes an offer
25 ___ on thick
27 "Citizen ___"
28 Nest eggs, briefly
29 Like some women's dresses
30 Film director Stanley
32 Proceeds
33 N.Y.C. subway inits.
36 Configuration of six places in this puzzle's answer
38 Family docs
39 Like most table salt
41 Scoop holders
43 Coercer
44 Cottage site
45 Big mouths
49 Pop-ups, e.g.
50 Slant
51 Gift getter
52 "Johnny ___"
53 Was trilling
54 Oklahoma athlete
55 Lovelorn group
58 Infatuated with
59 Mine, to Monet
60 Egg warmer
61 Come out
62 Odd look
63 "You bet!"

DOWN

1 Something brewing
2 Strand
3 Like some knees
4 Asks for alms
5 Make a scene?
6 1993 film that had Oscar's Best Actress and Best Supporting Actress
7 Recovering patients consume them
8 Early Cosby series
9 Like one in a series
10 "You just missed her!"
11 Pesky
12 "Go, man, go!"
13 Some board members: Abbr.
17 ___ vaccine
18 Maiden name preceder
19 Sci-fi figures
24 Afghan or Tibetan
25 River barrier
26 Ball-bearing group
28 ___ self
29 Pasta choice
31 Slimes
32 Cons
33 Tick off
34 Machine shop area
35 Poet Rich who wrote "Diving Into the Wreck"
37 March Madness feature
40 Alcoholic product popularized in the 90's
42 Kissy-faced
44 Like regal succession
46 American Shakers founder
47 Tiny tots
48 Dweller along the Morava River
50 "Poppycock!"
51 Affairs
53 New Year's Eve word
54 Arouse
55 Big: Abbr.
56 Keep a record of
57 Spawn

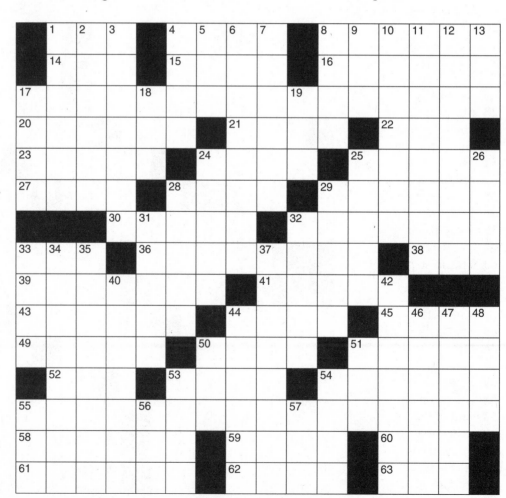

by Manny Nosowsky

ACROSS

1 Oil company acronym
5 Univ. dorm supervisors
8 Opening word?
14 One receiving orders
15 Dug in
17 First line of a couplet pertinent to this puzzle
19 Prefix with sex
20 War story
21 Word with buff or buffa
22 Guiding light
24 "I ___ you!"
26 Many a drive-thru feature
27 Failing grades
28 Great Laker
32 It's good for the teeth
36 Stout
37 Raft material
38 Poison warning
39 Greenfly, e.g.
41 Magazine accompanier
42 Chemical substance that hastens aging
45 Boom support
47 Mary ___ Evans (George Eliot's real name)
48 Sound investments, for short
49 Old Dodge
51 Buckeyes
55 It's a wrap
58 Start of a children's rhyme
60 Baby's first word
61 End of the couplet
64 "Really?"
65 Costa ___, Calif.
66 One of Paul Revere's message options
67 China's Sun Yat-___
68 Starts (off)

DOWN

1 Misbehave
2 Zoo heavyweight
3 Rhodes of Rhodesia
4 "___ in the Stilly Night" (Thomas Moore lyric)
5 Go over again
6 Nay sayers
7 Portico
8 Tre + tre
9 TV journalist David
10 Scenic views, briefly
11 Woeful words
12 Former Israeli P.M.
13 13th-century literary work
16 Comedian born John Elroy Sanford
18 Curved pipe feature
23 Motorists' clubs, in brief
25 Faulkner's "___ Lay Dying"
27 1-Across competitor
29 Otto who helped discover nuclear fission
30 Settled
31 Logical conclusion
32 Where Samson died
33 The Bushes, collegiately
34 Clinton and Blair, for two
35 Boys
37 Cadge
40 El ___, Tex.
43 Amounted (to)
44 Motto of the Prince of Wales
46 "See?!"
50 Quark plus antiquark
51 Earth tone
52 Match
53 It may be white
54 Tonics, to some
55 Tar
56 Naturalist Roger ___ Peterson
57 Russian city on the Oka
59 Heater stats
62 Birth control method, for short
63 You can set your watch by it: Abbr.

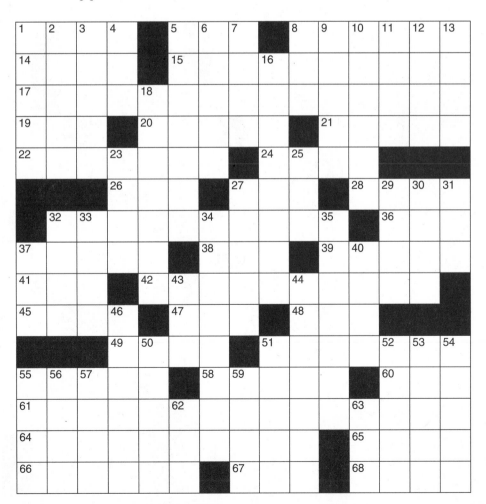

by Daniel C. Bryant

ACROSS

1 Banned pollutants, briefly
5 Suckers
9 Writer ___ Rogers St. Johns
14 Gamblers' letters
15 Finish with loops
16 Make merry
17 "Don't procrastinate"
19 Traction aid
20 Hunky-dory
21 Oklahoma city
22 Hammerheads
23 Counsel best heeded
26 Muggers
27 Scattered
28 Invitation heading
30 It'll grow on you
32 Took a card
36 Flapper's wrap
37 Stir-fry pods
40 Something that may need massaging
41 Con
43 Wearers of wool coats
44 Pigeon's perch
46 Itsy-bitsy biter
48 Yacht spot
49 Caution against neglect
54 Secure
55 Feels fluish
56 Part of a byte
58 ". . . ___ man put asunder"
59 Lethal stingers
61 "He's ___ nowhere man" (Beatles lyric)
62 Man, for one
63 Clark's partner
64 Leif's language
65 Freshman, probably
66 Jacket feature

DOWN

1 Type size
2 Après-ski treat
3 A Little Rascal
4 Retired flier
5 Shells out
6 Public company's requirement
7 Locale for a Velázquez
8 Slippery
9 One who takes a bow?
10 Late
11 "___ Heartbeat" (Amy Grant hit)
12 Sievelike
13 Mtn. stats
18 Carrier of orders from Zeus
22 Tacky?
24 Paddle
25 Jaunts
28 Ring org.
29 Snookums
30 Bookstore section
31 Overwhelming emotion
33 Award for second place
34 Deviled item
35 Misfortune
38 Not o'er
39 Puckered fabric
42 Tropical lizards
45 Shoebox letters
47 Designer Miller
48 Common allergen
49 In ___ (unborn)
50 Give voice to
51 Up the ante
52 De Gaulle's birthplace
53 Leg bone
54 King of comedy
57 Recipe amt.
59 Word with mess or press
60 Literary monogram

by Steven Kahn

ACROSS

1 Where people move 31-Acrosses back and forth
6 "Qué ___?"
10 1969 movie with an exclamation point in its name
13 Rich alumnus, perhaps
14 What a folder doesn't say
15 Portuguese king, 1861–89
17 Hemingway novel, with "The"
20 Bully
21 Place for a drink
22 Unconvincing
25 "Congratulations!"
27 They're in
29 Beehive State native
30 ___ Nast
31 See 1-Across
34 ___ purpose
38 Org. in old spy novels
39 Hit sitcom of 1994–2004 whose name can follow the first word of 17-, 25-, 51- or 61-Across
42 Support provider
43 Detective's need
45 Unfair?
46 Only sch. to win both the men's and women's N.C.A.A. basketball titles in the same year
48 Crimson rival
50 Charlotte ___ (Caribbean city)
51 2000 "mockumentary" about dogs
57 Fr. holy women
58 Stomach woe
59 Drive-in worker
61 "Not quite"

66 Sediment
67 Prefix with logical
68 Modern workout system
69 Harris and Asner
70 Fence's utterance
71 A wee hour

DOWN

1 Stir
2 S. Amer. land
3 Further
4 Speak highly of
5 "Dies ___"
6 Bench site
7 Obstetric test, for short
8 Allied (with)
9 Hill dweller
10 Dropped charges against
11 Impudent girl
12 Children's song refrain
16 Actress Pitts
18 Bothers
19 Knee-slapper
22 Silver maple leaf wearer: Abbr.
23 Stood
24 Smart set
26 Warner Bros. cartoon name
28 Cool, in 80's slang
31 Famous
32 Electric ___
33 Whichever
35 Fastener
36 "L.A. Law" lawyer
37 Bowling sites
40 Destroy

41 Adder's product
44 More than 55-Down
47 Volga's outlet
49 Pre-euro money
50 Seuss's "Horton Hears ___"
51 Tampa Bay players, for short
52 "Dallas" Miss
53 Upbraid
54 Mideast missiles
55 Has no love for
56 It can precede or follow "to be"
60 Numerical prefix
62 Heart monitor sound
63 "How about that?!"
64 Advocates' org.
65 CD-___

by Kevan Choset

ACROSS

1 Go on a vacation tour
5 2004 historical film, with "The"
10 Stench
14 Popular soap
15 Truman's Missouri birthplace
16 Latin oils
17 Wading bird
18 Unmoving
19 One who's always moving
20 Without ice
21 Rock music's Blondie, e.g.
23 Grp. whose mascot is Eddie Eagle
24 Country singer Tubb and others
26 Thingie
28 Creek
29 Grammarians' topics
31 Hotel guest
35 Gulliver's creator
38 Saturn model
39 Spot remover?
41 Performed
42 ___ fours
45 Calls up
48 Certain crustacean
50 Attacker
51 Fish hawk
53 Rabble-rouser: Var.
57 Org. in a Jeannie C. Riley song
58 Deli machine
61 "___ Williams," 1985 action flick
62 Once, long ago
64 Doo-wop song, today
65 ___ the buzzer
66 Congresswoman Lowey
67 One who says "uncle"
68 Short-billed rail
69 Otologist's recommendation
70 Calls at home
71 Is cultured

DOWN

1 Ticket buyer's concern
2 Cossack's weapon
3 Eau source
4 Asian
5 Late journalist Cooke
6 Strike zones?
7 Business sect. heading
8 Place of commerce
9 Sandinista leader
10 Mire
11 Next to
12 Name on a mower
13 Suspect foul play
22 Makes "it"
25 Bro's sib
27 Glistening beads
29 Pristine
30 Flower holder
31 "Psst! Smarty Jones in the fifth!"
32 Wade's opponent
33 Some appetizers
34 Saarinen of design
36 Douglas, for one
37 Six-pointers, for short
40 Ring leaders?
43 Mideast land: Abbr.
44 Shoe tips
46 May honoree
47 Pessimistic
49 Air race markers
51 Public proceeding
52 Minute groove
53 Prepare for winter takeoff
54 Origin of some salami
55 Baseball's Vizquel and others
56 Saw what it was like
59 Pelvic bones
60 Scale start
63 Smidgen

by Patrick Merrell

ACROSS

1 Inter-island conveyance
5 Ivory source
9 Map feature
14 Asian nursemaid
15 Con
16 Cutting tool
17 Alaskan cargo ship
20 About 1% of the atmosphere
21 Settle down for the night
22 Quarters
25 Start of an inventor's thought
29 Negative space
32 None too pleasant
34 Singer Braxton
35 Common feature in comic book dialogue
39 Asian occasion
40 Disney frame
41 Short order, for short
42 Preserve, in a way
43 Fond farewell to Honolulu and environs
47 Fictional hunchback
48 "Bonanza" brother
49 They share keys with exclamation points
50 Computer menu choice
53 Method
55 Sir Georg with a baton
57 Beguile
61 California park worker
66 Deck out
67 Whizzes
68 Some servers
69 Igloos, basically
70 Looks over
71 Makes lace

DOWN

1 Indian king
2 Russia/Manchuria boundary river
3 Poison injector
4 Provable proposition
5 Ancient cross
6 Spanish count starter
7 Agitates
8 2.2 lbs., approximately
9 Drastically reduce
10 Bach specialty
11 "Shoot!"
12 General at Antietam
13 Drop the ball
18 Four seasons in Sonora
19 Post-breakdown need
23 Bone: Prefix
24 Scratch
26 Colorful bird
27 Totally out of the question
28 Troublemakers
29 Empty promises
30 Testy
31 Moisturizer
33 Full-flavored
36 Prefix with pressure
37 Beethoven dedicatee
38 "___ a small world . . ."
44 Complete removal
45 Women's wear department
46 Miss the boat
51 Io and Ganymede, e.g.
52 Ivy Leaguer
54 ___ Club of old TV
56 Emergency medical kit item
58 "___ Breckinridge"
59 Locked (up)
60 Hardy heroine
61 Blue
62 Shogun's capital
63 City SW of Tehran
64 A Stooge
65 Letter add-ons, for short

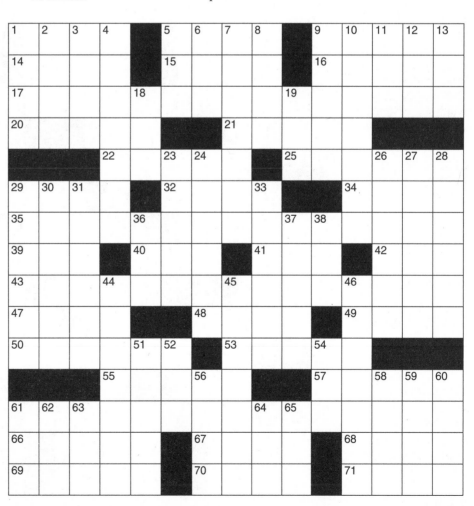

by Greg Staples

ACROSS

1 Reds Hall-of-Famer Tony
6 It holds a yard
10 Kind of pet
14 Historic mission
15 Northern capital
16 Kennel enclosures
17 Wardrobe malfunction at a restaurant?
20 Result of some bathing
21 Actress Vardalos
22 Bacon or Lamb product
23 With 48-Across, wardrobe malfunction at an auto repair shop?
27 Wash against, as the shore
29 Payment penalty
33 Duvet filling
34 Wink, nudge, etc.
36 Third qtr. starter
37 Wardrobe malfunction on the job?
41 Undermine
42 Knee-slapper
43 Subs
44 Figure seen at an intersection
47 Wampum
48 See 23-Across
51 Lock problem?
54 Get into a stew?
55 Amts. of meds
58 Wardrobe malfunction on a promenade?
63 Dench/Winslet title role of 2001
64 It may hold a spray
65 1967 hotspot, with "the"
66 His poem "Fleas" reads, in its entirety, "Adam / Had 'em"
67 Involuntarily out of a job
68 Unilever brand

DOWN

1 Over
2 2004 film "___ Enchanted"
3 Pour
4 Great Brit., once
5 It features creatures
6 Unifying theme
7 Comparable to a pig
8 ___-mo
9 Overlook point
10 One who might say "T.G.I.F."?
11 Barbarians at the Battle of Chalons
12 Andean ancient
13 Wan
18 Module
19 Neighbor of an Estonian
23 Work detail
24 Quaint cry
25 "___ My Heart at the Stage Door Canteen" (1942 hit)
26 Org. with far-out goals?
27 Kew bloom in a Noyes poem
28 Customize
30 15-Across is on one
31 French or Italian bread
32 Service group
33 "The sign of extra service" sloganeer
34 Woods varmints
35 Popular tabloid subj.
38 Restaurateur Toots
39 Which train to take, in song
40 Depreciation consideration
45 Over
46 Put a coat on
47 Title girl in a 1976 Kiss hit
49 It may be perfect
50 Like some playgrounds
51 Tibia
52 Writer Ephron
53 With dents and all
55 Kid's plea
56 Fan sound
57 Street wear?
59 Fraternal twins come from two different ones
60 Batiking need
61 Atty.'s title
62 Comic

by Cathy Millhauser

ACROSS

1 Result of a handshake, maybe
5 Athlete's foot symptom
9 Musical ability, slangily
14 Yours, in Tours
15 It borders Mayfair
16 Behavior pattern
17 Start of a quote by 9-Down
20 Oz visitor
21 For each
22 Natl. Humor Month
24 Norms: Abbr.
27 Some wool
32 Argentine aunt
33 Guest welcomers
35 Hodgepodges
36 Glossary part
38 Western tribe
39 Skater Lipinski and others
40 Eastern tribe
41 "___ as a winter swallow": Balzac
42 Connect with
43 Read
44 Like this puzzle's grid
46 Not bad, as an argument
48 One of the family
49 Overused
51 Teamster
56 Dummy
59 Mailing to a record exec
61 Like a bialy
62 Like a decal
63 One of four in 80
64 Bicycle buyer's request
65 "The Ladykillers" star, 2004
66 Construction ___
67 Finish (up)

DOWN

1 Fed. Election Commission registrant
2 ___ Z
3 One who doesn't do what's expected
4 Popular video recorder
5 Second half of the quote
6 Little one
7 A.L. and N.L. city
8 Bucket
9 See 17-Across
10 Shakespearean prince
11 Middle piece of Tokyo?
12 Locale in a Poe story
13 Pork place?
18 S.A.T. administrators
19 Cultural org.
22 Swear
23 Puncture
25 Computer program input
26 News feature
28 Part of R.S.V.P.
29 Broadcaster
30 Cousin of a raccoon
31 Like some profs.
34 "It ___ to me . . ."
37 Highway sign
45 Nearest the center
47 Pickling solutions
50 Emends
52 Roman road
53 Quo ___ ?
54 Lyric poem
55 Take up again
56 Snack
57 ___ Trail in the Andes
58 Noun suffix
60 ". . . ___ saw Elba"

by Mike Torch

ACROSS

1 Jest
5 Chekhov's "Uncle ___"
10 "Ape"
14 Actor McGregor
15 Acid/alcohol compound
16 Long ago
17 "Use brighter colors!"?
20 Cape Sable locale: Abbr.
21 Classic 1950 film noir
22 "Mack the Knife" composer
23 Like "Water Music"?
28 Leachman who won an Oscar for "The Last Picture Show"
30 Seep
31 High, in couture
32 Feeling of elation
37 Puts on . . . or things that are put on
38 Person who kneads
39 What a 38-Across needs
40 Teeny
42 What "yo mama" is
43 Bluesy James
44 "The Princess Bride" director, 1987
45 Multicolored yarn?
49 Georges who wrote "Life: A User's Manual"
50 Net alternative
51 Reliever's stat
54 What an old sci-fi comics fan might see?
59 Wept (for)
60 Spritz
61 Inspiration
62 ___ Trueheart of "Dick Tracy"
63 Cleveland nine, with "the"
64 Attorneys' degrees: Abbr.

DOWN

1 Bridges in Hollywood
2 Illegal way to go
3 Trysters, perhaps
4 Basic school subj.
5 Nixes
6 Take ___ at
7 Utmost
8 "___ haw!" (cry of delight)
9 Dada "daddy"
10 Snooped
11 Free
12 Immune system agent
13 Cut one's losses, maybe
18 Haskell of "Leave It to Beaver"
19 Bearded, as grain
24 Pretentious
25 Embryonic attachment
26 Poppycock
27 Côte d'___
28 Spiced milk tea
29 Milk, abroad
32 Subtly mean
33 "Truth!"
34 Three-time U.S. Open winner
35 Hawaiian goose
36 M.I.T. grad: Abbr.
38 Nosh
41 Sir Toby of "Twelfth Night"
42 Clinch
44 LAX to J.F.K. choice
45 Rumble
46 Some 47-Down
47 Exams
48 People kick things here
49 Go ___ (fizzle)
52 Cattail, e.g.
53 "___, how love can trifle with itself!": Shak.
55 Suffix with Mao or Tao
56 "Car Talk" carrier
57 Part of TNT
58 Be indisposed

by Paula Gamache

ACROSS

1 Cry from the block
5 Welcoming
9 Dust bits
14 "If I ___ . . ."
15 Et ___
16 See 29-Down
17 Pay back
19 Main male
20 Provoke
22 Biblical shepherd
23 Already off
24 Be indisposed
26 Blocks
29 Of an atrioventricular valve
30 Phil who sang "I Ain't Marching Anymore"
31 Sensitive things
32 Court call
35 Noted guerrilla
36 Scram . . . or a hint to solving 17-, 20-, 50- and 57-Across and 11- and 28-Down
38 Words of promise
39 Light source
40 ". . . ___ and hungry look": Shak.
41 Nabokov novel
42 Comparatively compliant
44 Composer Prokofiev
46 Spot to order a spot
48 Farm unit
49 Goals
50 "Understand?"
55 Go around
57 Be a hindrance
58 Pointer mover
59 Symbol of Apollo
60 Percolate slowly
61 Substitute (for)
62 Rowers' muscles, for short
63 Cub or Red, briefly

DOWN

1 Clinic fluids
2 In charge of
3 Forebear of one of Israel's 12 Tribes
4 Shifts
5 46-Across vehicles
6 Unalaska inhabitant
7 Run amok
8 1980 Andrzej Wajda film in which Lech Walesa appears
9 Inits. on N.Y.C. buses
10 "Verrry sexy!"
11 Star
12 Waters of jazz
13 Are going to
18 Not e'en once
21 Dos
25 Originally, once
26 Shot orderers
27 Parrot
28 Move it
29 Large 16-Across
31 Marathoner's challenge
33 Actress McClurg
34 Novelist Morrison
36 Bad cut
37 "Middlemarch" author
41 Not call it quits
43 Umbrian town
44 Things between cuts
45 European tongue
46 Heat and Lightning
47 Short concluding stanza
48 Lifeless, old-style
51 "The Memory of Trees" Grammy winner
52 Truant, in a way
53 It may be steely
54 Viewer
56 Habitable hole

by Robert H. Wolfe

ACROSS

1 Doubled, a Polynesian capital
5 Animals of the species Pan troglodyte
9 Doubled, a 1969 #1 hit song
14 The Phantom of the Opera
15 Make way?
16 "Century"
17 Figure in a math function
19 Replies to a host
20 Partly doubled, a call in a game
22 Explorer ___ Anders Hedin
23 Working in a galley
27 Doubled, a Hollywood star
30 Guess: Abbr.
31 "Well, let me think . . ."
32 Part of a roller coaster
33 Center of Florida?
35 Pro shop item
36 ___ Ridge (1972 Derby winner)
37 Partly tripled, a lyric from a 1964 #1 pop song
41 Head of Haiti
42 Resident's suffix
43 Ottoman Empire title
44 Sooner than
45 ___ Ten
46 TV component: Abbr.
48 Doubled, a drumbeat
49 Kind of bridge
51 Boxer Spinks
53 Partly quadrupled, a 1963 comedy
59 Orphan of old comics
62 Yarn spinner
63 Peckish?
64 "My Way" lyricist
65 Mystery author Buchanan
66 Doubled, home of Whitman College
67 Revel, in a way
68 Doubled, a pen

DOWN

1 Gourd fruit
2 Asia's ___ Sea
3 Miss
4 Approves
5 Mountaintops
6 Brainchild protector
7 Unexcitable
8 Feudal drudge
9 Laugh riot
10 Four-time Indy winner
11 Geo. Bush, once
12 Chem. neurotransmitter
13 ___ judicata
18 Relocate in
21 Beau
24 Most reserved
25 Kind of blanket
26 Coarse flour
27 Added spice to
28 Realm
29 Winning card combo
31 Tripled, Yogi Bear's catchphrase
34 Vaudevillian Olsen
35 Doubled, a tropical menace
36 Scandinavian rug
38 Perfume bottles
39 Tripled, a line from "The King and I"
40 Stylish and expensive
45 Old film
46 Knocking sounds
47 Some hardwood
50 Formed by inflow and outflow
52 Scribblings
54 Show horse
55 "Give that ___ cigar!"
56 Quick, in trade names
57 Sally ___ (teacake)
58 Zip strip?
59 Cousin of a crow
60 Oocytes, eventually
61 Nothing

by Patrick Merrell

ACROSS

1 Gobbled
6 "___ Lisa"
10 Press down
14 Deep performer
15 Parts of Japanese bridal costumes
16 S-shaped curve
17 Reunion group
18 It comes out of a trunk
19 Monthly expense
20 Was evasive
23 Spleen
24 Good news for an angel
25 Emulated Ethel Merman
33 Old Chevys
34 "Time's a-wastin'!"
35 Salon application
36 Outstanding
37 Oozes
39 Robin Cook thriller
40 Material for a whitesmith
41 Arizona river
42 Having more karats
43 Stake
47 Wedded
48 Colorado native
49 Worse than slapped
58 Toll unit, sometimes
59 "Got it"
60 Wedge drivers
61 Sinn ___
62 Plumlike fruit
63 Plumbing fitting
64 Grandson of Adam
65 Setters
66 Snappish

DOWN

1 Primer material
2 Make a deal with the feds, say
3 Actor Morales
4 "Back in the ___"
5 Document attachments
6 Worked by hand
7 Final notice
8 "The Secret of ___" (1982 animated film)
9 Danger in old homes
10 Some sculptures
11 Seemingly forever
12 Remote control button
13 Fountain of music
21 "A little ___ the mightiest Julius fell": Shak.
22 Bit of Kurdistan
25 ___ State (Arkansas nickname)
26 Roulette bets
27 Shaver
28 Main
29 Person in a mask
30 They're released
31 Shea player, for short
32 A mask, for a 29-Down
33 Punishment for some kids
37 Beans or rice
38 "Bingo, ___ Yale" (fight song)
39 Nod, maybe
41 Characteristic carrier
42 Bump
44 Some coins
45 Pupils
46 Biblical verb ending
49 Dependable
50 Alternatives to mules
51 Advertiser's award
52 Beach site
53 Gaudy sign
54 "Six Feet Under" son
55 "This Love of ___" (1945 film)
56 Thin strip
57 Glimpse

by Nancy Kavanaugh

ACROSS

1 "You wish!"
5 Win every game
10 The gamut
14 A Turner
15 Babe Ruth's was retired
16 Actress Anderson
17 Earthy deposit
18 Arabian Sea sight
19 Capone's nemeses
20 Start of a quip
22 Like most sonnets
24 Thousand ___, Calif.
25 Home of Pottawattamie County
26 Quip, part 2
32 William ___, attorney general under Bush the elder
33 Plug away
34 Swell place?
35 Wild revelry
36 "Bye Bye Bye" band
38 Bank holding
39 "The Matrix" role
40 He broke with Stalin in 1948
41 20 providers
42 Quip, part 3
47 Gross
48 When Hamlet dies
49 Smallest of the U.S. Virgin Islands
52 End of the quip
56 Faucet brand
57 Samuel Gompers's org., informally
59 Presidential ___
60 Tangelo trademark
61 Madame Tussaud
62 All alternative
63 Rash treatment
64 Switches around
65 Flag feature

DOWN

1 Michigan's ___ College
2 Auto import
3 Crucifix inscription
4 Hawking
5 See 40-Down
6 During the time that
7 Peer of Agatha
8 Letters on some pumps
9 Like a planetary orbit
10 "The Long Goodbye" director, 1973
11 Dead center?
12 R.E.M.'s "The ___ Love"
13 Much of a penny
21 China's Sun ___-sen
23 Gone wrong?
25 Barge ___
26 Seven-time A.L. batting champ
27 Vacuum tube filler
28 "Look ___!"
29 Question in Matthew
30 Swarms
31 Without
32 "With or Without You" singer
36 Handle
37 Dog command
38 Some dwellers on the Baltic
40 With 5-Down, some volatile investments
43 Not entirely human
44 Deemed appropriate
45 Lycées, e.g.
46 Old communications giant
49 Skin flicks and such
50 Forum wear
51 Become definite
52 Shapes with holes
53 Hilarious one
54 Novelist O'Brien
55 A couple of bucks, say
58 It's in one year and out the other

by Scot Ober

ACROSS

1 Artist Chagall
5 Put on hold
11 Internet letters, and a hint to this puzzle's theme
14 It's sold in bars
15 Two-legged salamander
16 Source of heat
17 Nirvana, essentially?
19 Potassium hydroxide
20 Right and left
21 Anonymous
23 Dealership that sells old Troopers?
27 Handsome prints?
29 Easy win
30 It ends in Oct.
31 Question from Miss Piggy
32 Tissue: Suffix
34 Handwriting on the wall
38 Hollywood favorite
40 Socialite Brooke
42 Memorization technique
43 Withhold from
44 Vaughan of jazz
46 "On the double!"
47 ___ draft
50 "Au revoir!"
51 Small colonist
52 Long forks, for example?
57 1967 Oscar winner Parsons
58 Toys sometimes stuck in trees
61 Shoe part
62 Certain Hawaiian instrument?
66 2002 British Open champion
67 Freud's home
68 Number for one
69 Shooting site
70 Went for a bite
71 Dermatologist's concern

DOWN

1 Mineral hardness scale inventor
2 Others, in Latin
3 Certain delivery
4 They may be cracked
5 Western Athletic Conf. school
6 Home for a hermit
7 Shogun's capital
8 Constellation known as the Hare
9 Like marble
10 Herd in Africa
11 Buck Rogers's lady friend
12 More twisted
13 Groundskeeper's bane
18 Assume
22 One with a part
24 Defender of Manet's work
25 Minutemen of coll. sports
26 Like Albany and Chicago
27 In the thick of
28 Went on
33 Capone rival known as Bugs
35 Quiet home, usually
36 Royal educator
37 Witches' brew necessity
39 Old "Hollywood Squares" regular
41 "Doggone it!"
45 Three-line work
48 "One great face deserves another" sloganeer, once
49 Café specification
52 Swanky dos
53 "___ Mio"
54 Explosive trial
55 Snicker
56 Purple shade
59 George and George W., e.g.
60 Musical chairs goal
63 Game with a 108-card deck
64 Burma's first P.M.
65 Kit ___

by Greg Staples

ACROSS

1 Testing centers
5 Connections
8 Large marine herbivore
14 Yellow spread
15 Short flight
16 State admitted during the Civil War
17 Eyesight impairer
19 Ready to be hung up, say
20 "Simon says pretend you're on a trampoline"
22 "Give it ___!"
23 Calamitous
24 Mischief-maker
27 Club ___
28 Seine feeder
29 High-rise member
30 "Simon says imitate a soldier"
34 Slanting
37 Last name in sharpshooting
38 "Simon says act like a bird"
42 Playwright who coined the term "lothario"
43 Patch up
44 Orlando Predators' grp.
47 Pay off the mortgage on
48 Milk source
49 Kind of lily
51 "Give me a round of applause"
55 Curmudgeon's greeting
57 Ballet featuring the evil magician Von Rothbart
58 Respectful
59 Get into a stew?
60 Strong server
61 Said "one club," e.g.
62 Sung syllable
63 Congressional mtg.

DOWN

1 Lumbering problem
2 Enticement
3 Appeared triumphant
4 Stock options?
5 Breakfast chain, for short
6 Like Bedouins
7 Florida colonizers, with "the"
8 Disparaging
9 Architect Saarinen
10 Acknowledge
11 Friday, for one
12 Work with feet
13 Mouthful
18 Studio shout
21 Eins + zwei
25 Stalker deterrent
26 Stalked one
28 Name on a wafer
29 Sorts
30 Have a long face
31 P.D. alert
32 Direction opposite sud
33 Kitchen spray
34 "The Mod Squad" do
35 School zone warning
36 Result of a house cleaning, maybe
39 1947 film noir starring Dennis O'Keefe
40 Fast-food worker's equipment
41 Pacifistic
44 French border region
45 Some breakfast cereals
46 Hens, e.g.
48 Trifled (with)
49 Aaron Brown's employer
50 World book?
52 High-handed remark?
53 Captain's aide
54 Figures
55 Mailing ctr.
56 Alley ___

by Patrick Merrell

ACROSS

1 Tie with a cord
5 Bouts
9 Stop running
14 Nike competitor
15 A Swiss army knife has lots of them
16 Musical featuring "Little Girls"
17 Author of this puzzle's quote
19 "There you go!"
20 Text enhancer
21 Clown's prop
22 Golf cousins
23 Start of the quote
26 Miss Mexico, e.g.: Abbr.
29 Pinch
30 Move through a crowd, say
32 Quote, part 2
38 Oil-rich province
41 Northerly locale
42 Quote, part 3
44 Became rampant
45 1970 World's Fair site
48 Impertinence
49 Quote, part 4
55 Slips by
56 Big A.T.M. manufacturer
57 "Eureka!"
60 Polytheist
61 End of the quote
64 Handling badly
65 Left-handers can't play it
66 Karate skill category
67 Game with a board
68 At any time
69 Combines

DOWN

1 Alta's opposite
2 In preference to
3 Good feeling
4 Bonehead
5 Box sets?
6 Say yes
7 Prefix with graphic or metric
8 Form W-9 info: Abbr.
9 Pack rat
10 U.S. security
11 Baker of renown
12 Pastel shade
13 Get a line on?
18 Book after Galatians: Abbr.
22 Syrupy drink
23 Have second thoughts
24 Even so
25 "From Here to Eternity" island
26 Influence
27 Realtor's specialty, for short
28 Off-limits: Var.
31 Stumble
33 Two turns, maybe
34 Modern treaty violation
35 Disk contents
36 Songwriter Blackwell
37 Wetlands
39 Pixar creations
40 Lhasa ___ (dog)
43 Corrode
46 Ignite
47 Object intentionally dropped on the floor
49 Halfhearted
50 One of Donald's exes
51 Gung-ho
52 Rework
53 Smallville family
54 Grp. involved in "the Troubles"
57 Like fine wines
58 Set aside
59 Kitchen pests
61 "The Naked ___" (1960's best seller)
62 All Souls' Day mo.
63 Org. whose members use the press?

by Seth Abel

ACROSS

1 Ball
6 Not docked
10 It may be herbal
13 Blitzed
14 Sports page news
15 ___ Cenis Tunnel, in the Alps
16 Radioer's words
18 Swear words
19 Serial story line
20 Winter worry
21 Mame, for one
23 Kind of hold
24 Disney collectible
25 One who makes rounds
26 Blues alternative
27 Compass heading
29 Rescues
30 The Governator
33 How actors respond
35 2000 site
40 Build ___ (settle down)
41 Assigns
42 "Ugh!"
45 Higher degree?
47 Bull's partner
48 Grated
50 Emergency ___
52 Police blotter letters
53 Package
54 Plastic ___ Band
55 "A Woman Speaks" writer
56 Actor Morales
57 Garment with a lot of pockets
61 Muffin choice
62 S-shaped molding
63 Big name in digital software
64 Fat letters
65 Oenologist's interest
66 "The Asparagus" painter

DOWN

1 Miracle-___
2 Washroom
3 Length of a quick fight?
4 1992 site
5 Seventh in a series
6 Mystifies
7 1988 site
8 It flows through un fleuve
9 Russia's ___ Republic
10 Precisely
11 Uncut
12 With 42-Down, 2004 site
15 1976 site
17 Eagles div.
22 Stretch out
26 Flier to Helsinki
28 Naval rank: Abbr.
31 You can see right through them
32 Change from bland to blond?
34 Loop group: Abbr.
36 Figure on an ancient Egyptian headband
37 Visit briefly, as someone who's sick
38 "I don't believe this!"
39 Show curiosity
42 See 12-Down
43 1996 Ron Howard thriller
44 Jack Nicholson has three
46 Home run, in baseball slang
49 Undercover cop, maybe
51 Overly
58 Francis Bacon said it "will not be defied"
59 Popular cooking spray
60 Stiffen

by David J. Kahn

ACROSS

1 Fair-sized garden
5 Tater
9 Cue user
14 "Mon ___!"
15 Garr of film
16 Carrying out the garbage, e.g.
17 Impugn
19 "My Friend" of 1950's TV and others
20 What Satan gets from poison ivy?
22 With 45-Across, book title with a hint to this puzzle's theme
24 Chinese dynasty of 2,000 years ago
25 Underground facility
26 Foreshadowed
27 Like some lines
29 G.I.'s address
30 Orderly phrase that can follow one, two or three
34 Money earned by a hospital worker?
39 When there may be censorship
40 New Deal agcy.
42 Corps member
45 See 22-Across
47 Spray target
48 Big name in ISP's
51 "Aieeeee!," e.g.
52 Donation for crackpots?
55 Film director Kenton and others
56 Pertaining to the lower skull bone
59 Hardly accepting
60 Truckful
61 Architect Saarinen
62 Clipped
63 Alternatively
64 Vitamin amts.

DOWN

1 Word on a dipstick
2 Year in Trajan's reign
3 Used as a chair
4 Cheat, slangily
5 They may be Irish
6 Prefix with cab
7 "Spenser: For Hire" star
8 Bears Hall-of-Famer Mike
9 It has a low pH
10 Name
11 Wren, for one
12 Answer provider
13 Like work horses, often
18 Matting material
21 Salad leaf
22 I.B.F. rival
23 Kachina doll maker
28 Cockney's residence
30 State of lateness
31 Blaster
32 Uris hero ___ Ben Canaan
33 Pro ___
35 Majorettes, e.g.
36 Suffix with Euclid
37 Like some stocks
38 Second planet past Merkur
41 In perfect condition
42 Product introduced in 1908 "for the great multitude"
43 Renée of silents
44 Painting aid
45 Trounce
46 More pretentious
49 "___ Mio"
50 Rank above maj.
51 Sarcastic
53 "___ sow . . ."
54 Wood sorrels
57 Coach Parseghian
58 ___ Alamitos, Calif.

by Ed Early

ACROSS

1 Prevalent
5 ___ & Whitney (aircraft engine manufacturer)
10 Flake material
14 Book of the Book of Mormon
15 Nouveau ___
16 College in New Rochelle, N.Y.
17 Barks up the wrong tree
18 Rhode Island, with "the"
20 See 34-, 42- and 55-Across
22 Rakes in
23 Mme., across the Pyrenees
24 Subj. of a 1984 Stephen Ambrose political biography
25 Daycare charge
29 Speed demon
34 19th-century writer/lecturer who advocated 20-Across
38 Like "der," in Ger.
40 "Lorna ___"
41 Inspirer
42 19th-century dress reformer who advocated 20-Across
45 Attacks
46 Trollope's "Lady ___"
47 It may give you a charge
50 Fed. bureau with agents
53 Walk down the aisle?
55 19th-century author/hymnist who advocated 20-Across
60 Needle holder
62 Rear end
63 Retained
64 It has bands with music
65 Morales of "N.Y.P.D. Blue"
66 Division preposition
67 Idyllic spots
68 Proceed

DOWN

1 Passed through, as a rope
2 Encroachment
3 Strongholds
4 German steel city
5 Univ. V.I.P.
6 Wealthy, in Juárez
7 Whiz of a tennis server
8 Détentes
9 ___ sax
10 Snack
11 Flecked horse
12 Six-footer
13 Dundee denial
19 Sassy
21 Grounded jets
26 When said three times, "et cetera"
27 Tree or door feature
28 Dreaded virus
30 "Alas!"
31 Place to get hitched, perhaps
32 Dash lengths
33 Certain whiskey
35 Bruins home, for short
36 Like many a quip: Abbr.
37 "Open all night" sign, maybe
38 ___-jongg
39 Grp. with a famous journal
43 Author Calvino
44 Antarctica's Queen ___ Mountains
48 "Seinfeld" character
49 Fearful
51 Feline in un jardin zoologique
52 Measure of capacitance
54 Nag
55 Elbow hard
56 Word processor command
57 Baseballer Boggs
58 Neat as ___
59 Fraternity letters
60 ___ Beta Kappa
61 Setter

by Stella Daily and Bruce Venzke

ACROSS

1 Tumbler's need
4 Palme of Sweden
8 Airport parking area
13 Got down
14 Major exporter of coconut oil
16 Crackers
17 Silver on the silver screen
18 With 20- and 55-Across, description of 60-Across
20 See 18-Across
22 Rig
23 Bean products?
24 Bite lightly into
28 Wife of Osiris
32 Place for a miss
36 Hide-hair link
38 News for the Wall St. Journal
39 "Is that ___?"
40 Investigator's question
41 Team in 1969 headlines
45 Ginsberg classic
46 Pizazz
47 Montreal university
51 Deli wares
55 See 18-Across
60 Western tourist attraction
61 Menu phrase
62 Knocked down
63 Give access to
64 Jiffy
65 Defeatist's words
66 Wisconsin natives
67 Put to the test

DOWN

1 Teammate of Mantle
2 Observe Yom Kippur
3 Brunch time, for some
4 Bone: Prefix
5 Retreat
6 Bygone science magazine
7 Nickname for San Francisco
8 Beginning
9 Do a fraternity prank, maybe
10 Much more than a snicker
11 For ___ (on this occasion)
12 Bill ___, the Science Guy
15 "When I was ___ . . ."
19 Lamb's dam
21 Sweeper's target?
25 "___ to please"
26 Insect stage
27 Completely
29 Embroiders a bit
30 Suffix with book
31 Place for shoats
32 Suds
33 Lingo
34 "___ Own" (song from "Les Miz")
35 December air
36 Extreme
37 "Really, now!"
42 Draws
43 Vacation spots
44 Kind of paper
48 ___ Triomphe
49 Letters on a brandy bottle
50 Popular shaver
52 It helps your dough grow
53 One on a conger line?
54 Keach who played Mike Hammer on TV
55 One in a mare's nest?
56 Colorless liqueur
57 Canzone melody
58 Stoltz of "Pulp Fiction"
59 Retired fliers
60 When many banks have extra hrs.

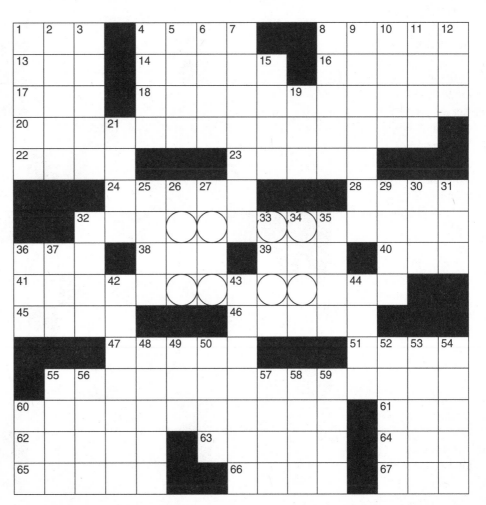

by David J. Kahn

ACROSS

1 Smudge
5 Quiet times
10 Hole maker
14 Call's companion
15 One in search of a tin can
16 Parrot
17 Hesitation by actor William?
19 Fats Waller's "___ I'll Be Tired of You"
20 Peeved
21 Rustling sound
23 Peanut Butter Lovers Mo.
24 River of Hesse
26 Abed
28 Garden figure
30 Don't just stand there
33 Piz Bernina, e.g.
34 Suffix with modern
36 Reason for a citation: Abbr.
37 A large order
38 Contract term for a 1930's heavyweight champ?
41 1974 Gould/Sutherland spoof
43 Farm cry
44 Select, with "for"
45 Neither's partner
46 Handle clumsily
48 Crocheted item
52 Bit of nostalgia
54 Leaves home?
56 Key opener?
57 Vivacity
60 Straddling
62 Org. with eligibility rules
63 Actor Russell's Oscar win?
65 Is beneficial
66 Trade fair-goer
67 Greatness
68 Travel plans: Abbr.
69 ___ Yello (soft drink)
70 Went down

DOWN

1 "The Thrill Is Gone" hitmaker, 1970
2 Use for support
3 Book specification
4 Ducats: Abbr.
5 One of a team of eight
6 Lessener
7 Cardinals great ___ Brock
8 It may be high in church
9 Do a slow boil
10 "Ditto"
11 Biography of a noted newspaper publisher?
12 Comic book hero since 1962
13 Babydoll
18 Cause for a blessing
22 Ft. Erie's home
25 Revolutionary War soldier
27 Later afterthought: Abbr.
29 G.I.'s not accounted for
31 Leather sticker
32 "Later!"
35 First name in humor
37 Job preceder: Abbr.
38 Famed admiral's concurrence?
39 Spread
40 Tournament shockers
41 ___-Jet (winter vehicle)
42 Skunk
46 Apiece
47 Mason's aid
49 Attorney's filing
50 Introspective query
51 Stole
53 Bridge declaration
55 Summer time in Buenos Aires
58 Long-range weapon, for short
59 Align
61 Switch positions
62 Popular news source, briefly
64 Olive ___

by Peter Abide

ACROSS

1 "O Captain! My Captain!," e.g.
6 What some watches display: Abbr.
10 Watch things, for short
14 "All ___" (1967 Temptations hit)
15 Choice for small toiletries
16 Company whose name is derived from a passage in Hosea
17 Watch
19 Musher's goal in March
20 Places for roots
21 "Hmmm . . ."
23 It began in A.D. 800: Abbr.
24 Town in east Umbria
26 It may get licked: Abbr.
27 Pioneer in scholasticism
30 Part of un opéra
31 One doing garden work?
32 1969 film character who said "I'm walkin' here! I'm walkin' here!"
33 Bond
34 "As I Lay Dying" family name
35 Montana's ___ National Park
37 Writing of St. Basil the Great
39 "A Dream" artist
40 Physics Nobelist Fitch and others
42 Jackal genus
43 Third of September?
44 Shakespeare's Gertrude, e.g.
45 Violent upheaval
46 Clark's "Mogambo" co-star
47 Bromide
49 It follows a chain in the military: Abbr.
50 Carrier of Bellerophon, in myth
52 Having a richer white hue
55 Hydrocarbon endings
56 Goose-pimply
58 Something Eric the Red read
59 Georgia O'Keeffe's "___ Pueblo"
60 9000 cars
61 "La Scala di ___" (Rossini opera)
62 Some lifesavers
63 Hiding place in "Hamlet"

DOWN

1 Service enders
2 It doesn't include customs
3 Bathroom shower, at times
4 Pentagon fig.
5 Snorri Sturluson story
6 Yooks' and Zooks' creator
7 Announcement over the P.A.
8 Script extras
9 Skirt
10 See-through item
11 "Almost!"
12 Toasted singer?
13 Summery attire
18 Unit of fat
22 Wed
25 "A wild sort of devil" in song
28 Verb ending
29 Napoleonic law
33 Sweeping success
34 Old overlord
36 Weigh
38 First person in Frankfurt?
41 Baudelaire's "___ fleurs du mal"
44 Recommended behaviors
45 Dweeb
48 Build a reserve of
51 Where liners go
53 Soprano Saffer
54 Bump on a log
57 Great deal

by Sherry O. Blackard

ACROSS

1 Antediluvian
16 What "they" have been saying
17 Helter-skelter
18 Jazzman Adderley
19 "Flashdance" director Adrian
20 Some records, for short
21 Rusedski of tennis
23 Break
25 "Adventures in Good Music" host Karl ___
29 Mideast map abbr.
32 Little bit
35 Melt alternative
36 Present for a picky person?
41 Hangover sufferer's lament
42 It often has islands
43 N.Y. neighbor
44 List keeper
45 Tip of one's tongue?
46 Big name in foreign news
48 Good source of antioxidants
50 Indian improvisation
54 Little bit
57 Sommer of Berlin
60 Three in a season: Abbr.
61 Biblical battlers
66 Extremely rare
67 Holistic health remedies

DOWN

1 Blowing away
2 Whale spotter
3 Captivate a crowd, perhaps
4 Carrier of "bad" cholesterol, briefly
5 Sugar
6 "Only the Paranoid Survive" author ___ Grove
7 A criminal may be caught in one
8 Successfully navigate a narrow passage
9 Part of a bray
10 Suffix with opal
11 Modern address starter
12 Dander
13 Regulus is in it
14 Gridiron great Ford
15 City planning concerns: Abbr.
22 Beginnin'
24 Goes where one shouldn't, maybe
26 Basic counters
27 E'en if
28 A Dutch master
30 Give what for
31 Make more secure
33 "___ worse than death"
34 One with a special touch
36 Leg of lamb
37 ___ Zelnicek (celebrity's maiden name)
38 Fun or song followers
39 Charged
40 Do the dishes?
47 Moundsman Dave
49 Cold
51 At full throttle
52 Perplexed pronouncement
53 Some remains
55 1998 Sarah McLachlan hit
56 Mark Twain's jumping frog
58 First name in diplomacy
59 A.C., e.g.
61 Schnook's cry
62 Chemical suffix
63 TV/___
64 Vet's service spot
65 "Lord, is ___?"

by Bob Peoples

ACROSS

1 Isn't nice to
8 Reception amenity
15 Rumless daiquiri
16 Author of "Miracle Mongers and Their Methods"
17 Cooler
18 Take the blame for
19 It's seen offshore in France
20 One of the family
22 Kit and caboodle
23 Make one
25 Opposite of sluggish
26 Tennis star Mandlikova
27 Middle ear bone
29 Bob and shag
30 Photo finish?
31 Butcher's hanger
33 Shoot
34 Lulu in "Lulu," e.g.
36 Not one-track
39 When to get revenge, proverbially
43 Many an e-mailer
44 Army E-3
45 Proctor-___ (small appliance maker)
46 Santa Maria Maggiore locale
47 Nesters
49 End notes
50 Big Ten powerhouse, for short
51 Portion of an editor's mail
53 London's Old ___
54 Like some trials
56 "Soup's on!"
58 Superhuman
59 Learned
60 Dropped off
61 Charged

DOWN

1 Lock-picking tool
2 "Attaboy!"
3 Song with the lyric "My heart with rapture thrills"
4 Wrestler's rippler
5 ___ Centre, Minn. (Sinclair Lewis's birthplace)
6 Mad Ave. profession
7 YM cover subject
8 Kayos
9 Rodgers & Hammerstein's "All I Owe ___"
10 Ex-Senator from Georgia
11 Internet address ender
12 Red Baron's transport
13 Willa Cather heroine
14 What gets read to rabble-rousers
21 Reserved
24 Hazel, for one
26 Doctrine doubter
28 Less forward
30 Fancy embellishments
32 Ear: Prefix
33 Henhouse threat
35 Opposite of charged
36 Some beachwear
37 Prematurely
38 Madrid daily
40 "Wonderful!"
41 Help settle
42 Took by force
44 Victimized, with "upon"
47 "A Vindication of Natural Society" writer, 1756
48 Tractor handle?
51 Memory jogger
52 Check mate?
55 Best-selling album of 2001
57 Military inits.

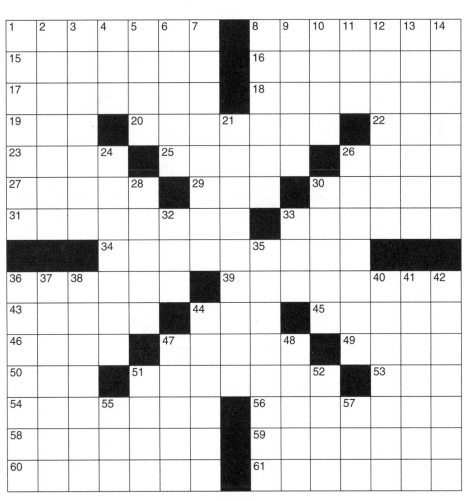

by Manny Nosowsky

ACROSS

1 Old trail terminus
8 Public hangings
15 Pushes
16 Race place
17 Test-of-time passer
18 Ends, e.g.
19 "The Piano" co-star
20 Supporter of a drop leaf
21 Keep someone awake, maybe
22 Order in the court
23 Bit of elementary Latin
25 Free
27 About to explode
28 Nonconformists
33 They're related
34 Kind of affiliation: Abbr.
35 Stars, e.g.
36 One raising Cain
37 Municipal council mem.
38 Something a company won't reveal
40 Beersheba locale
42 It may be between the seats
43 Horned rock climber
44 Times, e.g.
46 Some are shaded
50 Be granted
52 Garam __ (spice mixture in Indian cuisine)
53 Fast, agile runner
54 Mrs. Grundy
55 Where oils may be produced
56 Over
57 Going on the least
58 Pass up

DOWN

1 Draws (on)
2 "One for My Baby" composer
3 Marsh of mystery
4 Beta release, essentially
5 Product line
6 Abbott, to Costello, e.g.
7 Collier's, for one: Abbr.
8 "Call to Greatness" author Stevenson
9 Day's "The Pajama Game" co-star
10 North Sea feeder
11 Like an inscribed pillar
12 Martha Stewart Living reader
13 It's rarely found in the hospital
14 Like some complexions
20 A toy it isn't
22 "I Wanna Be Bad" singer __ Ford
24 Rule to live by
26 N.E.A. member
27 "Something's not right here"
28 Kharg Island resident
29 Observe
30 Coot
31 __ coming
32 Old name in news
39 Knocking off
41 Doesn't do just O.K.
44 Folder fodder
45 Open
47 San __
48 Something to resort to
49 Kind of blond
51 Medicine Nobelist Metchnikoff
52 Remote option
53 Rod
54 Mate

by Sherry O. Blackard

ACROSS

1 Triter writer?
5 Old toy trademark
9 Got through
14 Comics canine
15 Lottery cry
16 Santa Anna target
17 Apologetic words at the end of a meal
20 No-brainer
21 Call to a crew
22 Horse of the Year, 1960–64
23 Disadvantaged
25 Considers barely dignified enough
29 Go up and down
32 Hair implant?
34 Provide for
35 Smart ___
37 Marks for a score
39 Storyteller's challenge
40 Space
42 Great Lakes city
43 "Throw thine eye / On ___ young boy": "King John"
44 Polite turndown
46 Siege deterrents
49 Clip for TV
51 Clip joint figures
55 Lead-in to "goodbye"
59 "That's a shame"
60 Lend ___
61 Sleep activities
62 River rising in the Cantabrian Mountains
63 Level connectors
64 "In principio ___ Verbum" (biblical phrase)
65 Film private

DOWN

1 Popular snack cakes
2 Show flexibility
3 Lawyer, often, in court briefs
4 Partial to
5 Groundbreakers
6 Outstanding
7 Bit of parental buck-passing
8 With 18-Down, like some corrupt officials
9 Is blind
10 Numismatist's interest
11 Law assistant, for short
12 Birds with dark green eggs
13 Over
18 See 8-Down
19 ___ Hornie (Satan)
24 Charity
26 Mate's cry
27 Canceled
28 Pen with eggs
29 Hay there!
30 Spread
31 It travels at the speed of light
33 The Dixie Chicks, e.g.
36 Humbug
38 Sandbank's spot
41 Zacharias and others
45 Purely academic
47 Marvel Comics superhero
48 Certain volleyball player
50 English sculptor Henry
52 "Being There" director
53 Triple crown, for one
54 Attack
55 Foe of communism
56 Mrs. Chaplin
57 City south of Salt Lake City
58 Main idea of un libro

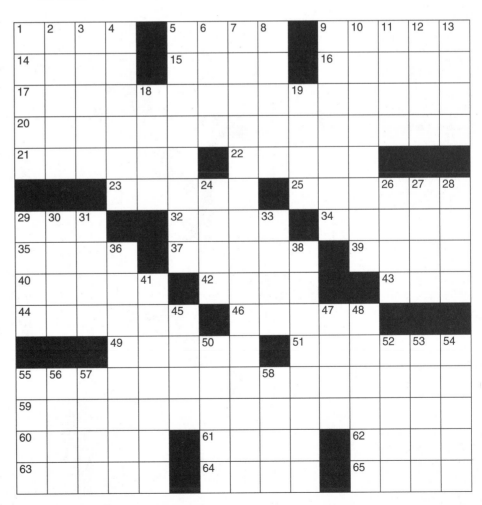

by Manny Nosowsky

ACROSS

1 Galoot
7 Come undone, as a robe
15 Israeli author of "Where the Jackals Howl, and Other Stories"
16 Possible psychotic symptom
17 Sort of
18 Food on which Charles Lamb wrote an essay
19 Architect's add-on
20 Bars
22 ___ meeting
23 Throw for ___
25 Tempting spot
26 Face
27 What many a word has
28 Film "Angel" player
29 Hall of Fame jockey Earl
30 Deliberate
31 Not necessarily real
34 Roof adornment
36 Men's fashion accessory
40 Galena
42 Miss O'Neill
43 Nag
46 Seabiscuit jockey ___ Pollard
47 Lets mistakes pass
48 Pick up
49 Unprosperous time, metaphorically
51 Press conference sights
52 Dot follower
53 Breezy competition
55 Evil spirit
56 Bronzes
58 Unkeyed
60 Delta Center team
61 Destroyer of the town Nicolosi in 1669
62 It's off-limits
63 Make fun of

DOWN

1 They're seen with T-shirts
2 "Sorry, none left"
3 Escaped
4 Hair color
5 "The only poor fellows in the world whom anyone will flatter": Pope
6 Book that tells of the reign of Cyrus the Great
7 Pumped
8 Dig deeply
9 Rimes of country music
10 Off
11 Literary adverb
12 1992 U.S. Olympic Dream Team member
13 Went out
14 Void
21 Like butterfly wings
24 Brown competitor
26 1909 Physics Nobelist
28 1970 Kinks hit
29 Inquire (about)
32 Still
33 Having colored patches
35 Bench
37 Check out
38 Popular
39 Bomb, for one
41 Lining material
43 Bygone military leader
44 Regarding this point
45 Disheveled
49 Cover again, as a road
50 Staring
51 "What'sa ___ you?"
53 Indian royal
54 Press down
57 Cable choice
59 "___ courtiers' knees . . .": Shak.

by Joe DiPietro

ACROSS

1 Phony
11 Endowment
15 Flat turndown
16 Fertile Crescent's place
17 Do a performance
18 Depression
19 Chef d'état
20 Not so strict
21 Unoccupied
22 ___ Fyne, Scotland
24 "___ me!"
26 Fraternity chapter
27 Went slowly
31 U.S. code and cipher grp.
32 Pack animal
33 Attunes
35 Honky-tonk player
37 Gossip's question
42 Nonsense
43 "Mother Goose Suite" composer
44 Part of a guffaw
45 Super power
48 W.W. II bond designation
52 Canada's ___ Island National Park
53 Zip
55 Was appealing
56 Jumble
58 Thingum
62 Lab offering?
63 Sign in the dark
64 Risqué display
66 Clip
67 Person at a foundation
68 Old World duck
69 Chug-a-lugs

DOWN

1 Complications
2 Cover made of silk
3 Ancient Greek state
4 Where pins are made
5 Really smart
6 Bird whose male hatches the eggs
7 Memorial Day solo
8 Grant-___
9 Filter
10 Colorful fish
11 Ship's spar
12 Volunteer's confident declaration
13 Make just right
14 "Congratulations!"
23 Soprano's note
25 Two-edged sword
28 Passed illegally, maybe
29 Put away
30 Dr. ___
34 Camera inits.
36 West ___, Long Island weather station locale
37 They're intriguing
38 Hurdle for a doctoral student
39 Job setting
40 Carrier to Tampere
41 Time before
46 One who's hurting
47 "Now!"
49 Title city in a 1960 #1 hit
50 Gentle underwater creature
51 Player of the Texaco Fire Chief, on old radio
54 Hullabaloos
57 Hasenpfeffer, e.g.
59 Animal shelters
60 "Hard ___!" (helm command)
61 Darkens
65 Hardly a girl's dream date

by Manny Nosowsky

ACROSS

1 Item on an auto shop checklist
11 Court grp.
15 Buoyancy
16 Nair rival
17 Tenderfoot
18 Taunt
19 "Lord, is ___?"
20 Forgo
21 Soft drink brand
23 Lowdown
25 Slip on
27 1957 Oscar winner Miyoshi
28 "Felix Holt" novelist
30 Time set, maybe, after a 7-Down
32 Negative principle
33 Library extension
35 Thingies
37 Korea Bay feeder
38 Bandar ___ Begawan, capital of Brunei
39 Determined
42 Gardening job
46 Special connections
47 Bill Haley and His Comets recorded for it
49 Big picture
50 Thrash
52 Drill sound
53 Minute opening
54 Many a trailer
56 Magicianlike
59 Program begun under F.D.R.
60 Solid ground, in Stuttgart
61 College student's filing
64 Garry Trudeau's "Check Your ___ at the Door"
65 Fresh start
66 Den
67 Healthy dose of reality

DOWN

1 Hairstylist, maybe
2 Despicable sort
3 1897 Felix Hoffmann discovery
4 White wine apéritif
5 K, for one: Abbr.
6 Over, overseas
7 Informal invitation
8 Accord
9 Transportation regulator of old: Abbr.
10 Bad marks
11 Correct, as a feeding problem
12 With 24-Down, agrees
13 Diagnostic tool
14 Realizes
22 Dreary
24 See 12-Down
26 Personal, e.g.
29 Rot
31 Fishing spot
34 African lily
36 Make more exciting, in slang
39 Bart Starr wore it at Green Bay
40 On a big scale
41 Tic-tac-toe
43 Rule without exceptions
44 Tell
45 Harvest helper
48 Club
51 Explanatory words
55 Year that Clement XI became pope
57 Lowlands
58 Emmy winner John
62 "Don't Bring Me Down" grp.
63 The U.N. recognized it in 1974

by Bob Peoples

ACROSS

1 Little people
10 In-box filler
15 Black Sea borderer
16 Kind of group, in chemistry
17 It's hard to handle
18 Montana, e.g., once
19 Credit card disclosure: Abbr.
20 Half of quatorze
21 Bounded
22 Island rings
24 Vets, once
26 As expected
28 When to vote, often: Abbr.
29 Mule feature
30 M.'s opposite
32 Chow
34 Football positions: Abbr.
35 Hunters' representation in "Peter and the Wolf"
39 Running times
41 Kind of Dr.
42 Clique
44 Unhelpable in the E.R., maybe
45 Pit-___
47 Thin fastener
49 Seventh heaven
53 Supporter of Victoria's Secret
56 Sports figure
57 Ear of Indian corn
58 Experienced
60 Canny
61 Landed
62 Popular weight-loss program with colored food cards
64 Ride
65 "The Hunchback of Notre Dame" woman
66 Banana oil, e.g.
67 "Almost there!"

DOWN

1 Hawaiian thank you
2 Annual sports event
3 ___ acid
4 Part of some uniforms
5 Humana and others, for short
6 Ones that are strung along?
7 Sulky
8 "You're lying!"
9 Letters of success
10 Enthusiastic to a fault
11 2002 Oscar winner for the song "Lose Yourself"
12 Gas station adjunct, often
13 Part given by the pious?
14 Cause for a massage
21 Two-___
23 Water hole
25 Fricandeau, e.g.
27 Webzine
31 Empower
33 Supercilious sort
35 One wearing the same colors, perhaps
36 Apart
37 Notable ancient landfall
38 Topic lead-in
40 Misses
43 Confab
46 "Fame and Obscurity" author
48 Wishful thinking
50 In ___ (per se)
51 Twinings alternative
52 Pen-shaped
54 Hot or cold drink
55 He co-founded Microsoft with Gates
59 Member of the arum family
62 Of the, in Venice
63 Pin cushion?

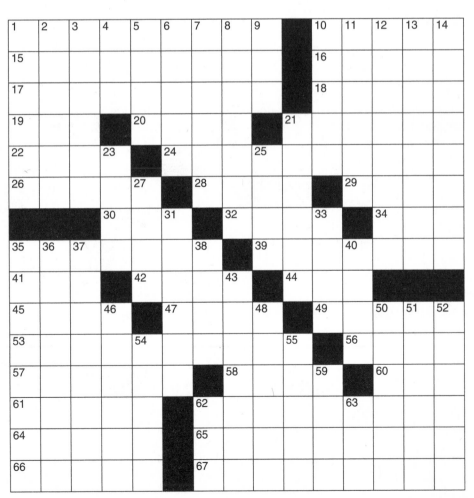

by Myles Callum

ACROSS

1 Some hotel adjuncts
16 Old plugboard plug-ins
17 One may be decorated
18 Pea jacket?
19 1980's proposal: Abbr.
20 Bounce
21 Kind of job
23 Makes fast
26 Home of Jorge Luis Borges: Abbr.
29 Mad modifier
32 Purlieu
33 San Joaquin Valley city
36 Cannes film festival's Camera ___
37 Small inventions
38 High place
40 Low places
42 Vein site
43 La lead-in
45 Just
46 Stopping points
47 Bothers
49 Race sponsor
50 Ancient manuscript
51 They have tight headbands
55 Arrow alternative
57 Presidential appointee: Abbr.
60 With 30-Down, zero
61 It may be eaten with chopsticks
66 Browner
67 Home of the Cougars of college sports

DOWN

1 Barracks sites
2 Electrolysis particle
3 Three-time Masters winner
4 Canadian poet Mandel
5 Breaks down, in a way
6 Victorian outburst
7 Save, and then some
8 Miniature
9 "Ti ___" (Pavarotti album)
10 Like a free agent
11 Patriot Putnam of the American Revolution
12 Poisonous Asian plant
13 Pit holder
14 Quarter of dodici
15 Bygone pol. unit
22 Landings
24 Fact follower?
25 ___ before
27 Riot
28 Bloated
30 See 60-Across
31 Like New York City's Sony Building
32 Something original
33 Removes
34 Something going on
35 Potential sources of poisoning
39 Well-___
41 Tannery sight
44 Tankard filler
48 Precise, in Méjico
50 "Rocky" score composer
52 One of the Pointer Sisters
53 "Haystack at Giverny" artist
54 About a quarter of a cord
56 "Scrubs" co-star ___ Braff
58 Unstable particle
59 Objectivity spoiler
61 Esther, notably
62 Like
63 Milano Mr.
64 Outside, at the outset
65 Retired cruiser

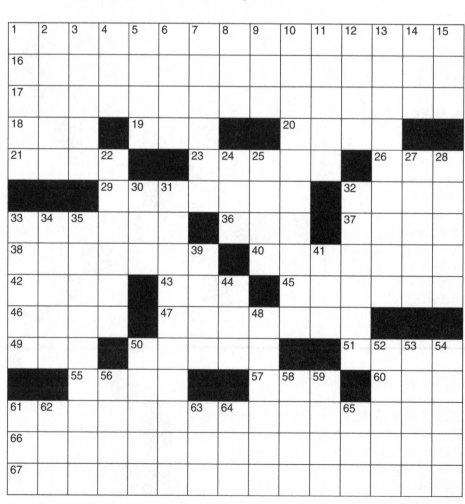

by Gary Steinmehl

ACROSS

1 Java man?
9 Base
15 Farm youngster
16 Spain's ___ Real
17 Tiny Tim sang in it
18 Solicit aggressively
19 Motor add-on
20 Scuttlebutt
21 Selling points
22 Suffix with neur-
24 Standard
26 ___ about (circa)
28 Perdue rival
30 Upright features
33 Lively songs with humorous, improvised lyrics
35 "Mazel ___!"
36 Singer of the aria "Largo al factotum"
39 Consumes with gusto
41 Ankara title
42 Reporting
46 Attendance counter
48 TV puppet
52 Saarinen of Finland
53 Note
55 Lake Wobegon's locale: Abbr.
56 Trig functions
59 George W. Bush's birthplace: Abbr.
61 "You Bet Your Life" airer
62 Runs a test on
63 News anchors often face this
65 Chemistry test topic
66 Undoes a breakup
67 Introverts
68 Locale identifier

DOWN

1 "Yeah, right!"
2 Property
3 Strait of Dover sight
4 Workplaces with openings: Abbr.
5 Got out of Dodge
6 Mesh
7 Tendency toward chaos
8 Vanity case?
9 Jacuzzis
10 "Yow!"
11 Put back in the oven
12 Fishing aids
13 "Darling, that dress looks divine!"
14 Flyspeck
23 Pioneer of TV comedy
25 Some family heads
27 Tell the host yes or no
29 Some feds
31 The "She" in Spike Lee's "She's Gotta Have It"
32 Bagnell Dam river
34 Booty
36 Horoscope revelation
37 "Well, perhaps . . ."
38 Fort
40 Make waves
43 Energy
44 Sister of Orestes
45 Eraser
47 Generic
49 51 past
50 Existing at birth
51 Protect, as with plastic
54 In a timely way
57 One with good looks?
58 They broke up in 1991: Abbr.
60 Favored caretaker
62 Feel fluish
64 Tape player port

by Elizabeth C. Gorski

ACROSS

1 Turkey heart?
7 Pronto
15 "The Last Samurai" extras
16 Begin energetically
17 Oodles
18 What many an addict is
19 Nail holder
20 Leaves
22 G squared?
23 Bunny's pace
25 Pool division
26 One reconciled in Gen. 33
27 Water ___ (oral-hygiene product)
28 Misogynist, e.g.
29 Flushing
32 Some are rattled
33 Takes off on one's own
35 Commercial charges
38 Venue for a smoking car
42 Is tiresome
43 Wee wee?
44 "Holy smokes!"
45 Peggotty girl in "David Copperfield"
46 Devout
49 Note
50 Beat in a debate, say
51 "___-Pan" (1966 best seller)
52 Cousin of Erse
54 Wrap
56 Site of the Mokuaweoweo crater
57 Carriage trade groups
58 Marching order
59 Most judicious

DOWN

1 "Hit me," in blackjack
2 Like some salads
3 Bit of football gear
4 1977 double-platinum Steely Dan album
5 A to Z, for one
6 Loan security
7 Envious wit's remark
8 "___ of the North" (1922 film)
9 Total
10 Paws
11 Alabama's Civil Rights Memorial architect
12 Enliven
13 Furniture worker
14 Cries out loud
21 Novel subtitled "A Peep at Polynesian Life"
24 Hype
25 Drudge
28 Light ring
30 Some pintfuls
31 U.S.S.R. successor
32 Lush
34 Infection-fighting drug
35 More than cool
36 International young men's club
37 Become payable
39 Shake up
40 Hors d'oeuvres
41 Most provocative
43 Many
46 Cunning
47 Someone ___ (not ours)
48 Cub Scouts leader
50 Something to explain your way through
53 Ties
55 Semi

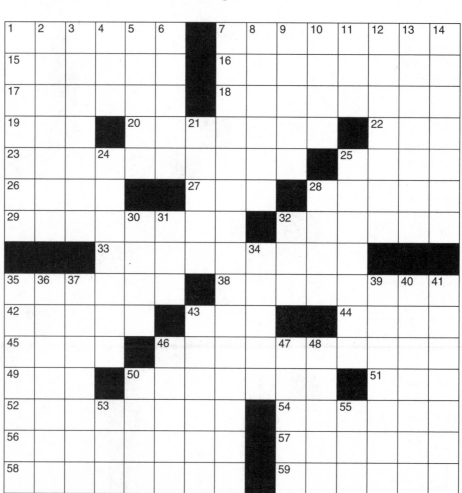

by Manny Nosowsky

ACROSS

1 Disarrange, in a way
8 Is able to 38-Down money
15 "There Is Nothin' Like a Dame" follower
16 Be there before
17 Detainee's entitlement
18 Lay elsewhere
19 Rare driving result
20 One might support a foundation
22 Dating consideration
24 "My Life" singer, 1978
25 Thea's daughter, in myth
26 Certain print
31 One way to see
33 Italian librettist Gaetano ___
37 They don't make it
38 Oil source
40 Dawn
41 North and others
42 One with a thick skin
45 Hit maker?
48 Tap trouble
49 Witch's brew
52 Mary's charge, in verse
57 Come out on top
58 Stand tall
59 Run down
61 Propitiate
62 Suspiciously
63 Went into first, maybe
64 Not so far along

DOWN

1 W.W. II predator
2 Drew on a case
3 Ever-energetic
4 Quirky behavior
5 Obsessed captain
6 Cartel city
7 Grouches
8 Comparatively quick
9 Small biological interstice
10 Part of an internal network
11 Writer Ferber
12 Figure in the French avant-garde
13 Unborn, after "in"
14 "For the Future of Israel" author
21 Orchestra alternative
23 "Take your pick"
27 It may be chipped
28 Fell
29 Sen. Mark of Arkansas
30 Hang out (with)
31 "Music for Films" musician
32 In the distance
34 Unable to decide
35 Córdoba condiment
36 Clout providers
38 See 8-Across
39 Shout of support
41 Scuttle contents
43 Be bad to
44 Essential
45 Some cakes
46 ___-null (math figure)
47 Hedren of "Marnie"
50 Potential heiress
51 Rear-___
53 Not kosher
54 One way of fitting
55 Prefix with America
56 Capital of Azerbaijan
60 Didn't fight, say

by Nancy Kavanaugh

ACROSS

1 9-Across's sidekick
9 1-Across's sidekick
15 Domestic
16 It may be full of junk
17 Fit behind the wheel
18 Cabbage
19 Noted sports retiree of 1951
21 Morning glistener
22 Lead-in for breath or tears
25 Bust figure
26 Sugar suffix
27 Certain bazaargoer
28 Yank
31 Virginia suburb of Washington
33 Thin-skinned one
34 Its flag consists of one white star on a blue background
36 "Stay!"
40 Enlisted personnel
42 Crunchy snack food
43 Bells may indicate them
47 South American city of 2 million
48 Brief rule?
49 Paradigm of patience
50 Bygone tale tellers
51 Suffix with 57-Down
52 Revelation subject
54 Had a problem with
56 Native lingua
60 Get through
61 Widespread
62 Neptune, e.g.
63 Chinese restaurant offering

DOWN

1 Geom. figure
2 "Beautiful Boys" singer
3 Stop on a line: Abbr.
4 Crib collection
5 "To __ human . . ."
6 British rocker Gallagher
7 "__ Run" (classic sci-fi novel)
8 Sauce ingredient
9 Hard things to break
10 Pep
11 Sure rival
12 Due from, as a bill
13 Weatherspoon of the W.N.B.A.
14 Mortar spreader
20 Heist unit
22 Loud hits
23 Big energy supplier
24 Bee __
28 Like some puns
29 Island near Mull
30 Now and then
32 Regrettably
35 "__ of Loving" (Stan Barstow novel)
37 Old salt's adverb
38 Symbol of goodness
39 Medical suffix
41 Rapping
43 Record listings?
44 James of the Met
45 Slate of affairs?
46 Film worker
50 Southern __
52 Architect Saarinen
53 It connects to the neck
55 Thought was really cool
57 Do lines?
58 Scot's denial
59 Suffix with play

by Gilbert H. Ludwig

ACROSS

1 Holdup cover-up
8 Joins the fray
15 Legally binding
16 Check out thoroughly
17 "Simple"
18 Seized hold of
19 Front
20 A lot of Oceania
22 Really moved
23 Ring data
25 Slight
26 W. S. Gilbert's "The ___ Ballads"
27 Kind of artery
29 Former item
31 Long-bearded type
32 Variety of penguin
34 Out of one's mind
36 Background noise
38 "Whew!" to an office worker
41 Wound up
45 In good shape
46 Market figures, briefly
48 It lies on the celestial equator
49 Court alternative: Abbr.
50 Parting need?
52 Work across the board?
53 Word
55 Take to the limit
57 Whittier war poem "Laus ___"
58 From the beginning
60 Out of control
62 W.W. I rifle
63 They have gripping roles
64 Outside the solar system
65 Vatican government

DOWN

1 Founder of Reprise Records
2 Bad-mouthed
3 Journalist who wrote "The Trial of Socrates"
4 Make shorter, in a way
5 It may be restricted
6 Beats it
7 Camphor, e.g.
8 More than intent
9 Cancels
10 Waxing offerer
11 Some climbers' conquests
12 Carrier
13 Primitive period
14 Sleeping bag alternative
21 Not just any old seats
24 Pay tribute to
28 "Singin' in the Rain" role
30 Drive off
31 Cutting remarks
33 Ancient literary work
35 ___ time
37 Pop music, informally
38 Struck with a resounding blow
39 Server's suggestion
40 Woman who makes the rounds?
42 Symbols of royal dignity
43 Cracked
44 Back
47 Smack
51 Con game
54 Cutlet?
55 Formula, essentially
56 Looked up to?
59 Some microwaves
61 Longest river in Scotland

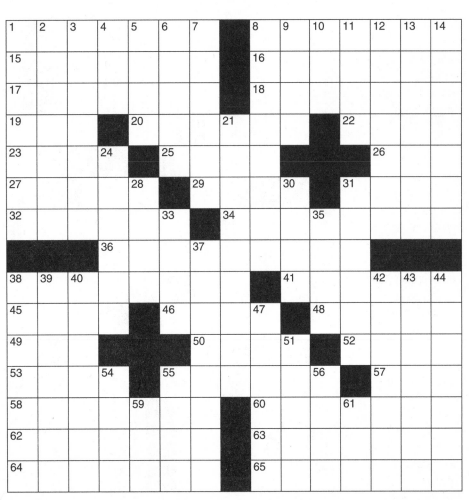

by Bob Peoples

ACROSS

1 Take the wrong way?
10 Kansas City university
15 Budgeter, in a way
16 55-Down's opposite
17 With 39- and 63-Across, a divorce lawyer's guarantee?
18 "___ Funny Feeling" (song from "Skirts Ahoy!")
19 Italian summer resort
20 Lottery winner's address?
22 Louisiana's ___ Cajuns
24 The Clinton years, e.g.
25 Local area network members
29 1598 edict site
33 Market event, briefly
36 Some mouths
38 ___ d'Azur
39 See 17-Across
42 Director Rohmer
43 Shoot for the moon
44 Chickadee relative
45 Series finale?: Abbr.
47 Vocal individual
49 Wobbly walker
50 Old-time actress Palmer
54 Dip's target
61 One with notions
62 Book club name
63 See 17-Across
65 Ringer of some necks
66 ___ Springs, Fla.
67 Strawberry, e.g.
68 Product manufacturer, at times

DOWN

1 Last name in the meat industry
2 Lon's "Frankenstein Meets the Wolf Man" co-star
3 Cast
4 Internet subdivision
5 Site of some serious hookups: Abbr.
6 Level, in London
7 Italian suffix meaning "little"
8 Inner ears?
9 Four's inferior
10 Dancer in a Grieg suite
11 Bum's offense
12 Thought about the Rhône
13 Not so heavy, informally
14 Lilian Jackson Braun's "The Cat Who Smelled ___"
21 Like some input
23 Gives a heady answer?
26 Actually
27 "Y" sporters
28 Way up
30 "Out of my way!" indicator
31 One with notions
32 Palais des Nations muralist
33 Solicitous response
34 A quarter, e.g.
35 Suffix with narc
37 1998 Sarah McLachlan hit
40 Glide
41 Cousin of a hornpipe
46 Cane accompanier
48 Certain prize
51 Was biased
52 Prefix with protein
53 Signatory
54 Schmo
55 Height
56 Make final preparations?
57 It's a mouthful
58 ___ nut
59 ___'acte
60 Get moist
64 Singer Sumac

by Ed Early

ACROSS

1 Interest amounts
9 Show astonishment
15 Bargain for leniency
16 Unlikely to judge
17 Exit indicator, e.g.
18 "Grand" place
19 Cab alternatives
20 ___ Sea, near the Greater Barsuki Desert
22 London production
23 Don't dawdle
26 "Whew!"
29 Drop-off point
30 Nevada's second-largest county
33 Gob
35 First name in Hollywood dirt
37 Rehearsed
38 Get to know
41 Sammy Cahn/Jule Styne's "___ Never Forgotten"
42 Kind of bean
43 Opposite of fluster
44 Tax, in Britain
46 Symbol of domination
48 G.I.'s reply
49 Ashen
52 Noted diamond family
54 Casa part
55 End of a parent's order
58 #39 in a series
60 Final proposals
63 Protect
64 Makes a party to
65 Excavate
66 Do some courtroom work

DOWN

1 Some of a lot
2 Hip
3 They often fill out schedules
4 90's kids' catchword
5 Good times
6 Criminal's creation
7 Stowe villain
8 Source of some serious shaking
9 Tittle-tattle
10 Rial spender
11 "Get out of here!"
12 Quarrying locales
13 Pathetic
14 It's known for its security
21 What some surfers do
23 Put on cargo
24 Switch words
25 Inclines
26 With 52-Down, microscopic staining compound
27 Pitch
28 Aggravates
31 Blues singer McDonald
32 Survey category
34 Payola
36 Not separately
39 Wallflower producers?
40 Club option
45 "Zip it!"
47 More fanciful
50 Alpine river
51 Malicious
52 See 26-Down
53 Track assignment
55 Baby spoiler, perhaps
56 Platte River people
57 Draw to a close
59 Cartoon canine
61 "What ___ Man?" ("Pal Joey" tune)
62 Hearing aid, briefly

by Alan Olschwang

154 FRIDAY

ACROSS

1 __ bit
5 Brought off
8 Scream inducer
14 One way to be wounded
16 Certain battery
17 Founder of the last Japanese shogunate
18 Deciphers
19 Image receiver
20 Finest examples
21 Base line?
22 Contract specs
23 Car since 1949
25 Facility
26 Disposed (of)
29 Hungarian-born mathematician Paul
31 Books about the Mounties, e.g.
33 Feature of many banks
35 Cared
36 "The Quiet American" star, 2002
37 Check out
38 Tries to win
39 Homer Simpson's hangout
40 Lush
41 Abyssinian greeting
43 Surface
45 Not at all curious
47 Want
48 Like the Crusades
50 In order
51 "Them"
52 __ worth
53 Bro's partner
54 Dosage abbr.

DOWN

1 Small criticism, slangily
2 __ around
3 Plummets
4 Better than
5 Lane with lines
6 Skunk River locale
7 Kind of test
8 Handheld cutter
9 One seeking signs of life?
10 Anti-__ (airport equipment)
11 Question or answer in "__?" . . . "__!"
12 Forest rangers
13 "Weir of Hermiston" author, in brief
15 Exclamation around a water cooler
20 Insignificant one
22 Yellowish pink
23 Umbrella plant, e.g.
24 Marshal
26 Program carriers
27 Combined
28 1925 Nobel Peace Prize winner
30 Shipshape?
31 Go for
32 Shortly
34 They may be gathered
40 Like some suits
41 Statistical figures
42 View from the Rock & Roll Hall of Fame
43 Architect Saarinen
44 Cardinal
45 Beverage brand
46 Light
47 Coolidge or Roosevelt
48 Chain parts: Abbr.
49 River at Ghent

by Kevin Hagen

ACROSS
1 Hold on (to)
7 On a par with
15 Expensive wheels
16 Right on
17 Bewitch
18 Stop suddenly
19 Bumper cars and such
20 Put down
21 Put on
22 Chapter 11 issue
23 Albéniz's "Iberia," e.g.
24 Game-ending word
25 E-mail suffix
26 Stock yards
27 Rocking toy, to a kid
28 Old comics girl
30 Male delivery?
31 Be indifferent about
36 Suffix with duct
37 Deep blue
38 Volunteer's phrase
41 Level connections
42 "Illmatic" rapper
43 "Caro ___" ("Rigoletto" aria)
44 "Mmm, mmm, good!"
45 Shower
46 Follow
47 Steinbeck characters
48 Vacation concern
49 Lyric sung three times in a row in the Beatles' "Michelle"
51 Beyond standard
52 Giving
53 Rings
54 All it takes to convince you, in some ads
55 Connection providers

DOWN
1 South Dakota city
2 Kept from
3 Ram
4 Irish revolutionary Robert
5 1930's Royales
6 Go wrong
7 Unobtrusive
8 Weightlifting exercises
9 Pretense
10 Promising words
11 Fictional ogre
12 Himalayan cedar
13 Gives out
14 Gateway to Australia
20 Rather
23 Wozniak who co-founded Apple Computer
24 Billing cycle
26 Forte
27 Gym game
29 Gazellelike
30 Mawkish
32 Beer brand
33 Tweak
34 Dentist's procedure
35 Fidgety
38 Deep blue
39 Like a beret, usually
40 "Later!"
41 Waste
44 They may give you many happy returns
45 Punted
47 Vindictive goddess
48 Paladin
50 Thoroughly investigate
51 It's water resistant

by Manny Nosowsky

ACROSS
1 Delivery aid
8 Bondage
14 Intimate
16 Query to a cow
17 Comes back, in a way
18 Bind
19 Kind of steak
20 Actress Pfeiffer
22 That vessel
23 Elemental form
26 Wild Bill Donovan's org.
27 Old D.C. team member
28 Cointrin International Airport locale
29 Foam ingredient
31 See 37-Down
33 Work, physically
34 Not on this side
40 Not go near
41 Part for the plate
42 Duck
45 Ruling units
50 Second person
51 Go off
52 Without anyone knowing
53 One with sharp teeth
54 Surface anew
56 Liquido vital
57 Pig
59 Bathroom bar option
62 Something done while running around
63 Mark
64 SuperDome site
65 Eggs, e.g.

DOWN
1 Full-figured
2 Be cruel to
3 Anticipate
4 Run, as an exhibition
5 Dedicated lines
6 Paris's Pont ___ Arts
7 Technique improver
8 Last word before someone is shot
9 "I kid you not!"
10 Little puncher
11 Entangled
12 Uninteresting progress report
13 Least dry
15 "And when I ___ my lips . . .": Shak.
21 Breed of sheep named for an English county
24 21-Down's genus
25 3, 4 and 5, but rarely 6
29 Not in
30 Part of O.H.M.S.
32 Bewhiskered fauna
34 Charges
35 Dead thing, according to some
36 Bit of indelicacy
37 With 31-Across, some clubs
38 Kicker's object
39 You might have a stake in it
43 Collected
44 In
46 Free of stains
47 Billy
48 Draw parallels
49 Smallest bone in the human body
52 Rx abuse
55 Harem room
58 It often has sliding doors
60 Suffix with Shakespeare
61 Sellers's foil in "Pink Panther" films

by Robert H. Wolfe

ACROSS

1 Title character in an Aesop fable
10 Palace, in Hindi
15 Modern mall feature
16 Ancient mall
17 Person of some account
18 Domestic comedy of 1983
19 "The X-Files" topics, for short
20 Discontinued coin
22 Record label inits.
23 Maintains, as a violin
26 Coupling
27 Bruno, e.g.
28 Conned
29 Letters at Camp Lejeune
31 Fundraising grp.
32 Exceedingly, with "so"
34 "King Kong" attire
36 Boxing outcome?
39 Never
40 Wife of Theseus
41 1856 Stowe novel
42 Cry sometimes made with hands on one's head
43 River known anciently as Obringa
45 On the right and left
49 Alternative to Pl. or Ct.
50 The 21st, e.g.: Abbr.
51 Actress Kazan
52 First name in tyranny
53 Monthly
55 Capitol V.I.P.
56 Backed
58 Befuddle
61 Seating sections
62 Baroque
63 Inscribed stone
64 New in the area, maybe

DOWN

1 Dessert, in Dover
2 Trixie of 1950's TV
3 Possible rebuttal in a childish argument
4 Food stat.
5 It turns out lts.
6 Fancy finishes
7 Loss leader, e.g.
8 1974 hit subtitled "Touch the Wind"
9 Singer with the 1980 #1 album "Guilty"
10 "Oh, ___!"
11 Cabinet dept.
12 Folksy
13 Like roses
14 Protect, in a way
21 Part of the brain associated with memory
24 "If ___ you . . ."
25 Place name that in Spanish means "covered in snow"
30 It's usually abbreviated "c."
33 See 48-Down
35 "Same here!"
36 They might be written on a blackboard
37 Classic 1868 novel set in St. Petersburg
38 City west of Knoxville
44 Store on a farm
46 Open
47 Nothing, in Napoli
48 Like a car, after a 33-Down
53 Stock: Abbr.
54 Botanist Gray and others
57 Unagi, at a sushi bar
59 Go bad
60 N.Y.C. subway

by Eric Berlin

ACROSS

1 Television portmanteau word
7 Question to a consumer watchdog
15 Treetop whistler
16 Like some relations
17 Ill-fated
18 Caterpillars, maybe
19 Fashion model Wek
20 Opinion leader?
22 Deserved
23 Take a flier?
24 TV monitor?
25 Study grant named after a Rhode Island senator
26 Call up
28 ___ Plaza, former Calgary landmark name
30 Draws on
31 Disciplined
33 Grayish brown
35 Is a pro
40 A fourth of what's left?
41 Award for Neil Armstrong
42 Prefix with graphic
45 Certain voice
47 Setting for "Androcles and the Lion"
48 Neighbor of Swed.
49 One-eighty
51 Water gate?
52 Do-say link
53 Tool for Edmund Hillary
55 Lily who debuted as Lakmé
56 Hokum
58 Biblical miracle worker
60 Water
61 No put-on?
62 Treasure Stater
63 Patronize, as an inn

DOWN

1 One whose work is counter-productive?
2 "The Stepford Wives" author
3 "See you later"
4 Go pffft, with "out"
5 Pennsylvania's ___ Bull State Park
6 "M*A*S*H" extra
7 Theater question
8 Peels
9 Shiraz locale
10 Sticker
11 Chow order?
12 Certain terminals
13 Schoolmaster's child-punisher
14 "E-cars"
21 Kofi Annan's bailiwick
24 Frost lines
25 Less significant
27 Truckle
29 Something you might turn up your nose at
32 Mrs. Chaplin
34 Emasculate
36 Little Bighorn fighters
37 Schiller poem used by Beethoven
38 "Hey Jude" chorus
39 Possible goal
42 Stuck
43 Square dance figure
44 Armenia's capital, old-style
46 Fashion designer Bartley
50 Makes a big stink
53 "___ boy!"
54 "Misery" co-star, 1990
55 Tucson's county
57 One concerned with matters of the heart: Abbr.
59 On

by Manny Nosowsky

ACROSS

1 "Blitzkrieg Bop" group, with "the"
8 Carrier's carrier
15 Chapter
16 Old-time actress Taylor
17 Be docile
19 Hit too high, say, with "out"
20 Diamond status
21 Logos and such: Abbr.
22 Bats
23 Hägar the Horrible's dog
24 Wool gatherer?
25 Mehmet ___, builder of Istanbul's Blue Mosque
26 Tests the waters, in a way
27 Dutch treat
28 They've been known to cause a stink
30 Praised loudly
31 Super bosses?
33 Drink since 1961
36 Wall Street workers
40 Rodgers and Hart's "___ Love"
41 How golf's Gary Player was named?
42 Make tracks
43 Knock-down-drag-outs
44 Letter opener?
45 Northumberland river
46 N.Y.C. subway
47 German boulevard
48 It's rolled in a bar
49 "Calm down!"
52 Sent with a click
53 St. Louis's ___ Airport
54 Legal paper
55 Definitive answer

DOWN

1 Danger sign
2 Quarrel stopper, maybe
3 TV news tool
4 Prefix with plastic
5 L'Étoile du ___, Minnesota's motto
6 ___ Period, depicted in "The Last Samurai"
7 Like some motions
8 They may be running along a street
9 Comparatively warm
10 L.A.-to-Jacksonville route
11 Syr. neighbor
12 Obscure
13 See 50-Down
14 Blows one's stack
18 Good one
23 Lyon's river
24 Punk
26 Lynyrd Skynyrd's "___ Your Name"
27 Pietistic
29 Snakes' eyes
30 Skipping notes
32 Behind one's back
33 This won't work
34 "Call!"
35 Instance of unfairness
37 Pettifogger
38 Small potatoes player
39 X-ray, for example
41 Refer
44 Fugard's "A Lesson From ___"
45 Supercharger
47 "The Shelters of Stone" heroine
48 Saxophonist Zoot
50 With 13-Down, a diner order
51 "O Tibbie, I ___ seen the day": Burns

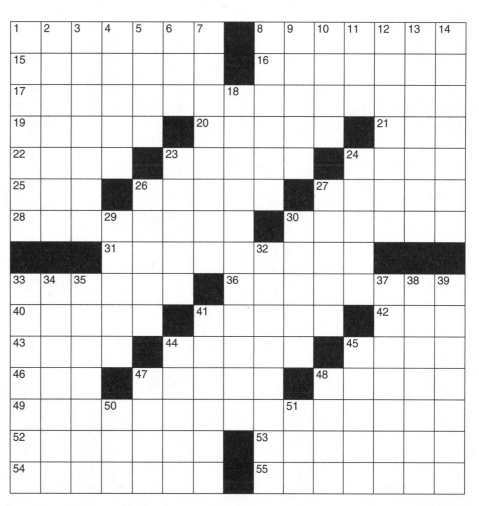

by Sherry O. Blackard

ACROSS

1 Gets ready to play
8 All done, as a movie
15 Last stops
16 Billboard listing
17 Adriatic port
18 Close enough
19 Claim
20 Having one's nose to the grindstone
22 Org. that publishes Playback magazine
23 El ___
24 Reserve
26 Time abbr.
27 With 44-Across, part of a children's song refrain
29 "___ Dinah" (1958 Frankie Avalon song)
30 Determinedly following
31 Gist
33 Was a bad influence on
36 Cause of delirium in farm animals
39 TV station inventory
43 "___ Cinders" of old funnies
44 See 27-Across
47 Fruity drink
48 Debut
49 Shrink
50 La ___, port near Buenos Aires
52 College Park player, informally
53 Arise (from)
54 Dovetail (with)
56 Flipper
58 It might accompany a pan
59 Unconventional delivery of supplies
60 Candy counter selection
61 Ebbs

DOWN

1 Staple of campaign oratory
2 Soothing medicine
3 Emulated Mikey in the cereal ads
4 Kind of room at a hosp.
5 Family nickname
6 Remove, as a notice
7 Oven container
8 Big wave
9 Thousandth of a yen
10 Popular razors
11 Mom-and-pop grps.
12 Like tickets and some stomachs
13 "Get ready!"
14 Really far-out?
21 Confused
24 "Yeah, you're right"
25 Funny business
28 Medium brown
29 "Well, lah-___!"
32 Cereal box stat.
34 Certain preowned vehicle
35 Ones making house calls
36 Go after, as a rebound
37 Reactionary
38 Suitable for gripping
40 It's uncultivated
41 Level
42 Sheets with stars
45 On the back
46 Up-and-coming type
48 Totaled
51 Cookbook author ___ Boyle
53 Benchmarks: Abbr.
55 Make a doily
57 They're rolled in Mexico

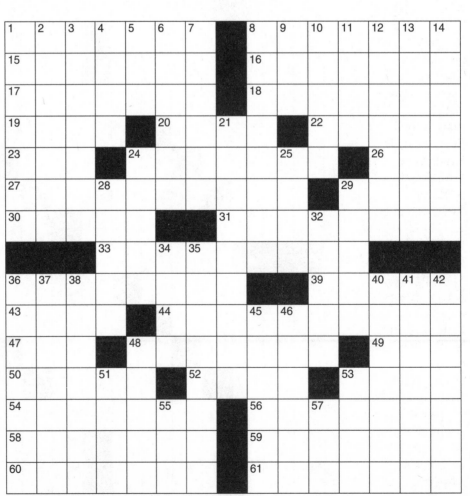

by Sherry O. Blackard

ACROSS

1 1995 Robin Williams film
8 Exalt
15 That's what you think
16 NASA, e.g.
17 Kind of table
18 It has its outlet in the East China Sea
19 Onetime Camaro alternative
20 Dump
22 Book before Neh.
23 Language from which "galore" comes
25 Rash decision?
26 Starr and Thompson
27 Control, symbolically
29 Bar stock
30 Electronic control system, for short
31 ___ chicken
33 Clinton, e.g.
35 Need to make a difference
37 Noted Carmelite mystic
40 Having more bass
44 Pool accessory
45 Football playoff grp.
47 Pit
48 Brief bylaws
49 Palm tree locale
51 Opposite of adios
52 Schubert's "The ___-King"
53 Some resins
55 Unit of 100 ergs per gram
56 Mutinied ship of 1839
58 Leaders in pits
60 Detail
61 Less than stellar
62 View
63 Reproduces, in a way

DOWN

1 Band on the run?
2 Stuck
3 Basic cell division
4 Chemical suffix
5 Sight in Memphis
6 Down Under youngsters
7 Ready to roll
8 Terminal headaches?
9 "See if ___"
10 Neighbor of Eure-et-Loir
11 Beaten punch
12 Completely overjoyed, perhaps
13 Tropical insect whose name is the last word in the Official Scrabble Players Dictionary
14 "Nature" essayist
21 Wily
24 Gives a protective cover
26 Poet Rexroth
28 Smug expression
30 White-haired types
32 Course setting: Abbr.
34 Yeaned youngster
36 Debut of 9/15/1982
37 Riots
38 Due to heat
39 Identifying phrase
41 Some Monopoly players pay it
42 Swell
43 Primes
46 High
49 "___ of Blue Eyes" (Thomas Hardy novel)
50 Split
53 Woman's name suffix
54 One with future prospects?
57 Juliet, to Romeo
59 Breaking capacity, briefly

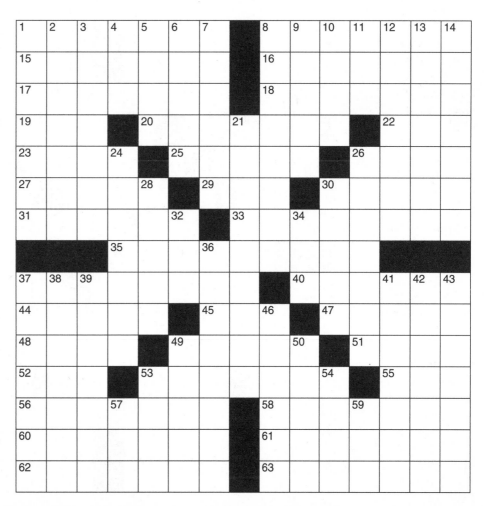

by David Quarfoot

ACROSS

1 Barefaced
8 Some air lines
15 Greasy kid stuff
16 Boutros Boutros-Ghali, by birth
17 Where to get in on the ground floor
19 Equate, in a way
20 Staff notes?
21 Tidy sum
22 Mother of Horus
23 Some hats
24 Innocent
25 Affirmative action?
26 Fields
27 Swiss canton or its capital, old-style
28 Stick out
30 Goes back over
32 Now unemployed
34 ___ hole in (corrodes)
35 Got off topic
38 Great desire
41 Late actress Uta
42 Twists in a bar
44 "___ favor, amigo"
45 Mullah Muhammad ___
46 Four Holy Roman emperors
47 He loved Lucy
48 "___ for Innocent" (Grafton novel)
49 Bang up
50 Monopolize
51 Hard to grasp
54 The Crossroads of America
55 Hug, maybe
56 Itty-bitty
57 Soft tissue

DOWN

1 Knot that won't slip
2 Link
3 "Seriously . . ."
4 Small fry
5 Not accepting nohow
6 Security Council vote
7 Just so
8 Short paradegoer's complaint
9 Nostrils
10 Little birds
11 Ready for combat
12 Watch closely
13 Dignify
14 Living room furniture
18 Like the end of the world
23 Liberator
24 Boito's Mefistofele and others
26 "I Love a Parade" composer
27 They may be drawn
29 Dairy outlet?
31 Not just aversions
33 Alpha particle's emission
35 Reply to a knock
36 He wrote "You and I have brains. The others have fluff"
37 Lightheaded
39 "Big deal . . . I was wrong"
40 Multiscreen cinema
43 De Niro's do in "Taxi Driver"
46 Warning signals
47 Class underachiever
49 Cross words
50 Make a bundle
52 Sticker
53 Salt, in Sauternes

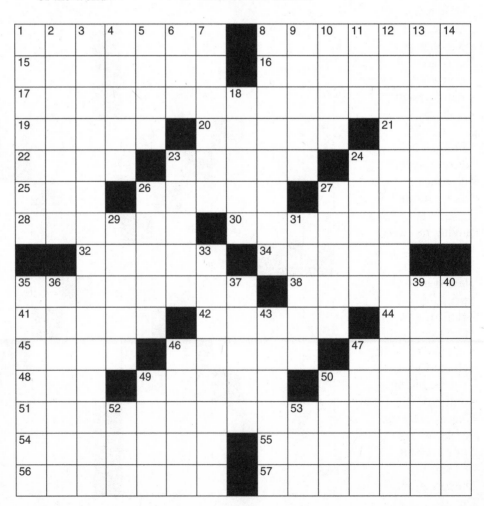

by Manny Nosowsky

ACROSS

1 Many a Standardbred
8 Aid in raising cane?
15 San Remo setting
16 One who's trying
17 Member of NATO
18 Hard at it
19 Like some checks: Abbr.
20 Rodgers and Hammerstein musical setting
22 Inner: Prefix
23 ___-El (Superman's birth name)
24 It may interfere with delivery
27 10 marks, once
29 Tank top
30 "Just because"
32 City where Mark Twain is buried
36 Foundation, often
37 People known to have germs?
38 Noted Hollywood exec
39 Refuse to change
40 Imposts
42 In headlinese, say
43 Minor expenses
47 Spanish pronoun
48 Baseball's Drabek
49 Man who's taken vows
50 Cottontail's tail
51 RCA rival
54 Catch
56 Target of a flick
57 Moped
58 They send up jets
59 Things fault-finders study

DOWN

1 It may require joint checking
2 Popular side
3 Rulers' rulers
4 The earth is on one
5 Kind of service
6 Novelist Jünger
7 Fireplace alternative
8 Austrian physician whose work laid the foundation for hypnosis
9 Digital communication?: Abbr.
10 11-member grp.
11 Be on easy street
12 Checking out
13 Kappa's position
14 Cereal killer
21 Pull ___ on
24 Jelly plant
25 "Band of Gold" singer Payne
26 Lets up
28 Broadway sights
31 Assist
33 Curse
34 No longer worried
35 Hill predators
37 Statement made with a tsk, tsk
39 ___ record
41 Cloisonné clusters
43 Label
44 Wild West justice
45 Hardly hard
46 Cavalry soldier
50 Judgment passer, perhaps
52 Boiling blood
53 Tender place?
55 "___ wise guy, eh?"

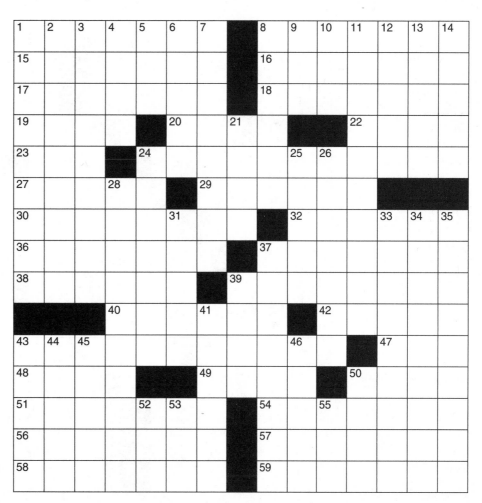

by Sherry O. Blackard

ACROSS

1 Once popular Bravo series, informally
9 Quaint hairstyle
15 Outraged
16 Insight
17 "Servant of the Bones" writer
18 "This I gotta hear"
19 It's flaky
20 Like a certain complex
21 Per ___
24 March sound
25 Weeklong holiday
26 "The Wizard of Oz" co-star
27 Of the bicuspid valve
29 Annual contributions may be made to them
30 One of 52 in Las Vegas
34 First name in horror
35 Dries up
36 Maupassant's "___ Vie"
37 Where a specialist has expertise
39 Develop
40 Develop
41 Develop
42 Way off
44 Like Brahms's Symphony No. 3
45 Workers' incentives
46 Things included in a count
48 Bristol locale: Abbr.
49 Join forces?
50 It may raise the roof
54 Hebrew title of respect for God
55 Rosary bead representation
56 Zapper
57 Serves

DOWN

1 In the capacity of
2 Broadcaster since Jan. 1995
3 Article of Cologne
4 They may be sworn
5 Hole-in-one, e.g.
6 Pine Valley soap siren
7 Place to work out
8 A storm heading: Abbr.
9 Caused to swell up
10 Snake or eel, e.g.
11 Assign an alias
12 Delicate breakfast item
13 Bravura
14 Break
20 Performed better than, in a way
21 Kind of powder
22 R.B.I. recordholder
23 Annual, e.g.
24 Dialectal pronoun
27 Bidding doers
28 Oils and such
30 Baking holder
31 Masters
32 ___ side (askew)
33 Axolotl look-alikes
35 Bug-eyed cartoon character
38 Irish game resembling field hockey
39 Charging
41 They come from Mars
42 "9 to 5" co-star
43 Fusion
45 Title girl in a Left Banke hit
46 Kind of nectar
47 Levi's uncle
48 VCR alternative
50 Monetary unit?
51 The Rams of the Atlantic 10: Abbr.
52 Yes, in São Paulo
53 Martial arts word meaning "trample" in Korean

by David Liben-Nowell

ACROSS

1 Not blocked
5 Knocked completely off one's feet
15 What a card reader may do?
16 For love or money
17 Dejection interjection
18 It's used to make carbon black
19 Pool opening
21 Like some hands
22 It's nice when prize winnings come with lots of these
23 Meddle managers?
24 Town near Perugia
27 Blazed
28 Wars of the Roses battle site
31 Coupe complement
34 Permanently undecided
35 Gallery item
36 1969 target
37 Head up North?
38 Noted 2003 Eton graduate
42 Pan, e.g.
43 Peak
44 Application after a break
47 Reason to put on a collar
49 Sash accompanier, maybe
50 War game
54 Line of sight?
56 Inter ___
57 Events for potential bidders
58 Artery
59 Using big words?
60 Lively

DOWN

1 Moore verse opener
2 Counseling, e.g.
3 Bring up
4 Expanding
5 Punch with punch
6 Aviator ___ Balbo
7 "Princess Caraboo" star, 1994
8 Currency unit in Harry Potter tales
9 Strathclyde port
10 Some earth movers
11 Francis of old TV
12 Probe
13 Florida's ___ National Forest
14 Exploits
20 Make a home
23 Thither
24 Contemporary of Emerson
25 Bellow in a library
26 Send down
27 Barber's supply
29 Cut off the back
30 Crib
31 Reason to press a suit, perhaps
32 Sported
33 Black
36 Nougat-filled treats
38 Dash
39 Progress preventer
40 Superlatively smooth
41 Pressure
42 Activity on a range
44 Milker's aid
45 Browning title character
46 "Ciao!"
47 Persian
48 Rouse
50 Fear, to François
51 Cockeyed
52 Iago, e.g.
53 Disney dog
55 Letter lineup

by Craig Kasper

ACROSS

1 Home of America's first automatic traffic light, ca. 1920
16 Declaration of independence
17 Store something away, in a way
18 Raised rumblers
19 "One Mic" rapper
20 Western N.C.A.A. powerhouse
21 Workout unit
22 Southpaw Shawn
24 N.S. clock setting
27 ___ Drake, longtime illustrator of "Blondie"
30 Actor Corey ___
34 Mrs. Reed's creator
39 "That's my final offer"
40 It's surprising when played
41 Record problem
42 Shift very carefully
43 Fronted
44 Personal assts. keep track of them
48 A question of self-examination
51 Follower of Christ?
52 Cartoon hit
55 Sun Devils' sch.
58 Superpowers often have them
62 1959 pop hit that asked "Why?"
63 Infatuation situation

DOWN

1 Element of change
2 Series follower: Abbr.
3 "Bad!" sounds
4 Explorer of the Canadian Arctic
5 P. D. James's "Death ___ Expert Witness"
6 "Garfield" waitress
7 Tight ends?
8 What androphobes fear
9 Metrical stress
10 Vacation locale, with "the"
11 Mozart's portrayer in "Amadeus"
12 Vacation spot
13 Classic cars that were the first to have Ram Air engines
14 Giotto's work
15 Reply put in by Putin?
22 Some like them hot
23 Be rude in line
24 Be temporarily
25 Radio___
26 Original "Star Trek" actor
27 Bad thing to have showing
28 Threatener of Miss Gulch
29 Buckets
31 Slippery as ___
32 Stick-to-___
33 Dealt
35 Commits to another hitch
36 The lady in "The Lady From Shanghai"
37 Former first lady's first name
38 Breathing abnormality
45 Firing places
46 Zhou ___
47 Think fit
48 Politico Hutchinson and others
49 Slugger Williams
50 Virginia willow
52 Universal Postal Union headquarters
53 Japon's place
54 Range: Abbr.
55 "That's not ___!" (parent's admonishment)
56 Golf's Ballesteros
57 Handles
59 Suffix with cannon
60 ___ Fabi of auto racing
61 It contains about 6% alcohol by volume

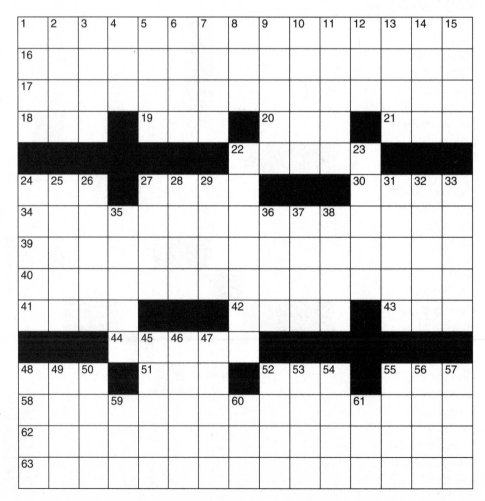

by David Levinson Wilk

ACROSS

1 Much-seen figure on a security cam
10 "Look out below!," e.g.
15 Going
16 Mann who sang "Save Me," 1999
17 Ninnies
18 Quintain rhyme scheme
19 Make a face
20 Pound sound
21 Old-fashioned news announcer
22 Got down
24 "No kidding!"
26 A or B in blood typing, e.g.
29 Kin of hagfish
30 Kick, in a way
31 Usual
33 Nice amount of moola
36 Eur. kingdom
37 Hardly the screaming type
38 Let go
39 Off one's feed
40 Fuel type, informally
41 They have plans, for short
42 Longtime Delaware senator William
43 Place name in 90's TV
45 Kid's taunt
49 Feature of an exit strategy?
50 "The African Queen" co-star, informally
51 Farm male
53 Bang up
56 ___ Corning, fiberglass maker
57 Integrated with
59 Amtrak station west of Grand Forks
60 Drawing room?
61 First name in sewing
62 [See above]

DOWN

1 Goes up and down
2 Sometime soon
3 Zero
4 Beggar's bearing
5 Baseball hero called "Gibraltar in cleats"
6 Wear and tear
7 Not home
8 Transmit
9 Calling a Jaguar XK a jalopy, say
10 Certain battery
11 Fall guys?
12 Kind of address
13 Not stand for oppression
14 Demonstratively sad
23 Stretching quality
25 Flinched, maybe
26 Prefix with syllabic
27 Wassailer's song
28 Pretty good
32 Preschoolers?
33 Attorneys' productions
34 Some people cry when these are said
35 ___-humanité
38 Major export of Albania and South Africa
40 "No legacy is so rich as ___": Shak.
42 Three-toed critters
44 Was beaten by
45 Certain W.M.D.
46 "That hurts!"
47 Broker
48 Nymph in Muslim paradise
52 Paw
54 Energize
55 You can hang your hat on it
58 "Saving Private Ryan" craft: Abbr.

by Manny Nosowsky

ACROSS

1 Holder of a lot of hidden dirt
8 Cajun condiment
15 Basement feature, sometimes
16 Not quite direct
17 Took some of
18 Bass offering
19 Shellback
20 Swear
22 By and by
23 Big name in home furnishings
25 Accommodate, in a way
26 "The 5,000 Fingers of ___" (1953 film musical)
27 Emulates a wolf
29 Roller coaster feature
31 Quintillionth: Prefix
32 Implant deeply
34 One and only
36 Efficiency option
38 Available from, as a product
41 Winter weather wear with adjustable straps
45 Eliminates as unnecessary
46 Old Testament figure
48 Insinuating
49 Year in St. Gregory I's papacy
50 Old World grazers
52 Formerly, once
53 Duffer's obstacle
55 Isn't up
57 Bird of the genus Corvus
58 Approach in a hurry
60 Sure shot
62 Wearing
63 Get behind
64 Sports physicians' concerns
65 Coty fragrance

DOWN

1 Like some egos
2 Indicate
3 Molson product
4 Something to thank God for: Abbr.
5 Historic Hebrides monastery site
6 Mississippi senator's family
7 Gushed
8 News leader
9 Makeup course?: Abbr.
10 "Up the Down Staircase" novelist Kaufman
11 Like some salts
12 Keep at steadily
13 Development of the 1950's
14 Like some mules
21 It's not too bright
24 Baking by-products
28 Essential element
30 18-Across offerers
31 Renaissance edition of a classic
33 Every family has one
35 Cries of alarm
37 Optimist in "Candide"
38 Masters
39 Good-for-nothin'
40 Record player
42 Ones who pay attention to bills
43 "Sounds about right to me"
44 Linking
47 They have naps
51 Knackered, as a Brit would say
54 Long-lasting, in commercial names
55 Cold-cock
56 "Vic and ___" of oldtime radio
59 Samoan staple
61 Point of "view"

by Bob Peoples

ACROSS
1 Sports column?
5 Standard deviation symbol
10 War fare?
14 Like many a hurricane
15 Allege in defense
16 Coat or skirt preceder
17 Disappointing election results
19 Seasoned
20 Help
21 Equal
22 Channeled
23 Resolute advice to the hesitant
27 Stuff for surfacing
28 He painted clocks
29 Community contest
30 Stumpers?
33 Flags
34 Hal Foster comic character
35 One associated with honesty
36 No one special
38 Castilian hero
39 Expert on the rules
40 Good relations
41 Manages, with "out"
42 N.Y. minutes?
43 Fountain in New Orleans
44 Word for word: Abbr.
46 1985 sequel to a classic 1939 film
48 Donny or Marie Osmond, e.g.
51 Unit of nautical displacement
52 Tall topper
54 Gee
56 Like bats
58 Biblical book
59 Available
60 Small animal shelter

61 Short time out?
62 They follow cuts
63 Dict. offering

DOWN
1 First name in animation
2 "This ___ Youth" (Kenneth Lonergan play)
3 Just learning about
4 Discovery of Galileo
5 Comparatively quick
6 Long series of woes
7 Lee, e.g.: Abbr.
8 ___ wheel
9 Plugs
10 Burn
11 Gripping read
12 Brutally destroy
13 Season opener?
18 Miss, south of the border
21 Parsley relative
23 Fine accompaniment?
24 Promise, e.g.
25 À la Poe
26 Fractures
28 Exile of 1302
30 Kitchen gizmo
31 Really big
32 Rights shouldn't be taken from it
33 Frosty
36 No performers are found here

37 Red sky, maybe
41 Colorize, e.g.
44 Immerses
45 Draper's unit
47 Cad
48 Slight indication?
49 "What ___!" ("Hilarious!")
50 Like some habits
52 Numerical prefix
53 Overflow
54 Modicum
55 Insurance letters
56 Green-light indicator
57 Person

by James M. and James C. Jenista

170 SATURDAY

ACROSS

1 Tim Russert venue
5 Had an assignation
12 Tribune Company competitor
15 Have a tête-à-tête with
16 Store sign
17 Argues
18 Store sign
20 Matisse's "La Tristesse du ___"
21 Initiation declaration
22 Elton John and others
23 Like some floor polish
24 Center
25 Benjamins
27 Some princesses
28 Phil Niekro and others
29 Dip into
30 Eye parts: Var.
31 Fair to middling
32 One giving the silent treatment
33 "___ abed and daylight slumber / Were not meant for man alive": Housman
34 Tabloid topic
35 Not-too-spicy cuisine
39 She's a doll
40 In modern lingo, an urban male who devotes much time to his appearance and lifestyle
42 Provide a segue for
44 What's left
45 Sign-up
46 Places for pilots
47 Perfume ingredient
48 Something to shoot through

DOWN

1 ___ sum (Chinese flowering cabbage)
2 Spanish infants
3 Boito's Mefistofele, e.g.
4 CNN screen feature
5 Three-legged ornamental table
6 Fix, as a costume
7 [That is, like, so last week]
8 Driver's caution
9 Superlatively hot
10 Check mate?
11 Stops
13 Teen party
14 House wreckers
15 Heads (off)
19 Feminine suffixes
22 ___ headache
24 Imbroglio
25 Ones in joint custody?
26 Candidate of 2000
27 Christmas carolers often get them
28 "Music for Airports" composer
29 ___-Novo (Benin's capital)
30 Sticker
31 Missouri Compromise signer
33 Company that makes Othello
35 Prefix with grade
36 Panegyrize
37 Worldly
38 Put away
40 ___ soup
41 Exhibiting greater moderation
43 When repeated, a classic horror movie line

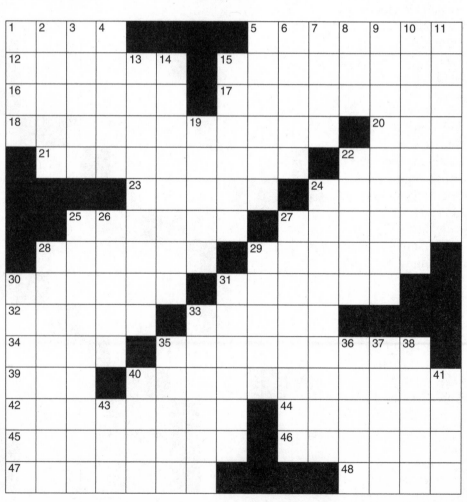

by Brendan Emmett Quigley

ACROSS

1 Tree that yields fragrant balsam
9 Club for wayward youths
15 High guy?
16 Miss ___ (teacher in "Peanuts")
17 Directed
18 Much-mistrusted name in news, once
19 Reels off
20 Steep rocky eminence
21 Name on a compact
22 U.S.N. functionary
23 Some rainwear
27 Secretly amassing
31 Place for candlesticks
34 Relief
35 Arena shout
36 First-nameless private eye in Robert B. Parker mysteries
37 Like some hotels, for short
38 It might receive feedback, briefly
39 1999 sitcom about a hockey player-turned-social worker
41 Finishes some of
43 Alumni ___: Abbr.
44 Single or double
45 Ringers in a ring
49 Huckleberry eaters
51 Not hiding much
53 Outgrowth
56 Tab, for one
57 Two-time U.S. Open champ
58 Filling choice
59 Practical school subject
60 Venus and others

DOWN

1 Messy snack
2 Sea, metaphorically
3 Decide on
4 Most peculiar
5 Some ad features
6 Cause of big smiles
7 Mountain West Conference team
8 Dieu et ___ droit (motto of England)
9 Ticketmaster event
10 Razor's handle
11 Title character in a 1997 ABC sitcom
12 Tag sale site?: Abbr.
13 "Carry the ___ that's born to be king" ("Skye Boat Song" line)
14 Period piece
20 Surveils
22 Shot the breeze
24 Flooded
25 1943 conference site
26 Actor von ___ of "The Seventh Seal," 1957
28 Like some codes
29 One who enjoys unlimited travel?
30 Sprouts
31 When repeated, Harold Rome song lyric before "I fear you reared me wrong"
32 Vacationing celeb's convenience
33 Goes parking
40 Betrays impatience with
42 Purpose
46 "The Mary Tyler Moore Show" character
47 Press product
48 Tons
50 "What ___?"
51 1962 Johnny Mathis hit
52 Count
53 Arena shout
54 Off-putting trait
55 Friend of Frodo
56 Clunker

by Patrick Berry

ACROSS

1 Like going in circles
12 Atlantic City, e.g.
14 Academy Award winner who said "I dream for a living"
16 Western bulrushes
17 Sch. that Roger Staubach played football for
18 Freshwater fish with bill-like jaws
19 Serving edge
20 "The Optimist's Daughter" author
22 Viva ___
23 Crisper
24 Chip flavoring
25 "Hotel de ___" (1959–60 TV western)
26 Camp seat
27 Moolah
28 Father ___, the leper priest of Molokai
29 Blue prints
31 Exotic stamp collectors, maybe
32 Keeps from
33 Gives the heave-ho
34 Org. with writing fellowships
35 Things seers see
36 Off one's trolley
37 Year that Eric the Red was born, traditionally
38 Place to dry tobacco
39 "Check it out!"
40 Park opened in 1964
41 Former MGM rival
42 Santa suit stuffing
43 Defensive play
44 It's dangerous for you to fly by
48 Stiffs
49 Roadwork equipment

DOWN

1 Full of vinegar
2 Mystery writer's award
3 Plays for a sap
4 It could be original
5 Stats on some backs
6 Put off
7 Longtime record label for Whitney Houston and Kenny G
8 Small
9 ___ Margarita, in the Caribbean
10 Head, slangily
11 They're always unaccompanied
12 2001's "Planet of the Apes" and others
13 Selenium and zinc
14 Openings for horse trainers
15 Healthful dishes
20 W.W. II volunteers
21 "The Intimate ___" (1990 jazz album)
22 "Hard Hearted Hannah" of song
24 Irving Berlin's "Blue ___"
25 Velvety plant
28 Packed
30 Affect in a subtle way
31 Place of hard knocks?
33 Kind of battle
36 Procrastinator's reply
39 Misstep
40 It can be icy
42 Laugh, in showbiz slang
43 Showcase lead-in on "The Price Is Right"
45 Your, in Roma
46 20-time Rose Bowl winner: Abbr.
47 Sorority letter

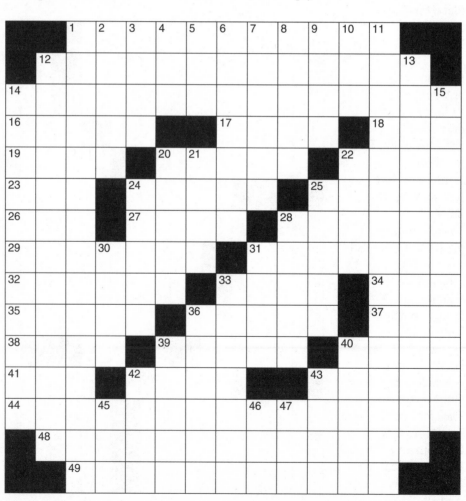

by Mark Diehl

ACROSS

1 Strategic Iraqi port just across the Kuwaiti border
8 Old green coats?
15 Paste
16 Home to Dyess A.F.B.
17 Before
18 Lagged
19 Fits
21 Like articles and blood
22 Steady devotion
23 1960's chess master
24 Starts to resemble
25 Fouls up
27 Map point
28 Like ink, in France
30 Where we live
32 Scholars
35 Some bargains
36 Disinclined
37 Decalogue word
38 Exact
39 Still
41 Go from here to there
45 Fat letters
46 PET scan particles
48 Northern forests
51 Loses focus
52 When coins came into general use
54 Get the last bit of suds out
55 Tower of faith
56 Less subdued
57 Parade times
58 Disburses

DOWN

1 Jazz enthusiast?
2 Personification of humanity's dark side
3 Title TV character played by Brandy Norwood
4 Pertaining to the present period in earth history
5 "Father Knows Best" family
6 Harshly criticize
7 Employees in the sugar industry
8 Grammarian, at times
9 Org. that the Indiana Pacers once belonged to
10 Moonroof feature
11 Not well
12 First or third quarter phenomenon
13 Animal with no teeth
14 Like some melons
20 Decent plot
26 "I thought I ___ . . ."
27 What a tough guy may not show much
29 Pair
31 Support, redundantly
32 Do a hurry-up job
33 Common wedding song
34 Competing narratives
35 Sad Sack's tormentor, in comics
37 Cry from a tickled person
40 Bouts of gastritis
42 "Don't stay out here"
43 Available
44 Ethyl acetate and others
47 Mountaineering aid
49 Small distraction
50 Europe's Gorge of the ___
53 E.U. language

by Byron Walden

ACROSS

1 Contributed
10 Dance in double time
15 Top-grossing movie of 1990
16 Out
17 No matter what
18 First major brewery to put beer in cans
19 Part of an office sched.
20 Screeches
22 ___ gestae (transactions)
23 Artist Mondrian
25 Finland's second-largest city
26 Point to the left
27 Rival of Venus
29 "Oh, really?"
31 Area of danger
33 Good way to go out
34 Energy producer
37 Cosmopolitan people?
39 Pounds, e.g.
40 Do taxing work
42 Souvenir shop item
44 Lines descending from a common ancestor
48 Kind of principal: Abbr.
49 Pussyfooted
51 Hall-of-Fame college swimming coach ___ Thornton
52 Diary
53 "Ta-ta!"
55 ___ piece (alike)
56 Subject of a commercial trade ban
58 Actor whose debut film was "The Russians Are Coming! The Russians Are Coming!"
60 Radios
61 Oversees, with "on"
62 Doctor
63 Hurricane origins

DOWN

1 Ticker-tape parade honorees
2 Major babe
3 Graphics machine
4 State ___
5 Is advantageous
6 A tightwad
7 Peddlers' stopping points
8 Flat
9 Boardroom worries
10 Breaks
11 Russell Cave Natl. Mon. locale
12 Text
13 Preoccupied one
14 Break points?
21 Studio site
24 Clipped the most
26 Desires to participate
28 "Sitting Bull" star, 1954
30 Davit
32 Behind
34 One who's resigned
35 Freezes
36 1976 hit by Hall & Oates
38 Earmarks (for)
41 Agate alternative
43 German self
45 Swindler
46 Spinning group
47 Carnival units
50 Fendi competitor
53 Skin problem
54 Place to hold hops
57 Fig. expressed in percents
59 Chi ___ (religious symbol)

by David J. Kahn

ACROSS

1 Signifies respect and sadness
16 Slipped
17 He said "In America, anybody can be president; that's one of the risks you take"
18 Service groups
19 Minds
20 Engineer in 2000 headlines
21 Masses
28 Alternative to Castilian
36 Place likely to have zoning restrictions
37 Factor in relationships between viruses
38 Mimics satisfactorily
39 Long and sharply pointed
46 "Speaking personally . . ."
47 Compound in fungicides
54 Pal of Pogo
56 Playground activity
57 Buying guides?

DOWN

1 Like some rates
2 Treasure-trove
3 Margarita, e.g.
4 Itinerary info
5 French silk
6 Without ___ (daringly)
7 "Touched by an Angel" character
8 Bygone presidential inits.
9 White poplar
10 1987 Tony-winning actress for "Broadway Bound"
11 Relatives
12 Sending a ___ the moon (1960's goal)
13 Noted Adams
14 Baked breakfast item
15 In danger of snapping
20 Flipped
21 Green stretch in Grenoble
22 Post-Passover period
23 Mexican mint product
24 Writer who created the writer Gideon Zadok
25 Blinkers
26 Pete Sampras, notably
27 One with a supporting role
29 Director Vittorio De ___
30 Dabs
31 Some Muslim men
32 Place to pray
33 Glad family
34 Bristle
35 Eponymous code creator
39 Uno and others
40 "___ in Her Ear" (classic Georges Feydeau farce)
41 Coveted award
42 Marathoner Waitz
43 Like inferior computer graphics
44 Prefix with molecular
45 "Lines on the Mermaid Tavern" poet
47 Some singers
48 Annual sports contests, for short
49 1988 Belinda Carlisle hit "___ Weak"
50 Pasternak heroine
51 Pack ___
52 Terse warning
53 Dyne-centimeters
55 Spanish article

by Frank Longo

ACROSS
1 Assembly area
6 Clinton's secretary of health and human services
13 Study
15 Developmental site
16 Start of a carol
17 Water
18 Saint usually depicted carrying the infant Jesus
19 TV control
20 French resort Villefranche-sur-___
21 Big name in women's wear
23 Smooth
24 Like some missiles
25 Betting game
26 Longevity
27 Gang
28 "Nice!"
32 Prima ballerina who married an ambassador
33 Noted TV war correspondent
34 "Hi-___, Hi-Lo" (1953 hit)
35 Some bays
36 Persevere and succeed
40 Verb with vous
41 Having columns set into a wall
43 Hang loosely
44 Charles Anderson ___, owner and editor of the New York Sun, 1868–97
45 Sexually attractive
46 Like sage or allspice
48 Interstice
49 1920's communication fad
50 Figure
51 Drunken
52 Bamboozles and how

DOWN
1 Lower
2 Lady of Coventry
3 Kind of band
4 Forwarded
5 Ones who'd never think of flying?
6 Head doctor
7 Star of the 1957 Broadway musical "Jamaica"
8 Going ___
9 Account
10 ___ Creek, N.C., site of a 1771 colonial battle
11 In a dormant form
12 North Sea oil industry center
14 Hair shirt wearer
15 Climbers' spikes
22 Zoo keeper?
23 Work with mail
25 Dollhouse collector's collection
27 Fall phenomenon
28 They name the seasons
29 Handel work
30 Awaiting punishment, say
31 Scrabble 2-pointers
32 Purveyor of luxury tableware Michael C. ___
34 Flowers in a Whitman verse
36 Surface coating
37 Noted Viennese composer
38 Melodic
39 Gutless
41 Crowns
42 ___ list
44 "Anthropomorphic Bread" painter, 1932
47 Satisfied

by Brendan Quigley and Patrick Berry

ACROSS

1 Like a versatile wardrobe
10 Excited about
15 Ill-advised place?
16 View from the Latin Quarter
17 Masked man's cry
18 It may be supplied by a draft
19 Part of a Spanish explorer's name
20 Attaching, in a way
22 Very slow-moving
23 Its seat is San Rafael
24 North Carolina's ___ River State Park
25 Problem while getting clean
26 Drove obliquely
28 ___ ester
30 Empty
32 Deal in
33 One who might count you out
36 Cousins of a 33-Across
38 Foundation producer
39 It's tricky to return
41 Saint of housewives, in France
43 ___ fever (was sick)
44 "___ lied!"
47 Be in a cast
48 Protector of Io
50 Runs across
52 Halfhearted
54 On something
55 Legal scholar Guinier and others
56 Sought acceptance from
58 Square things
59 Participate in military combat
60 Bad spelling?
61 Doesn't do anything crazy

DOWN

1 Bungled
2 Fixed
3 Bizarre cases
4 Not as cold
5 Teach on TV?
6 Service sign-off
7 Plus fours go-with
8 Cause
9 Bouncing off the walls
10 Noted Phila. facility
11 Menial
12 Rat
13 Intimate chat
14 Wrap giant
21 Nestor
23 Rumble
27 It began in 1968, for tennis
29 Dark side
30 Bit of headway
31 They have big bells
33 West Bank city
34 Clear out
35 Gold holder
37 Packaging suppliers' industry
40 Ballyhoo
42 Parts of ship bows
44 New Mexico's ___ National Labs
45 Freight unit
46 Needs no more work
49 Blades that are cut by blades
51 ___ Corner, part of Westminster Abbey
53 Start of a Mozart title
54 Fell
57 Source of a royal pain?

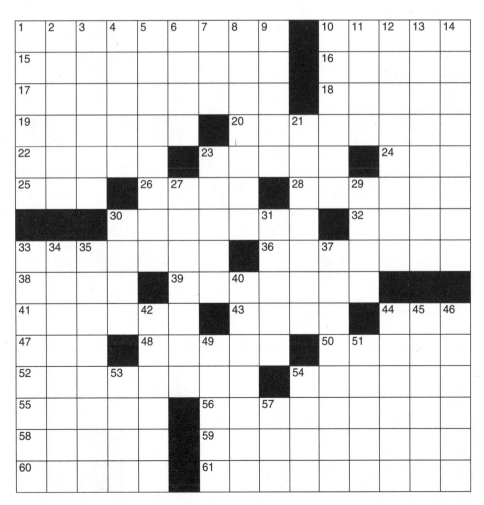

by Byron Walden

ACROSS

1 Physician Golgi, for whom Golgi bodies are named
8 Reader holder
15 Evangeline, e.g.
16 Pen
17 "Separate Tables" playwright
19 Muster
20 ConAgra Foods brand
21 Black Panthers co-founder
22 Half of a cartoon duo
23 Writer who coined the word "robot"
25 Lundi ___
26 Al Jolson's real first name
27 Italian colony, 1890–1941
29 Numerical prefix
30 Undoer
32 Barely runs?
34 One overseas
35 "Shake a leg!"
36 Stability enhancer
39 One may live on it
42 Student inside ivied walls
43 Was in no way happy
45 Old Egyptian title
46 Bad: Prefix
48 Deceives, slangily
49 Wind instrument
50 Low life?
52 Code word
53 They may be taken before drawing
54 It's set in a castle near Seville
57 Not as distinct
58 Like some heads
59 They often come in twos
60 Actress Taylor of the silents

DOWN

1 Dali, by birth
2 Needle-shaped
3 Union authorization
4 "Any ___?"
5 Wrinkled
6 Supérieur, e.g.
7 Hand holding
8 Obviously happy people
9 Where Stratford and Cambridge are: Abbr.
10 Fall times: Abbr.
11 ___ light
12 Couple in old pictures
13 One way to be happy
14 Opening
18 Caught up
23 Contradicts
24 Two-masters
27 Old liquid heaters
28 Holding one's piece
31 Bother
33 Many a hirer: Abbr.
36 Stops the progress of
37 W.W. II battle site, with "El"
38 Chicken servings
39 "The Ill-Made Knight" novelist
40 Campaign manager?
41 Dump
44 Horse : herd :: ___ : knot
47 Deposed Ugandan leader
49 Fuzzy
51 Longtime adviser to Saddam Hussein
53 Longtime British Tory P.M.
55 Sleep unit?
56 Hi-___

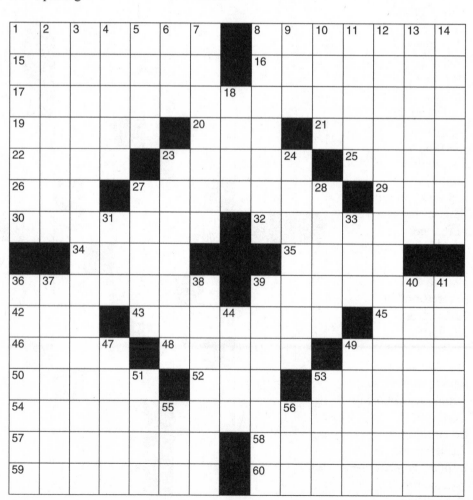

by Ed Early

ACROSS

1 Party promoter
8 Shows devotion (to)
15 Place for a comb
16 Thingies
17 Cover over
18 Ties up
19 Drinks made with Southern Comfort
21 "Where there's ___ . . ."
22 A story might be told in it
32 Paneling material
33 40-Down's birthplace
34 "I'll get this"
35 Lets have it
37 Shower
38 Marker
39 March subject
42 Part of a religious title
43 1990's TV detective drama
53 Villainous ones in the Bible
54 Brass production
55 Name on a cake
56 ___ Aigner, popular maker of shoes and handbags
57 Addiction accomplice
58 Gits in a scrap (with)

DOWN

1 Spelling start?
2 Debark?
3 Spice in a rap trio's name
4 Obsessive hunter of fiction
5 "Live!" co-host
6 A bead may represent one
7 Large amount of juice?
8 "Let's Eat Right to Keep Fit" author ___ Davis
9 Name associated with the Taj Mahal
10 ___ oak
11 Skimmed milk product
12 What hearts sometimes do
13 River of Hesse
14 Air hose sound
20 Something to build on
22 Poet Lazarus and others
23 "___ on me"
24 "Per Ardua ad ___" (Royal Air Force motto)
25 Termite, e.g.
26 Rare birds
27 Sperry who invented the Sperry gyroscope
28 Hedren of "The Birds"
29 Old political journalist with the newspaper column "Matter of Fact"
30 Admission of defeat
31 Spring times
35 Huge flop
36 Some threats
38 Year the oldest college in the Americas was founded, in Mexico City
40 "The Big Parade" co-star, 1925
41 Aswan Dam builder
43 Old stage actress Eleanora
44 "There ___ old saying . . ."
45 Subtle quality
46 Interest greatly
47 Charles II's mistress
48 Colleges, to Aussies
49 A.A.A. info
50 Twain's jumping frog
51 White-tailed bird
52 Explorer John and others

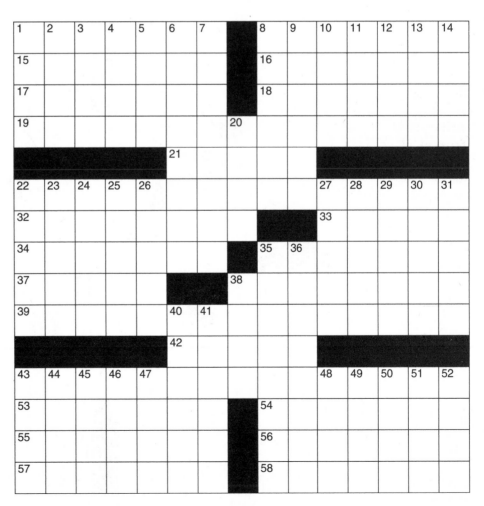

by Harvey Estes

ACROSS

1 Heavenly array
8 One way to leave a hair salon
15 Least fresh
16 What the first caller may be on
17 Film event
18 Goddess mentioned in Poe's "Ulalume"
19 Tie indicator
20 "Strangers on a Train" chase scene site
22 Short stroke
24 Cancel
25 Like a literary prince
26 Targets of some sprays
28 Federal Communications Commission target
30 Play thing?
31 King Gyanendra, for one
33 Eliciting a "So what?"
35 Old union member: Abbr.
36 It's topped with Roquefort dressing
39 No longer edible
42 Extra
43 Denouement preceder
47 European border river
49 Particles of the lepton family
51 Impound
52 "Zapped!" co-star, 1982
54 Chase of "Now, Voyager"
56 Rimsky-Korsakov's "The Tale of ___ Saltan"
57 Jeremy Irons film based on Proust's writings

60 Ziegfeld of the "Ziegfeld Follies"
61 Chemical salt in some black inks
62 Places for some rings
64 Customer
65 It needs three walls
66 Causes increasing irritation
67 Incessant

DOWN

1 Attach, in a way
2 Warm-up
3 Good viewpoint
4 Noël time in Tahiti
5 Get back
6 New Jersey county
7 Trial figures
8 Embryonic stage
9 Pros or cons, e.g.
10 Ready
11 Less muddled
12 Snack food brand
13 Catches in a trap
14 Catalog anew
21 Dope
23 Ford Explorer Sport ___
27 Eats, but barely
29 Sprinkler's need?
32 Doubter's scoff
34 "The Merry Drinker" painter
37 No-___ (snaps)
38 One may cheat on it

39 Be proud to have
40 Computer program that blocks pop-ups
41 Has to have
44 Put in the wrong place
45 Heath family members
46 Abnormal dryness
48 Milk curdler
50 Capital SSE of Belgrade
53 Web
55 For the birds
58 Aqueduct of Sylvius, e.g.
59 City near Vance Air Force base
63 Asian carrier

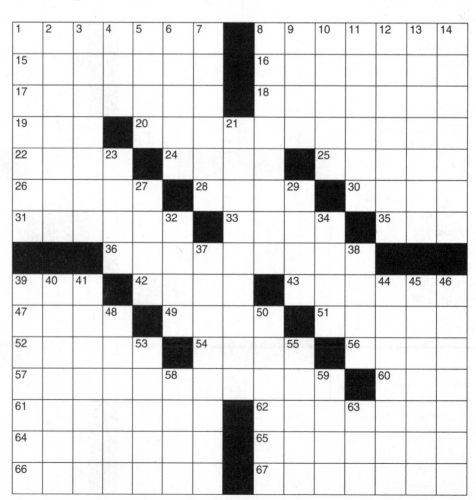

by Byron Walden

ACROSS

1 Not merely deep
8 Without stopping
15 Moon of Neptune named for a Greek nymph
16 Kind of ray
17 One waiting for an accident to happen
19 Animal that spits
20 Sees people
21 Part of retribution
22 Remain
23 Chopin's fifth étude is in it
24 No big thing
25 ___ voce (without dissent)
26 One may be fired up
27 Physics units
28 Base place
30 Take in
31 Jazz Age figures
33 Thin
35 Liner
38 Space ___
39 Isn't doing support work
40 Dr.'s order?
41 Wrestler Flair and others
42 Antique weapons
43 Shouts in a ring
44 ___ Mae (Whoopi's role in 26-Down)
45 Wear
46 Twist
47 Eliciting a "So what?"
50 Bust
51 One of the Kennedys, and namesakes
52 Set up
53 Like no human, according to the Bible

DOWN

1 Modern record
2 It can be taken down
3 Absolutely awful
4 Bubble up
5 Leon Uris's "___ 18"
6 Bibliophilic suffix
7 Wasted area?
8 Perfume ingredient
9 Be silent, in music
10 Jocks: Abbr.
11 Dance bit?
12 Reeled
13 Comes up with something
14 Most cheeky
18 Station identification
23 Recipe directive
24 Perfume ingredient
26 See 44-Across
27 Concern of some codes
29 Healing sites
30 Food stabilizers
32 Endowed individuals
33 One visited by 26-Downs
34 Treated
36 Punishes arbitrarily
37 Electric, say
39 High
42 Piped up
43 Newsman Roger
45 Caber caster
46 Detective who frequented the jazz club Mother's
48 Tolkien terror
49 ___ Transtulit Sustinet (motto of Connecticut)

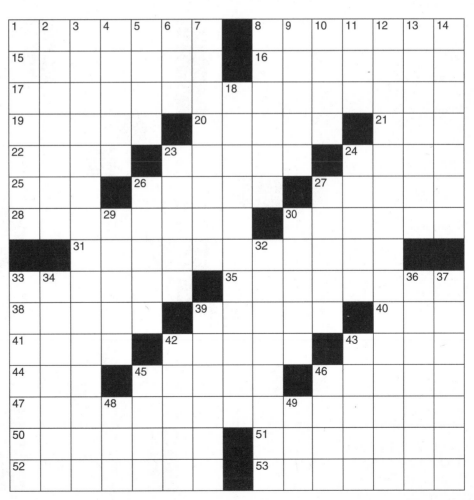

by Sherry O. Blackard

ACROSS

1 Plug in the sticks
5 The old you
9 Confuse
14 Musical form whose name means "color"
15 Streamlet
16 "Put me out of my misery!"
17 See 13-Down
18 "Something's not kosher"
20 Señor of old TV
22 Coffee mishaps
23 Substantial plates
25 Nephew of King Mark, in legend
28 Running things
30 Day-___
31 One with set goals?
34 Vat waste
35 End of a requiem title
36 Tic-___ (metronome sound)
37 Wasp's nest site
38 Short-lived particles
39 Easy
42 BBC rival
43 Night crier
44 It has a knot
46 To-do list
50 Up-to-date, in a way
52 Block houses
53 Part of a ship
56 First name in fashion
57 Real estate info
58 Friend of Masterson
59 Big name in magazine publishing
60 Hardly a 39-Across feeling
61 Old film actress who starred in 1950's TV's "The Pride of the Family"
62 Middle Earth creatures

DOWN

1 "Master and Commander" star
2 Port
3 Cut taker
4 Focus of some tribunals
5 Make a mathematical cut
6 Matching pair designation
7 Threatened flora
8 One sensitive to light
9 1965 Patty Duke film
10 Affected-sounding outburst
11 Low
12 Certain cells
13 With 17-Across, quit worrying about
19 Indication not to rush
21 Dark times in literature
24 Discovery team
26 Bayer brand
27 ___-um
29 Dig a lot
31 Belong
32 Sore and more
33 Sending up
34 Quit messing with
39 More sharp
40 Frugal
41 Famed puppeteer
43 Validate
45 Wrap-arounds
47 "A Tree Grows in Brooklyn" family name
48 Accomplish, archaically
49 Superiors of senior airmen: Abbr.
51 Frost
53 One with a supporting role?
54 Wine: Prefix
55 Pray, to Publius

by Jim Page

ACROSS

1 One of the crowd, perhaps
8 Vegetable matter
12 In condensed form
13 Devilfish
14 Be summarily lost . . . or what 30-Across might do?
16 Mean
17 Make inquiries
18 Susan who wrote the 1978 best seller "Compromising Positions"
22 Dishwasher, at times
23 Spots to spot Dalmatians
26 End of a flight?
27 1040 attachment
30 Moniker suggested by the pattern of white squares in this grid
35 Plied, as a dirty trick
36 Renowned chair designer
41 Most dear
43 Bulk up
46 Like some hard soils
47 Fine home decoration
50 Short respite
51 Dangerously positioned, like 30-Across, often?
55 Modern alternative to Hallmark
56 Actor Tom of "Top Gun"
57 Proofer's mark
58 Alpha ___ acids (cosmetic ingredients)

DOWN

1 Hit series whose pilot was the TV movie "Panic at Malibu River"
2 Investing opportunity, for short
3 Nashville sch.
4 Place
5 Ski resort near Snowbird
6 Cheers
7 Slogs far afield
8 Bear fruit
9 Off-road motorcycle competition
10 Penitent soul
11 Cheap
12 Like the winner in a guessing contest
13 Some MOMA holdings
14 Simple hairstyle
15 "Never Wave at a ___" (1952 military farce)
19 New York's ___ Stadium
20 Sci. class
21 Round at a snack bar
24 Give up, slangily
25 Swift sailing vessel
28 Get an ___ effort
29 Savory jelly
31 Kind of support
32 Peter Gunn's girlfriend
33 "It is the sea / Gone with the sun," wrote Rimbaud
34 Skill often touted but rarely seen
36 Spotted
37 Posthaste
38 You or me, e.g.
39 Flimflam
40 Mount
42 Letters
44 Right angle
45 Charlie Chan player of 50's TV
48 Pitch-black
49 It's more than a desire
52 Famous Bruin #4
53 Back
54 Jam

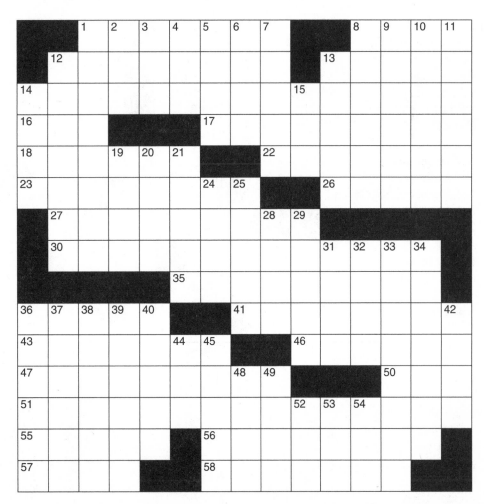

by Mark Diehl

ACROSS

1 Keep from practicing
7 A little hard to find
15 Prefix with bacteria
16 Brought to light
17 Some French wines
18 Like a cat's existence?
19 "Of course, what would I know?"
21 Place for a monitor: Abbr.
22 Excited
23 English sum?
25 Make (out)
26 6 letters
27 Speed
29 Eva's half-sister?
30 Beat
32 Plant used to prevent erosion on banked roadsides
34 Had a peak experience?
37 Start of a revival?
39 Clipped
40 Beats
42 Market purchase
44 Hi-tech bookmark
45 Tom Sawyer's half-brother
47 F.D.R. initiative: Abbr.
48 Bad from the start?
51 "Stupid me!"
52 Poles are in it
54 Treebeard in "The Lord of the Rings," e.g.
55 2002 upset event
59 Try to impress, in a way
60 Of a heart chamber
61 Dual
62 RNA constituent
63 Pressed hard
64 The beginning

DOWN

1 Gibson of pop
2 Fortunate
3 One may be standing at a fountain
4 Inclination
5 Early calculator of pi
6 1982 Toto hit that won Record of the Year
7 See 24-Down
8 Wood of Hollywood
9 Something easily forgotten
10 Does in
11 Break
12 Perfumery purchase
13 Stir hopes?
14 Roush of Cooperstown
20 Major irritant
24 With 7-Down, wasn't inane
28 Paper pusher's words
30 Anderson who directed "The Royal Tenenbaums"
31 Jubilant cry
33 Sheepish excuse lead-in
34 Starch source, informally
35 "The Men Who Tread on the Tiger's Tail" director, 1945
36 Bile
38 "Man!"
41 Milieu for John Muir
43 Praise
46 Novelist ___ Heyward
48 1992 Michener book
49 For nothing
50 "___ Nacht" (German carol)
53 Caught, in a way
56 Rapper Sandra Denton's stage name
57 Old English letters
58 Look into?
59 Kind of power

by Brendan Emmett Quigley

ACROSS

1 Clumsy lug
4 Bondsman
8 An urn, after an accident
14 Ammo named after its English inventor
16 Enter with care
17 Place to keep leaves
18 Dutch brewery
19 Retract
20 Makes a racket
22 Web-___
23 Sierra Nevada's location
25 Spring
27 Former organizer of senior field trips
30 Zap
31 Grace period?
32 Holm who played Bilbo Baggins
33 Question concerning an early arrival
36 Raincoat coating
38 Speed
39 California food fishes
41 "___ Blue?"
42 1979 Broadway hit set during the Industrial Revolution
46 Pioneering automaker
48 Little problems
49 Composer Siegmeister
50 Preeminent, slangily
52 Yields
53 Overlong
54 Lawbreaker with two partners
57 It's south of the Yucatán
58 Plantation figure
59 Moor growths
60 Locker sites
61 Sharp

DOWN

1 Not easily misled
2 "Hospital smell" chemical
3 Cleared
4 Alter
5 Top or bottom
6 Médoc, for one
7 Angle
8 Tentacled marine animals
9 Hanseatic League city
10 Atty. in the firm
11 Add new parts to, say
12 Well-known hymn
13 Chase vehicle?: Abbr.
15 Scholar
21 One in a suit
23 Doesn't really hit
24 Teflon and Plexiglas
26 Sharp-sighted animal
28 Brings in
29 Satchel Paige's real first name
33 "A grand, ungodly, godlike man" in fiction
34 Citrus source
35 Judge of film
37 Holds high
40 Organic fuel source
43 Radio genre
44 Big vehicle's need
45 1930's western hero
47 Woody Allen film set in the 1920's
51 Baseballer known as the Big Cat
52 A shopping mall has lots of these
53 Onetime "Stay curious" sloganeer
55 Creeper
56 Little masterwork

by Patrick Berry

ACROSS

1 Snapped
7 Arrowhead feature
11 E.T.O. carrier
14 Other direction
16 It may get you
out of a rut: Abbr.
17 56-Across's land
18 One might
be verbal
19 Waiting to exhale?
20 Dairy product
used in some
cheese plants
22 Asian capital
23 Saxophonist
nicknamed "the
Sound"
24 Enjoying
25 Tight (with)
27 Appearance after
an eclipse
31 Not treat seriously,
with "at"
32 Aesop's morals, e.g.
33 Pole length?
35 Mil. post in
Fayetteville, N.C.
39 Baseball
Hall-of-Famer
George and others
41 L'___-deux-guerres
(French era)
42 Cold side
45 "Goin' Gone"
singer Kathy
46 Demeter's mother
47 Memorial announcer
49 Self starter?
50 Noted early 20th-
century
writer/reformer
54 Collectible frames
55 Touch
56 Capital of 17-Across
58 Bad thing to invoke
59 "Civil dissension
is a viperous worm"
speaker
60 "This is ___"

61 Stationer's stock
62 Didn't go unfulfilled

DOWN

1 Bill's friend or foe?
2 Plenty
3 Suddenly revealed to
4 Drag
5 "Woe ___"
(best-selling
grammar guide)
6 Seasoned lightly
7 Show fluster
8 Make ___ (earn big
bucks)
9 Level, in London
10 Letters of invitation
11 Basic language
course
12 Reach on a cruise
13 Add
15 Biting
21 Like many a
dead letter
23 Fetching ones?
26 Marching to a
different drummer
28 Place holders
29 Kind of booster
30 It's been seen before
32 Boy/girl introduction
34 It's sometimes
wrapped in rice
36 Where sweaters
are found?
37 60's mantra
38 Mascot costume,
maybe

40 Breakfast order
42 Knocker
43 "Shoot!"
44 Hard to move
45 Basement problem
48 Not so hot
51 Golfer Isao ___
52 Crush
53 Statement issuer
54 Growlers
57 ___ mission

by Byron Walden

ACROSS

1 Fair
10 Paul Gallico title character
15 Peace Memorial Museum locale
16 Extinct Algonquian
17 A trust may reduce it
18 Dismay
19 "Hair" tune
20 Circulation aid
22 Grand Prix feature
23 Richard Gere title role of 2000
24 It turns out lts.
25 "Children of the Albatross" author
26 Stagnation
28 Abbr. before a number
29 It looks bad on the surface
30 Not flabby
31 Stand
33 Old-fashioned alternative
35 "Remain calm"
38 Rationed
42 Victim of Polyphemus, in myth
43 Name on an oval
44 Fillet
45 30-day span: Abbr.
46 Trash
47 Rapper MC ___
48 Port Huron Statement org.
49 Run into
52 A/C measure
53 Situation in which only 56-Across is occupied
54 Hardly relaxed
56 See 53-Across
57 Hard thing to fill
58 Takes nothing in
59 Discount clothing store chain

DOWN

1 Tops
2 Meets
3 Crafty one?
4 Druggist for whom some commercial pills are named
5 It's not exact: Abbr.
6 Cuts
7 Number-starting prompt
8 Taliban mullah
9 Gush, in a way
10 Opposite of deplete
11 They may be put in stitches
12 Noted Chilean island
13 Ezra Pound, e.g.
14 Honorable start?
21 "Not with ___ the heart is broken": Emily Dickinson
23 Styled
27 They branch off
28 ___ tree
29 Loser
31 Some office attire
32 Guys in promotion
34 Geological depression
35 Leave quickly
36 Totalitarian state in "1984"
37 Some playful pooches
39 Taqueria offering
40 Software developer's concern
41 What a loser may skip
44 Alaska's ___ National Park
46 Auto damage
47 "Good Times" star, on 70's TV
50 Place on duty
51 Surveyor's work
52 Landscaping screen
55 Host

by Bob Peoples

188 SATURDAY

ACROSS

1 Camper's food warmer
8 River to Lake Huron
15 Barely cook, say
16 "The little flower of Jesus"
17 Not as warm
18 Handled better?
19 Tangelo, e.g.
21 Dogs were sacred to him
22 In one's Sunday best
28 Conspirator against Caesar
33 Joining
34 Take a mortar and pestle to
35 Sneaker seller
37 Out, in a way
38 Dwell on negatively
39 Not fair
40 Roadblocks
41 Thus, in Trieste
42 Weirded-out feeling
53 Not hard to get on with
54 Former Italian colony
55 Appellate order
56 Pitcher Randy Johnson's power source
57 Appliance conveniences
58 Babe

DOWN

1 Astrological transition point
2 "___ victory!"
3 It may elicit a funny face
4 North Dakota senator Conrad
5 Governessy
6 Music halls
7 Spinning out of control?
8 "The River Wild" star, 1994
9 World Series champs, 1972–74
10 Some blackboard writing
11 Get ___ deal
12 San ___
13 Scene of heavy W.W. I fighting
14 D.W.I. opposers
20 Swimmer with a boxlike body
22 Like
23 "Once ___ midnight . . ."
24 Bar brand, briefly
25 Suppress
26 Decorative work
27 Expressionist Schiele
28 Queens, workers or soldiers
29 "The Maltese Falcon" actress
30 Treat rudely, in a way
31 Good doctor
32 Parrots
34 Bamboo Harvester "played" him
36 Sports figure nicknamed "the Big Easy"
40 They have their reservations
41 B another way
42 Beef
43 New World abbr.
44 Launch ___
45 C.B. equipment, to a C.B.'er
46 Play honor
47 Work detail
48 Overrun
49 Room add-on?
50 "Sicut ___ in principio" (doxology phrase)
51 Beautiful fairylike being
52 Very

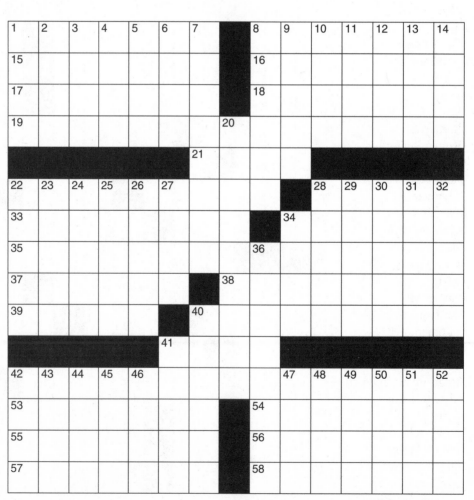

by Byron Walden

ACROSS

1 Possible source of big winnings
11 Introductory text
15 Words on some maps
16 Hubbard of fiction
17 Where errors are seen
18 Another white meat
19 Bit of granola
20 One can't do this
21 Port on the Vistula
23 Brave, for instance
25 Colony member
27 Seoul's Kyung ___ University
28 Straight
31 Sound off
33 Slower, musically
36 Buddy-buddy
37 Slippery ones
38 Cleanup target
40 Insane talker
41 Unprofessional film quality
43 Shop, for one
44 Familiarize
45 Chris's player in "The Magnificient Seven"
46 Kind of acid
48 Money-losing proposition
52 Texas/Louisiana border river
54 When repeated, a child's plaything
57 Treasure of the Sierra Madre
58 "Voice of Israel" writer
59 They build bridges
62 Further
63 Extreme
64 Archie or Veronica
65 Sedimentary materials

DOWN

1 Chicken giant
2 Not shy
3 Nasdaq listing
4 Nasser once led it: Abbr.
5 Put out
6 Indian bovine with a humped shoulder
7 Jackson moniker
8 Arms of the underworld
9 Skating legend
10 It can give a golfer a lift
11 Lady Bird's middle name
12 Ringbearer of Scandinavian myth: Var.
13 Meeting of the minds
14 Throw for a loss?
22 Pays a visit
24 Ancient Wonder site
26 "Eat to live, not live to eat" penner
29 Boston college
30 Rocky prominence
32 Puts on a coat
33 Resting place of God, in the Bible
34 Like the items shown on "Antiques Roadshow"
35 Guantánamo Bay, e.g.
39 Make, with "out"
42 Early American explorer
47 Weakly pronounced consonant, in phonetics
49 Jay follower
50 Rocky prominence
51 One ordered to take two tablets
53 Home ___
55 Cutlass maker
56 Final farewell
60 Santa ___, Calif.
61 Bed-In for Peace participant, 1969

by Mark Diehl

ACROSS

1 Good clean fun?
11 Bolted
15 Typical Scarlatti work
16 Bar ___
17 Public relations people
18 Leading ammunition maker
19 Film featuring Slinky Dog and Hamm the Pig
20 Waste time
22 One of a matched pair, maybe
23 Henpecks
24 Mount ___, highest peak in the Rockies
27 Most sexually alluring
28 Pick up from school
29 Was older than
31 Regrettable
32 Tosses it in
33 Pulse quickener, say
34 They snip and clip
37 TV show created by Steven Bochco
39 Fine
40 In an ugly way
41 Able to bear
42 Pink-slip
43 Castel Sant'___ (Roman museum)
44 Ajar
48 Old nick
49 Carnival game played with a mallet
51 Proctor's call
52 Drinks made with mixers
53 Husky burden
54 They're full of life

DOWN

1 Salt holder
2 Beehive, e.g.
3 Multitude
4 More impudent
5 Light case
6 Ford model introduced in 1981
7 What "Britney Spears" means in rhyming slang
8 It may go into action
9 Even finish
10 Stone Age relics
11 Stir-fry tidbit
12 Freezes
13 Done on one side
14 Precept
21 Bone-dry
23 Some trousers
24 "Anything ___" (Woody Allen film)
25 Number 2, e.g.
26 Cheating-woman-with-an-angry-husband con
27 Unwise undertaking
29 Historical author seen on PBS's "The Civil War"
30 ___-eyed (naive)
32 Restaurant hostess's command
35 Typed in
36 Final portion
37 Scrubbers
38 Retro restaurant
40 Like Ma and Pa Kettle
41 Some religious observances
42 Bets on
44 Good sign?
45 Stick
46 Low-grade?: Abbr.
47 1987 Costner role
50 Coca-Cola drink brand

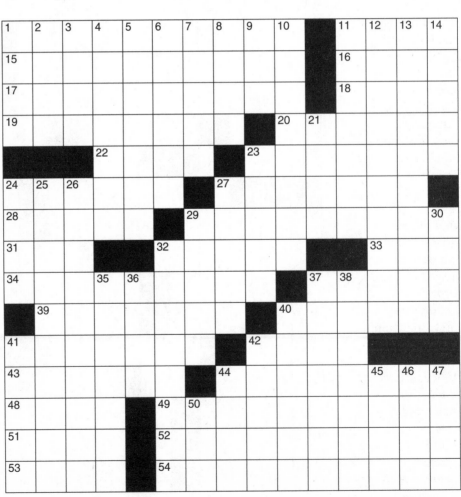

by Patrick Berry

ACROSS

1 Allures
8 Little angels
15 Exercises
16 Handout for tourists
17 Whitney Houston song used by NBC for the 1988 Summer Olympics
19 Nickname on the range
20 Wearing a small crown
21 Opening words of "Travelin' Man"
22 Schmaltz
24 Piano composer ___ Nancarrow
26 Contrary to the spirit of 37-Across
36 It separates Sicily from the rest of Italy
37 Football coach's admonishment
38 Start of some games
39 "Doughnut," in baseball lingo
46 Stink
47 Access the contents of
49 Popular apéritif
50 Dumber than dirt
54 Said one's piece
55 Mouth, slangily
56 Some poker players
57 They get left behind

DOWN

1 Anaïs Nin, for one
2 Like a pregnancy
3 French Beaux-Arts painter Cabanel
4 Common calculator button
5 Spanish bear
6 Tom and Jerry ingredient
7 Concrete proposals?
8 Prefix with linear
9 Lover of Eos
10 Alternative to bowties
11 Spreads
12 Puts out
13 Not electric
14 Cannonballed
18 Drama with lots of fans
22 Dinner companion?
23 Seconds, e.g.
25 Iago, notably
27 "The Sopranos" figure
28 Martian rover?
29 Confrère
30 Scottish seaport
31 "This ___ a drill!"
32 Onetime Aerospatiale products
33 Links strings
34 Not picked up
35 Scouting outings
39 So-called "royal herb"
40 Got off the dime
41 U.S. air base site in Greenland
42 Kind of fluid
43 English children's author Blyton and others
44 "___ help a lot!"
45 Lose it
47 Daredevil
48 Classic Bruin nickname
51 One at the kids' table, perhaps
52 This, in Thiers
53 Response when something hits you

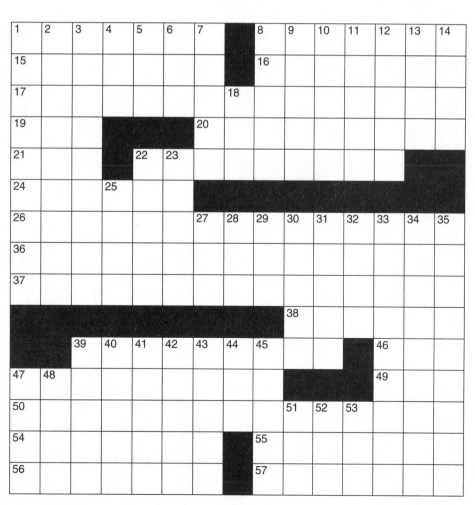

by Byron Walden

ACROSS
1 Makeup artist?
5 Paired: Prefix
10 "Woe ___ . . ."
14 Archipelago component
15 One of the Saarinens
16 "D"
17 Country legend dropping in?
19 Track
20 Rollerjam participant
21 Pincered insects
23 "Topaz" author
25 Prepares to propose
26 Onomatopoeically named legume
30 Break
31 Claiborne of fashion
32 Polar explorer dropping by?
37 Hip to
39 It may need stroking
40 Small combo
41 Supreme Court justice dropping out?
46 See 62-Down
47 "Ladders to Fire" writer
48 Gabby was his sidekick
50 Gregg experts
53 W.W. II villain
54 Western burg, unflatteringly
55 Smell in "Apocalypse Now"
59 Jon Arbuckle's dog
60 Labor leader dropping off?
63 Tops
64 Religion, to Karl Marx
65 Physical
66 Comic book supergroup
67 Droplets
68 Sixth-brightest star in a constellation

DOWN
1 They may be locked or sealed
2 "Out of Africa" name
3 Neighbor of Mont.
4 Get some sleep
5 Disparaged publicly
6 "___ be!"
7 It's just past three
8 Vichyssoise ingredient
9 David Mamet play
10 Not resting on the shoulders, say
11 Salad orderer's request
12 Salad maker's need
13 N.A.A.C.P. and others
18 ___ Buena (island in San Francisco Bay)
22 Unaltered
24 Unaltered
26 Dove home
27 Historical ship
28 Russia's Sea of ___
29 Almost
33 Origin
34 Sweater letter
35 Nada, across the Pyrenees
36 Steeple sound
38 It barely misses a score
42 Rat Pack nickname
43 Con
44 Those who lend their names
45 Oriental royal
49 Singer with the 1999 #1 hit "If You Had My Love"
50 Vice venue
51 Cord
52 Take potshots
54 Wheedle
56 Fire
57 Map figure: Abbr.
58 Baby's word
61 One of Frank's exes
62 With 46-Across, marsh-dwelling bird

by Henry Hook

ACROSS

1 Dainty piece of delicate workmanship
6 "A truer measure of man's ability" sloganeer, once
11 It has a variety of schedules: Abbr.
14 Nursery supplies
15 Nut source
16 Struggle
17 Dispirit
18 Not currently
20 Occupational ending
21 Site of some famous hangings
22 Consideration
23 Humanities degs.
24 Canadian capital?
25 "Angie Baby" singer, 1974
26 "The point being . . . ?"
27 Biker's bike, colloquially
29 Suffix with two
30 Line from a classic tongue twister
36 Lenape orator who inspired Pontiac
37 Anticipates an imminent disaster, maybe
38 Ten follower
39 Long haul
40 "___ Time transfigured me": Yeats
41 Owner of a famous thumb
44 Ricky Nelson's "___ Late"
45 Solution, on an Rx
46 Big benefit, say
47 They're impulsive
50 "Friends" actress, familiarly
51 Vaunt
53 Spent

55 Richard Gere title role of 2000
56 North Sea tributary
57 Dispatch boat
58 Emolument
59 Composer Warlock
60 Stately home

DOWN

1 Italian color
2 View from Calabria
3 "Medical Center" star
4 Taliban mullah
5 Salts are in it: Abbr.
6 It's free for a limited time
7 David George Gordon's "The ___-Bug Cookbook"

8 Polo competitor
9 Match game?
10 Paul Bunyan's blacksmith
11 Like some walls
12 Put a winter coat on?
13 Poorly kept
19 Doctor's order
21 Field worker
23 Yum-Yum, Peep-Bo and Pitti-Sing in "The Mikado"
24 Excoriate
25 Marinates more
28 Hospitality target
29 Hare hunters
31 Sink item
32 Laser Jet 2100, e.g.
33 Brought by dolly

34 Jocosity
35 Court citation abbr.
41 Staff lines?
42 Dance studio feature
43 Really turn on
47 Answer to the folk riddle "Worker in yellow clothes"
48 Strike
49 English river to the Wash
50 Mud
52 Increase, with "up"
53 Fix
54 Unknown name

by Brendan Emmett Quigley

ACROSS

1 Gets out of the way
11 Bass output
15 They don't react well
16 N.F.L. Hall-of-Famer Ronnie
17 Perilous thing to cross over
18 Prune
19 Tend to brood?
20 Mathematical extreme
21 Incurred
22 Grooming gizmo
24 Three-time 55-Down champs
25 What an optimist envisions
28 Quoits pegs
31 It can't be played on a trumpet, e.g.
32 Fire
33 Revelation response
34 18th-century French inventor of a temperature scale
36 Boric acid target
37 Common rugby score
38 Baseball, slangily
39 Estimate follower
40 Take a city bus, perhaps
44 Podiatric concern
45 Enthusiastic show of approval
49 Worked (up)
50 Persona non grata
52 Cry of horror, in poetry
53 Director Reitman
54 Statistical calculation
56 Campbell of "Wild Things"
57 Movie mini-marathon
58 Looking like rain
59 Passing events

DOWN

1 Thick
2 Pleasant way to walk
3 Twenty, in Trieste
4 Bit of work
5 One associated with fire
6 Goes along
7 Figures in major-league baseball
8 Protector of the dead, in myth
9 Something hammered out
10 Liverpool-to-Nottingham dir.
11 Some wool
12 Auto garage courtesy
13 Tuscan ancients
14 Boards
21 Weary worker's wish
23 "___ Brown" (Judi Dench film)
24 Its highest point is Huascarán
26 Holy Arks' homes
27 "Get your pretty self over here!"
28 Cooling one's jets?
29 Belle of Louisville's beat
30 Mountain-climber's hood
34 Rose on the hind legs, with "up"
35 "Odyssey," e.g.
39 Home to Queens U.
41 President Ford's chief of staff
42 Too
43 Less trusting
46 Column choice
47 Frère de la mère
48 Present times
50 It may be tribal
51 Set, Egyptian god of ___
54 Hdqrs.
55 See 24-Across

by Byron Walden

ACROSS

1 Better Business Bureau concerns
6 Hefty competition
10 What someone who is out might be in
14 Put through the mill?
15 Legal cover-up?
16 Robert Burns title starter
17 1986 rock autobiography
18 Member of a small family
20 "Six Degrees of Separation" family name
22 Suitor's presentation
23 Where to spend birr
24 John of Parliament
25 It's projected
30 Browsers' place
32 Sturdy building material
33 Pique experience?
34 Make a stink?
35 Density symbol, in physics
37 It may follow an etym.
39 Ottoman officer
40 Utter
42 Special ability
44 Burrowing animal
46 Mysterious letter writer, maybe
49 Lyricist Dubin and others
50 Come this close
53 Take, as a life
56 Humored
57 Curved wall used as a stage background
59 Actress Georgia ___ of "The Mary Tyler Moore Show"
60 "Flower Petal Gown" sculptor
61 Not easily angered
62 Surgical tube
63 Ones that may get ticked?
64 Gathering suffix
65 "Me, too"

DOWN

1 Sudden increase
2 Get the job done
3 Putting two and two together, say
4 Bring up
5 Pirate
6 "Beethoven" star, 1992
7 Time of many a fairy tale
8 Good enough to 2-Down
9 "The Partridge Family" actress
10 Collusion
11 Votes overseas
12 M.'s counterpart
13 Contributes
19 Swamp thing
21 Bad words
24 "Me, too"
26 See 51-Down
27 Not mincing words?
28 European capital
29 Virginie, e.g.
30 Dos into seis
31 "If a ___ is happy, it cannot fit too close": O. Henry
36 Mama bear, in Madrid
38 Keep
41 It can be semi-attached
43 "The Murder Room" novelist
45 Token
47 Kids' TV character voiced by Kevin Clash
48 One of "Them"
51 With 26-Down, it may be used in a pool
52 Longtime Chicago Symphony conductor
53 Sent a duplicate, briefly
54 Invention of Hermes, supposedly
55 ___ gratuit (something done without apparent motive)
56 Give up, slangily
58 Make calls

by Eric Berlin

ACROSS

1 Athletic supporter?
10 Electric meter inventor ____ Thomson
15 Viniculturist's sampling tube
16 Join securely
17 It remains effective until filled or canceled
18 Places to set geraniums
19 Hardly a Yankee fan
20 Flatten, in metalworking
21 Near
22 Brand in the freezer section
24 Prima donna
26 "The Neon Bible" novelist
28 Union foe
29 Shrimp
30 Those with 48-Acrosses
32 It may have reservations
34 Vital
36 Most numbers have two or more
39 Enliven
41 Gym amenities
43 Year in Severus's reign
46 Letterhead?: Abbr.
48 See 30-Across
49 Pros at increasing profits
52 Railroad necessities
53 Series finales
54 Guffaw
56 Setting for St. Paul: Abbr.
57 Country lass
58 Rush hour, in adspeak
60 1,000 millimes
61 Ride
62 Catcher
63 Horoscope data

DOWN

1 Affirmed in court
2 "Put a lid on it!"
3 Not as a group
4 TV dog
5 'Vette option
6 Bit
7 Those who wait
8 Play again
9 About 20% of the earth's land: Abbr.
10 Footnote abbr.
11 Disco-era duds
12 Rather than, with "of"
13 "Stalag 17" star, 1953
14 Still waiting to go out
21 They're changed frequently
23 Option for some long trips
25 "Terrif!"
27 One of die Planeten
31 Antique photos
33 Stink maker
35 Flashy basket
37 Seductive
38 Drummer
40 Male character in French pantomime
42 Some stanzas
43 Ochlophobist's dread
44 Finished
45 "The Third Man" setting
47 Three-person team
50 Three-time World Cup skiing champion
51 Hero, at times
55 Play directors
58 Infielders' stat.
59 Honey eater of New Zealand

by Bob Peoples

ACROSS

1 National service
9 Buggy
15 How some entrees are served
16 Cut aid
17 "Don't sweat it"
18 Palace figures
19 Mass apparel
20 Part of a column
22 Animal that Poseidon turned Theophane into, in myth
23 Year in Nero's reign
24 Land
25 Unrest
26 Lamp sites
28 All over
29 Biblical verb
30 Bash
32 Neutral shades
34 Fork-tailed bird
35 Ending of some plant names
36 Classic convertible name
39 Murphy's portrayer
42 Dredge (up)
43 They're all for it
45 A month abroad
47 Somalian-born supermodel
48 Swinger
50 "Cupid is a knavish ___": "A Midsummer Night's Dream"
51 Part of a footnote abbr.
52 Jewish village
53 Zaire's Mobutu ___ Seko
54 One to watch in a pinch?
56 Matter of course
58 Attach securely
59 Drinkers, at times
60 Magnetic induction units
61 Cruising

DOWN

1 Presidential first name
2 Unfolds
3 Wimp
4 Speaker of note
5 Cape Tres Puntas locale: Abbr.
6 ". . . but no ___"
7 Environmentalist's concern
8 Grooves on a coin's edge
9 Snack named for a Massachusetts town
10 Like Hawaiian shirts
11 Boise's county
12 Relative of a bug
13 Back to back
14 Takes off wrongly
21 Period of darkening
24 "Rich Man, Poor Man" actor, 1976
25 Recluse
27 Term of affection
31 Surprise court actions
33 Warwickshire forest
35 Accusatory question
36 Fair
37 "It's Too Late Now" autobiographer
38 Camel performers
39 Totals
40 Former name of Sulawesi
41 Sign of a slip
44 Mus. slow-up
46 Texas city named by Russian immigrants
49 ___ once
52 Old gathering place
53 1960's–70's Japanese leader
55 NATO member since 1999: Abbr.
57 D-Day vessel: Abbr.

by Rich Norris

ACROSS

1 Polo alternative
5 Food item whose name means "slice"
9 The "C" of C. S. Lewis
14 Composition of some ladders
15 Gray ode subject
16 Soda pop purchase
17 Abbr. that may precede a colon
18 Fast talker
20 Like some architectural designs
22 Checks
23 Leading the queue
24 Honolulu's ___ Tower
26 Pulls the plug on
28 Liberal
32 Executive attachment
33 Quaint taletellers
34 ___ mater
35 Divvy up
37 Old faces in workplaces, perhaps
39 Where to go in Gloucester
40 Schubert's "___ sentimentale"
42 In a safe place
43 Lamp locale
45 Pick-me-up
46 Time's partner
47 End of Missouri's motto
48 "The View" co-host
50 Lonely
54 Mom or dad
56 ___ jure (legal phrase)
57 Sipowicz player on "N.Y.P.D. Blue"
58 "What ___?"
59 Commend, as for outstanding service
60 Rosalind's cousin in "As You Like It"
61 Terrarium youngsters
62 Are, in Arles

DOWN

1 Gasconade
2 Learning may be done by it
3 Like a troublemaker
4 Not so tough
5 Spreads
6 It has its notions
7 Fantasia's cousin
8 Dove's helper, in an Aesop tale
9 Person likely to have a big closet
10 Unlike a plane
11 Point
12 Flashed signs
13 Need to be set straight
19 Legendary Irish princess
21 Really big show
25 "Mad Love" star, 1935
26 Red ___
27 Red ___
29 Laetrile source
30 Flower girl, sometimes
31 Stunner
33 Ruby's defender
36 Armor coverer
38 Sooner than soon
41 Dispatch
44 Falafel sauce
45 Plagues
48 Empty
49 Notably secure carrier
51 Put out
52 Town in the Euganean Hills
53 Pulls off
54 One overseen by a sgt.
55 Name associated with anonymity

by Dana Motley

ACROSS

1 1971 Bond girl portrayer
11 It's often given a red coat
15 Something that may be twisted apart
16 Deal
17 Fancied
18 Language of the 1983 film title "Koyaanisqatsi"
19 Contracted into folds
20 They may be blowing in the wind
22 Plus-or-minus fig.
23 1998 name in the news
26 Get set to shoot
27 It may put you in a difficult position
29 Modest
31 Thackeray's "The Book of ___"
33 "It's all ___"
34 Dungeons & Dragons co., once
35 Kind of story
38 G.E. co-founder
41 It may fill up your tank
42 Keep from desiccating
46 Jet-setters
49 Ballyshannon's river
50 Corn problem
51 Conical dryers
53 It's hard to get a grip on
54 Over
56 Shirt that leaves the midriff exposed
58 Applied oneself (to)
59 Request to a cabby
62 Capacity
63 Oscar nominee for "A Man and a Woman"
64 Soprano Ameling
65 Untold

DOWN

1 They're usually short . . . or shorts
2 Affixes, in a way
3 "Move on"
4 Senator who succeeded John Stennis
5 "Gladiator" director
6 Some cartridges' contents
7 Famed streaker of 1941
8 Let pass
9 Chart maker
10 Hardly classicists
11 Making a comeback?
12 Punching bag, so to speak
13 Kind of court
14 Expert, slangily
21 One who may marry repeatedly
24 Supercontinent of 200+ million years ago
25 1998 Ice Cube film, with "The"
28 Exerciser's pride
30 Plasma alternative, for short
32 Lift passages
36 Tied, in a way
37 Thou
38 Globe, e.g.
39 Send a jet over?
40 Dim sum selection
43 Correspondence request
44 Added numbers
45 Mobile homes
47 Something to play
48 Forty-niner's fantasy
52 Aid in removal of mines
55 Arch
57 "Buck Rogers" novelist Nowlan
60 Big name in Burmese history
61 Actor in Pink Panther films

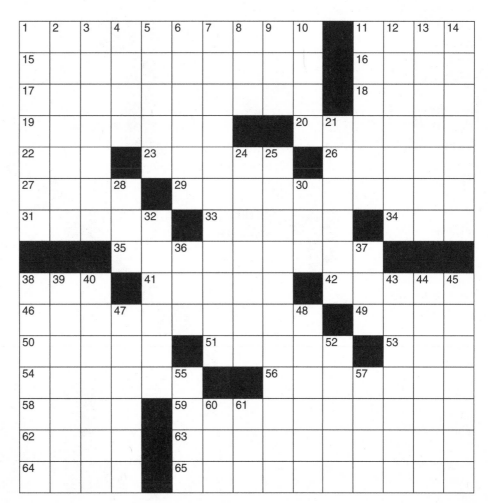

by Byron Walden

ACROSS

1 Xerophyte
7 Demands
14 Surfing, say
15 Outside-the-box
16 Nation with a red-crested crane on its flag
17 Strewn
18 Good things
19 So to speak
20 Oktoberfest duds
22 Talented
23 Song that ends "Bless my homeland forever"
24 Certain charity event
25 Supporter
26 ___ special
27 Like a junker's engine
30 Dumpster lifters
31 Free-for-alls
32 Blood line
33 Resin from ancient trees
34 Dead giveaways
39 Show of absolute power
40 Corresponding
41 Regrettable occurrence
43 Hand-decorated
44 Auto part you shouldn't tamper with
45 Preshow ritual
46 "___ is knowing that your worst shot is still pretty good": golfer Johnny Miller
47 Cover
48 Matricide of Greek myth
49 Record producers

DOWN

1 Dance team
2 Like hockey sticks
3 18th-century French artist Gillot
4 Decorative threads
5 Masks are worn here
6 Oldest known form of currency
7 Surfaces
8 Became widespread
9 William of TV's "The Greatest American Hero"
10 Some Amtrak employees
11 Vessel that pumps the water it's floating in
12 Sheets used in four-color printing
13 Cashes in
15 Upmarket
21 Lubricative
24 Bridge hand assessment
26 Morning routines
27 Note on the fridge, maybe
28 Relative of a bigeye
29 Certain club reservations
30 1965 #1 hit with an exclamation point in its title
31 Family member
32 Church committee
34 What a creed is composed of
35 Pronto
36 Mystery author ___ Jackson Braun
37 Despite what you say
38 Swamp grasses
40 Secure anew
42 Ding

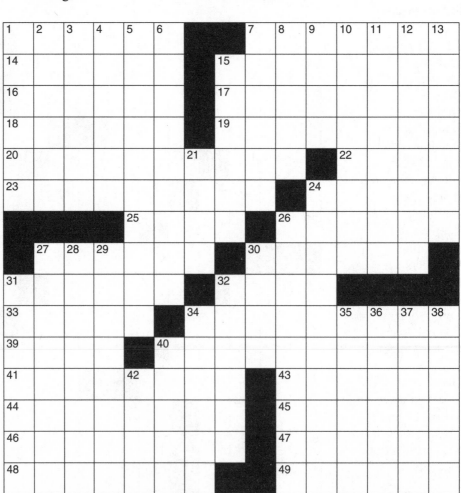

by Patrick Berry

The New York Times

SMART PUZZLES
PRESENTED WITH STYLE

  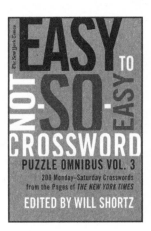 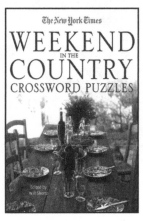

Available at your local bookstore or online at www.nytimes.com/nytstore

St. Martin's Griffin

1

```
S P A M   A C M E   S C H M O
T O G A   B A I L   A R E A R
A L E C   O R M E   L A M P S
P E N E L O P E C R U Z
L A D   I K E   T O T E B A G
E X A C T   T W I C E   A L A
      A H A   O O O   C L A M
S H A K E D O W N C R U I S E
K O B E   A R E   O E R
A P E   E G A D S   L E A R Y
T I T A N I C   I I I   L E A
      G R O U N D S C R E W S
M A R G O   L O N E   A X I S
A V A I L   A V E R   M E R E
J E W E L   R A Y E   P I E R
```

2

```
N E S T S   B O S S   E G A D
O N T A P   A L T O   N O D E
A D E L A   Y E A S   S L O T
H O T C R O S S B U N   D R E
    S R O   S E E D I E R
N E B   O N U S   M A I L
A R E   W A R M W E L C O M E
R O D E   A I R   E C O N
C O O L M I L L I O N   K A Y
  F L A N   E T T E   S T A
C A N A S T A   T W A
A M A   C O L D C O M F O R T
R U I N   N O R A   A I M E E
O S L O   E N O S   T R A N S
B E S T   S E P T   H E R D S
```

3

```
S T R A T A   Z A P   C L I P
T H E S I S   I M A   A O N E
R E D I N K   P B S   R I C E
A M O D E S T P R O P O S A L
F R E E   W O O   A L L
E S S   I D O   S A Y   A S H
    S S R   A I R L A N E S
P R I O R E N G A G E M E N T
M O N T A G U E   U S A
S E A   E S T   W E S   P J S
  S O L   C O W   A L A I
A M E R I C A N W E D D I N G
H O N E   U S E   D O M A I N
A L S O   L E N   E V I N C E
B E E S   L S D   N E T T E D
```

4

```
C L A S P   I C O N   F L A B
H A I T I   R O M A   L U L L
I D T A G   A M A T   U R G E
    L S D   P H I L   C A N
S E D A T E   L A V I S H E D
T R I C Y C L E   E M T
A N A T   A U T O   B A L D S
M I N I   F I E L D   L O R N
P E A T S   S C A R   A R O O
    E A R   O V E R G R O W
N U T S H E L L   G A M E L Y
E N E   L U A U   S R I
A L A N   B U M P   E T T A S
R I S E   E R N E   S E W E R
S T E T   N A S A   T S A R S
```

5

```
L A T H   U C L A   S T A I D
E C H O   M R E D   W A L D O
A L A S   B E A M   E N T E R
P U R P L E P R O S E   O A K
    E R E   N A P S
I P A N A   S H I V   M A S S
D I N E R O   I S O   E D N A
L A V E N D E R H I L L M O B
E N I D   E V E   R E T I R E
S O L E   S A S S   A S T E R
    D I S C   T A S
A H A   M A U V E D E C A D E
M A N I A   A E R O   H U R L
A L O N G   T I E R   E R A S
D O N N E   E L O N   W A G E
```

6

```
B O R E S   L A M A   C H A P
E L I T E   O W E D   R O S E
A G O R A   M O O D   O M I T
M A T E R I A L W I T N E S S
    E R N S   T H Y
P A R A D E   L I O N E S S
A M O S   S W O O N   A P E
S I G H T S E E I N G T R I P
T E E   H A T E S   A T R A
E S T E E M S   R A C H E L
    R I O   A M E N
O B S E R V A T I O N D E C K
T A L C   A L A N   A R L E N
T R O T   R O L E   L I S L E
O N E S   S E E D   S P A T E
```

7

8

9

10

11

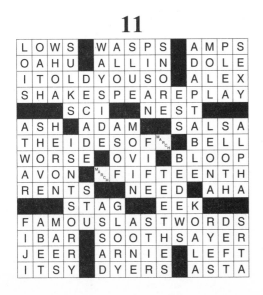

12

13

```
M A C S   H O U R   H A Z E L
U G L Y   E S S E   A V E R Y
N O O N   A H E M   M O U S E
C R U C I V E R B A L I S T
H A D   T E A   R U E D
    B E N   M A R T   J A B
A X I O M   B O N A   C O L A
C R O S S W O R D E D I T O R
H A W N   H O S T   I N S E T
E Y E   P E K E   U T E
    F I L M   T N T   D I S
  E N I G M A T O L O G I S T
G L E N S   K A T E   R O L E
U B O A T   E X E S   I D E A
M A N L Y   R I M S   D E S K
```

14

```
J A M S   M A Y O R   S E L F
O B O E   A R E W E   T R I O
T E N C O M M A N D M E N T S
S T O O L I E   D A V I E S
    N E E D E D   R E E S E
E G A D S   X E D I N
C L U E   P A P U A N   M B A
H U N D R E D A C R E W O O D
O T T   U S E N E T   H A Z E
    G L O P S   H I T O N
F A I R E   T E A M U P
A C C O R D   G A L L O P S
T H O U S A N D I S L A N D S
E O N S   F E I N T   S C A T
D O S E   T O N G S   H E S S
```

15

```
P A S T E L   T B A R   A L T
E L O I S E   I A G O   L E A
C O U N T R Y C L U B   B A N
S T L   E N O   D E E P E N D
    M O S E Y S     A R T E
M C A N   R O C K B O T T O M
P U T T S   H O Y L E
H E E H A W S   P E E R S A T
    E M A I L   S N A C K
R A P S E S S I O N   A L T O
O V A L   P R O W L S
L I L Y P A D   I T O   A E R
L A M   S W I N G B R I D G E
E T E   S A S E   A S S I G N
R E D   T Y K E   D E S P O T
```

16

```
L O B O   N A D I A   I M P S
A L U M   U S E R S   N A R C
M E R E   D I N E S   B R I E
B O R N A G A I N   S E D A N
    S K I   M E A L T I M E
B T U   I N C   S O W
L I V I N G O N T H E E D G E
E D E N   M E R   E I R E
D E A D A S A D O O R N A I L
    I W O   N Y E   L P S
R E V E R S E S   S P A
E D I F Y   T H A T S L I F E
U G L I   O H A R E   A L E X
S E L L   L E V E R   M I L E
E D A M   D R E S S   O A T S
```

17

```
F A R O   A R R O W   O P U S
O L A F   U H H U H   M E T A
W A I F   G O O S E   S T U B
L I L Y M U N S T E R   U R L
    E A S E   D I A N N E
D E P A R T   B I L O X I
O Z A R K   J I B E   E A T S
U R N   S L A K E R S   P O T
P A S T   A P E X   H A I T I
    Y A W N E R   D O D G E R
H E Y D A Y   B E A D
E L O   D A I S Y C L O V E R
M I K E   R H I N O   N O P E
A Z U R   D O N O R   T I E D
N A M E   S P E W S   O D E S
```

18

```
S W A M   R A S H   D A I S Y
O H N O   E S T A   O L D I E
N E A T   E S A U   A G E N T
G E T T O F I R S T B A S E
    O N E S   O L E
E S S   T R I R E M E   F I T
L O T T O   A L E   H I D E
B A L L P A R K F I G U R E S
O P E C   S U E   C H E A T
W Y O   T H E R M A L   S L Y
    S H E   U T E S
  O U T I N L E F T F I E L D
R U N O N   S A F E   X I I I
O R I N G   A S I S   T R E E
E S T E S   T E N T   Y E N S
```

19

A	P	T		C	H	I	L	I		G	O	R	E	N
D	A	Y		L	U	R	I	D		A	N	I	S	E
H	U	P	M	O	B	I	L	E		Z	A	P	P	A
O	L	E	I	N		S	Y	S	T	E	M			
C	A	S	S	I	S			A	B	A	S	E	D	
		O	N	E	L	U	M	P	O	R	T	W	O	
M	A	D		G	R	E	T	A		S	C	R	E	W
A	L	I	E		B	A	T	O	N		H	A	R	E
S	P	A	Y	S		P	E	R	I	L		Y	S	L
T	H	R	E	E	S	T	R	I	K	E	S			
S	A	Y	S	N	O			E	V	E	N	E	D	
	L	O	W	E	R	S		I	R	A	Q	I		
O	U	T	E	R		P	E	T	I	T	F	O	U	R
K	N	I	F	E		I	N	A	N	E		M	A	T
S	A	L	T	S		C	O	R	D	S		I	L	S

20

J	E	T	S		I	M	A		A	R	E	T	O	O
U	P	R	O	O	T	E	D		B	A	S	I	N	S
T	H	U	R	G	O	O	D		A	Z	T	E	C	S
	B	R	O	W	N	V	B	O	A	R	D			
S	P	R	E	E			E	A	R					
H	U	I	T		A	N	N	E		E	E	L	E	D
O	L	D		A	S	E	A		O	D	D	I	T	Y
P	L	E	S	S	Y	V	F	E	R	G	U	S	O	N
P	I	R	A	T	E		T	R	E	E		T	I	A
E	N	S	O	R		E	A	R	L		T	E	L	S
		O	P	T			B	I	N	E	T			
	O	F	E	D	U	C	A	T	I	O	N			
P	A	R	L	O	R		M	A	R	S	H	A	L	L
A	T	E	A	M	S		P	R	E	S	A	G	E	S
C	H	E	N	E	Y		S	T	S		T	O	D	D

21

D	I	R	E		T	R	A	M	P		C	A	S	A
I	D	O	L		R	E	C	U	R		A	V	O	N
R	E	D	S	K	Y	A	T	M	O	R	N	I	N	G
T	S	E		H	I	P	S		A	V	A	I	L	
		B	A	N	S		F	I	N	A	N	C	E	
S	P	R	A	N	G		S	O	A	K	S			
I	R	A	N		K	I	N	T	E		T	W	O	
D	O	G	D	A	Y	A	F	T	E	R	N	O	O	N
E	W	E		R	E	N	T	S		O	G	R	E	
	S	N	A	G	S		D	R	E	A	M	S		
T	E	M	P	E	R	A		H	E	A	L			
A	L	O	E	S		S	O	L	I		A	C	E	
B	L	U	E	S	I	N	T	H	E	N	I	G	H	T
L	E	N	D		B	E	A	U	T		R	E	I	N
E	N	D	S		N	O	T	M	E		E	D	N	A

22

L	O	Y	A	L		C	A	P	S		K	I	S	S
I	R	E	N	E		A	S	H	E		A	C	M	E
D	E	L	T	A		M	E	A	N		T	O	O	T
S	O	L	I	D	R	E	A	S	O	N	I	N	G	
		P	E	R		E	R	I	E					
L	I	Q	U	I	D	A	S	S	E	T		S	A	Y
U	S	U	R	P	S		H	I	S		Y	A	L	E
C	A	I	N	E		F	I	N		H	O	W	L	S
C	A	T	S		H	I	P		H	O	G	T	I	E
I	C	E		G	A	S	S	T	A	T	I	O	N	S
	P	O	S	H		I	M	P						
	W	H	A	T	S	T	H	E	M	A	T	T	E	R
J	A	I	L		L	A	I	R		N	A	I	V	E
I	D	L	E		E	I	R	E		T	U	N	E	S
M	E	T	S		S	L	E	D		S	T	A	R	T

23

S	A	U	L		T	H	I	N		C	H	A	N	T
W	I	N	E		R	O	S	E		O	I	L	E	R
A	R	E	A		A	L	E	E		I	N	L	A	Y
R	O	A	D	S	I	D	E	D	I	N	E	R		
M	U	S	S	E	L	S		C	A	S	I	N	O	
S	T	Y		M	E	T		M	E	G		G	E	N
	F	I	R	E	S	I	D	E	C	H	A	T		
A	L	S	O		A	H	S		O	T	T	O		
R	I	N	G	S	I	D	E	S	E	A	T			
T	E	A		P	R	Y		T	N	N		P	B	S
Y	U	P	P	I	E		H	A	N	G	O	U	T	
	B	E	D	S	I	D	E	M	A	N	N	E	R	
C	R	E	T	E		L	O	C	O		A	C	N	E
O	N	A	I	R		S	O	U	R		S	H	O	W
W	A	N	T	S		A	M	T	S		H	O	S	S

24

T	G	I	F		B	R	E	W	S		A	S	A	N
A	R	L	O		M	A	R	I	A		L	E	G	O
P	I	L	L	O	W	T	A	L	K		L	O	R	I
S	P	O	I	L	S		M	I	S	C	U	E	S	
	G	O	D		S	E	A		A	L	L	E	Y	
A	S	I	S		P	I	N		A	T	E			
B	I	C		S	O	F	A		D	E	A	C	O	N
B	L	A	N	K	E	T	C	O	V	E	R	A	G	E
A	L	L	O	Y	S		T	W	I	N		M	R	S
	F	L	Y		E	E	L		D	E	E	T		
L	A	U	R	A		A	D	D		S	U	R		
E	X	H	I	B	I	T		S	A	L	A	D	A	
D	I	A	L		S	H	E	E	T	M	U	S	I	C
G	A	U	L		L	O	R	N	A		T	H	E	M
E	L	L	S		E	L	E	C	T		H	Y	D	E

25

```
G R I D   D A T E   S T A L E
A E R O   O M A R   T I M E X
B L O C   R A V I   R E E V E
S Y N T H E T I C F A B R I C
    R A M       O N A
A R T I F I C I A L G R A S S
M O U N T   A N N I E   L E E
A R T E   O P T I C   M E N D
T E T   B U R R O   L O U S E
I M I T A T I O N B U T T E R
    A R R       A S H
C O U N T E R F E I T B I L L
H O R D E   E A R L   A L O E
U N S E R   E R I E   L I N T
M A A M S   L E N D   L A G S
```

26

```
W A V E   F A R M   M A R K S
A U E R   A R E A   I N A L L
X X X R A T I N G   R A D I O
      A R C   E N G A G I N G
S C O T I A   W A R C R I E S
P A P I S T S     I L A
O N I C E   A A A M E M B E R
R A N       B B B     R N A
E L E V E N E E E   A M A S S
      A X E   T A P E S U P
S T E N C I L S   R I N S E S
P E N D U L U M   A N D
A N D Y S   G E O R G E I I I
S T O K E   E L L A   R O A N
M O R E S   S T E T   S U N K
```

27

```
T A S T E   S W A M P   T I L
A N T E S   P A N E L   O N E
B Y Y E S T E R D A Y   U T E
      E R A S   W A T E R
S P O O N E R   P R O U D L Y
H E N L E Y   C H O O S E
R A T E S   R O A L D   S U N
E C H O   P U R S E   T U N E
W E E   M E L E E   B R I D E
    D O O L E Y   L O O T E D
A M O U N T S   F I N D E R S
B O U T S     A L O E
O R B   T H I S I N S T A N T
M E L   E E R I E   U R I A H
B Y E   R E E F S   P A R T Y
```

28

```
B A S H   C A B S   A D H O C
E L I A   O R E O   D R A W S
D E L I   F R E D   D O N N A
S E L L S F O R A S O N G
      S L E W   U N E A S Y
  A R T I E   A P E S   R O I
S W O O N   A R I D   S O U P
C H A N G E S O N E S T U N E
R I D E   L A S T   W A N D S
A R T   D U P E   W A R D S
P L O W E D     P E R T
    F A C E S T H E M U S I C
C R A V E   H O O D   R U S H
H E M E N   A N N E   N I L E
E X E R T   D Y E D   S T E W
```

29

```
R O C K   I N L E T   A B L E
U G L I   B O O T H   S L U G
B R O N Z E S T A R   T U N A
Y E T   E R E   L I P R E A D
    M L I       L E A R
P A G O D A S   S L A Y I N G
I L O N A   M I T E R   B O L
P O L K   F A D E D   A B O U
E N D   A A R O N   S H O N E
D E M E R I T   O C T A N E S
    E M I R     O R B
R E D C A P S   D R U   P S I
A L A E   L O V I N G C U P S
M I L E   A D O R E   O P A L
P A S S   Y A W E D   Z A N E
```

30

```
S T O R E   E S A U   S O A R
T R A I L   C H I N   Y U L E
O U T O F D O O R S   R T E S
W E S T   O N R Y E   I O T A
    E P C O T     N O N F A T
P O O D L E   L E T S G O
E M U   E N C Y C   M E R C I
R A T   A T A   R I O   D A D
T R O T S   P O U T S   E R E
    F E E D E R   S I E R R A
I M P E D E   B L E S S
T A R P   S T I L L   P A C S
E R I E   O U T O F S I G H T
M I N E   T R E S   E E R I E
S O T S   O K R A   A D A P T
```

31

```
WALKS ABEL  NATS
INERT CLIO  INIT
STEAL CANOPENER
PICKUPTHEPACE
  SHAKES    LEMON
   TEN  BAWL  ERE
ESSO  SERGEI  ABS
PUTAFIREUNDERIT
SIR  RODENT  VATS
OTO  ONED   ALI
MENDS    APOLLO
  GETTHELEADOUT
CUBBYHOLE  TORTE
SPOT  OMAR  HEARS
INXS  RENT  ERNES
```

32

```
TARO  ASTA  BABAS
ODOR  DAIS  AMIGO
NASA  OMNI  YODEL
SMALLPOTATOES
   ATA   HUB
AWARDS  TOE  ASST
CONED  MANIA  HIE
TRIVIALPURSUITS
ORS  ERIES  SPRAT
RYES  GIS  RISERS
  TOO   AES
  PETTYOFFICERS
ADULT  ANTE  AVOW
TULLE  LEER  LIMA
MOLAR  ERRS  FLAT
```

33

```
ADORE  SHH  TROOP
MOTEL  MIA  EARLE
FLIPFLOPSANDALS
MESA  ORPHAN  NIT
  SCREE  HINGES
RAPTOR  SASSY
EUR  WIDTH  SEDGE
FREEBEE  ASHTRAY
SAYSO  METOO  EER
  PYLON  MEDDLE
STROBE  CEASE
ARI  ONCALL  LPGA
BEDROOMSLIPPERS
LEGIT  DEA  CHEEK
EDENS  RDS  SINGS
```

34

```
DRUM  BAG   ACURA
ANNE  ODEA  MOTEL
MALCOLMMCDOWELL
  ACED  MOA  RIO
  STANLEYKUBRICK
TLC  OYL  EBRO
OOHS  GET  ABIES
BEETHOVENSNINTH
ESSAY  NAH  NEHI
  SPAT  NEA  SON
ANTHONYBURGESS
CIO  ESE  WERE
CLOCKWORKORANGE
RETRO  NERO  SCOT
ASSTS  TAD  EEOC
```

35

```
AWL  LESS  KARATS
SHH  ABUT  AMENRA
(H)(E)(A)(T)WAVE  RASTAS
EASILY  VIA  TICS
STALE  (B)(E)(A)TBACK
  SCI  NEAR
(B)(O)(A)TSHOW  BATONS
EWER  ALENE  ENNE
DESILU  (B)(O)(L)TDOWN
  LIFT  STR
(B)(O)(L)DFACE  EFLAT
CALI  EGO  EATERY
ORMOLU  (C)(O)(L)DSNAP
IRONER  OPIE  ABE
FESSES  ATAD  SYS
```

Note: The circled letters will show a "change in the weather."

36

```
MAIM  ALTO  ABACI
ALDA  LEAP  BASIC
NEON  OGLE  ELITE
  CLOSESCRUTINY
  REV   APT
PAT  WERE  CIGARS
ELIA  RANK  NADIA
CONSTANTNAGGING
KHAKI  TEEN  SOSA
SASSES  READ  SEN
  ORO   COO
  CONNIPTIONFIT
JODIE  TORN  FLED
ORONO  EGAD  ESAU
BARON  DONA  RARE
```

37

```
A R C H E R . S A L S . S H E
G A L O R E . I M A C . T A D
A D O N I S . L A V A T O R Y
T I S . E A V E . A M A N A S
H O E D . W I N G . A L E S .
A S T E R . S T A I R C A S E
. . N E O . L E S T . G E L
H O L Y C O W . A B I D E R S
A R I . E R R S . N S A .
T A K E S T E P S . T Y P E S
. T E A S . N O T O . O I L Y
T O N S I L . O D O R . N A S
A R E Y O U O K . H A C K I T
G I S . N A P E . E R M I N E
S O S . S U E D . R E D E E M
```

38

```
A L T E R . B O A T . S R T A
P E E V E . A B L E . C O I L
E A S E L . L I E S . R A R E
. T R I C K S C H R O D E R
O T S . E P A . A L I S T
T R I P V A N W I N K L E
T I T L E . I N R E
O B E Y . V O D K A . A T M S
. C I A O . A R R A Y
. T H A N K W I L L I A M S
S P O O N . G A S . P A T
T R U S S F E I N G O L D .
R A P T . A C T I . R O O M Y
A T E E . C H E T . A V O I D
W E E D . T O M E . N E R D S
```

39

```
A C D C . L I N E . B A T T Y
A R E A . I T E M . A L O H A
H E N R Y F O R D . D I N E R
S E T T E E . D A N G . E N D
. E N V S . S O U P
. W A L T E R C H R Y S L E R
V I D . A S T A . S I E G E
E L I S . T A I N T . S O Y A
I C E U P . N O U N . N P R
L O U I S C H E V R O L E T
. T Y P O . A N T I
L A D . C A T T . A C T S A S
E P O C H . B I G W H E E L S
A E I O U . E L I A . R E I N
F S T O P . D E N Y . S P A S
```

40

```
T I L . M E T A L . A C H E S
A C U . A M A N A . B U E N O
H E M . L U C I L L E B A L L
I D E S T . M A I L E D .
T I N K E R B E L L . S O N
I N S I D E R . A T H E A R T
. N E A . U R I A H
. T W O D O L L A R B I L L
T H I N E . I S E
W E N T B A D . S P A R T A N
A N D . C O T T O N B O L L
. P O C O N O . A I S L E
C H I C A G O B U L L . S P A
C O P T S . R A T I O . E R S
S T E A K . S T E I G . D O T
```

41

```
O L A V . E R A S . A C H E D
J A P E . X O U T . B O O T Y
A C E S . C O T Y . D U R A N
Y E R T L E T H E T U R T L E
S D S . E S S O . A L S O .
. O A T S . R O N . E N D S
D I N G S . S E G A . H O I
D R S E U S S . O O B L E C K
A M A . P L O T . S T A S H
Y A P S . A U G . B U R R .
. E L A N . E W E R . S A T
S P R I N G F I E L D M A S S
H O S E D . A S I A . Y W C A
A R O S E . Z E S T . T H O R
G E N T S . E L S E . H O T S
```

42

```
S T E A M . T N O T E . B A R
C R A V E . R O W E D . A M O
H E R E S J O H N N Y . G P A
E M T . S U P . S O B E R
M O H S . D E N S . F O R E
E L E A . O Z O N E L A Y E R
D O N A S . S E R A . S S S
. B I G C H E E S E .
A B O . M A H I . S N A G S
B A T H S P O N G E . O M A N
A T T A . O G O D . S I L O
S T O I C . V A N . A I R
H E M . A L I C E M A R B L E
E R A . K I N E R . V I L E R
S Y N . E P S O N . Y O Y O S
```

43

44

45

46

47

48

49

```
S P E C █ E B A Y █ C O M B O
H I L L █ D E L I █ O N I O N
A Q U A █ I D L E █ G L A Z E
N U D I S T C O L O N Y █ █ █
D E E R E █ H Y D R A █ S R I
Y T D █ D I E █ S E C T I O N
█ █ L A R C H █ █ █ I S B N █
B A R E N A K E D L A D I E S
A V O N █ █ P R E X Y █ █ █ █
J O U S T E D █ I D I █ P A L
A W E █ S W E L L █ O P E R A
█ █ T H E F U L L M O N T Y █
H A N O I █ I N R I █ S C U M
A R B O R █ L A I D █ S I R E
S C A N T █ E R G O █ E L O N
```

50

```
I B E R I A █ █ J A I █ S T A
D A N A N G █ C U T S H O R T
O N E D G E █ A L L E Y C A T
L E S I O N █ T I A █ P K W Y
█ █ A D D █ C A R P O O L S █
G O A T █ A S H █ G A S █ █ █
A C C E S S C O D E S █ F A B
L H A S A █ A F R █ T A L I A
S O D █ F O R T U N A T E L Y
█ █ F E R █ H M O █ L E S S █
C A M I S O L E █ N S A █ █ █
O L I N █ T E D █ S A N T A S
A L L E L U I A █ T U T O R S
T E N D E N C Y █ O N A P A R
S S E █ I D A █ P A N E L S █
```

51

```
S P A R E █ O F F E R █ J A M
A L L A N █ H A L V E █ U R I
N O V I C E S Q U A D █ N I L
S W A N █ M U S E █ T O K E N
█ █ F A I R █ █ S A D D L E █
N O T A B L E H O P P E R █ █
U V U L A █ A C R E █ A I R █
D A N L █ P A R T Y █ Y W C A
E L I █ T E M P █ C O E U R █
█ N O Y E S O F C O U R S E █
A R G Y L L █ █ R A N G █ █ █
R I F L E █ O B I S █ O O N A
G T O █ N O M A D H A T T E R
O E R █ O R A N G █ S M O R E
T S K █ L A R G E █ S E E D S
```

52

```
L A Y S █ P H O N Y █ A W A Y
O R E O █ R A D I O █ R I M S
G O A L █ E L E G Y █ E T A L
J U S T A S I T H O U G H T █
A N T I C █ T O T █ H O M E R
M D S █ T E E █ C B S █ A U K
█ █ M I A █ W A R █ N Y R O █
█ U P R I G H T P I A N O S █
A P E X █ E O S █ A W E █ █ █
B L T █ A R T █ S R A █ I F S
S I N A I █ C E L █ R A D I I
█ F A I R T O M I D D L I N G
A T M S █ I C I E R █ A D I N
R E E L █ L O T S A █ N I T E
M D S E █ T A S T Y █ S T E T
```

53

```
N O D █ A F T E R █ P O P U P
A L E █ D O N N E █ E L E N A
R E T █ D U T C H T R E A T Y
C O H E I R █ L E E S █ C I E
█ █ R A N T S █ A N O T H E R
W R O U G H T I R O N Y █ █ █
E O N █ S O S █ R A R I N G █
E V E R T █ A S S █ L O S E R
D E S I R E █ U A R █ V E E █
█ █ F U D G E F A C T O R Y █
C O R T E G E █ E C L A T █ █
E R O █ P A T S █ E O C E N E
C O L L A R S T U D Y █ D O E
I N L E T █ O L L I E █ I L L
L O A T H █ N O E N D █ N O S
```

54

```
T A B U █ K E E L S █ A S C H
A V E S █ A U D I E █ R O L E
P A T E N T R I T E █ T R U E
A S T R A Y █ F E S T E R E D
S T E I N █ C Y R █ A M Y █ █
█ █ █ D A D A █ █ R I S E R █
H I S S █ I M A M █ A S I D E
A S H █ T E E T E R S █ T I E
S P I T E █ L E N O █ S E E K
H Y P E R █ █ S E C T █ █ █ █
█ W A R █ S P A █ H I C K S █
P E R M E A T E █ C A L L I T
I T I S █ B A C K U P L I T E
E T T U █ A L A I N █ E V E R
S E E P █ B E N N Y █ D E R N
```

55

R	A	C	E	■	G	U	I	L	E	■	B	O	A	S
U	L	A	N	■	I	N	D	I	A	■	A	P	S	E
D	I	S	C	O	N	T	E	N	T	I	S	T	H	E
E	T	H	A	N	■	E	E	K	■	R	I	S	E	N
■	■	P	I	E	S	■	U	F	O	S	■	■	■	■
F	I	R	S	T	S	T	E	P	I	N	■	O	P	A
E	S	A	U	■	S	E	Q	■	N	I	C	H	E	S
T	E	L	L	A	■	D	U	B	■	C	H	A	O	S
O	R	L	E	S	S	■	I	A	M	■	A	R	N	E
R	E	Y	■	T	H	E	P	R	O	G	R	E	S	S
■	■	C	H	O	U	■	C	O	I	L	■	■	■	■
M	A	D	A	M	■	R	A	H	■	N	O	R	M	A
O	F	A	M	A	N	O	R	A	N	A	T	I	O	N
T	R	I	P	■	O	P	E	R	A	■	T	O	R	T
T	O	S	S	■	D	E	A	T	H	■	E	T	E	S

56

C	R	A	G	■	G	O	A	D	■	P	A	V	E	D
L	U	L	U	■	E	R	N	E	■	A	G	I	L	E
A	D	O	S	■	T	A	T	S	■	L	E	A	F	Y
N	E	U	T	R	A	L	Z	O	N	E	■	■	■	■
■	■	■	A	U	G	■	T	O	R	T	O	L	A	■
■	R	E	V	E	R	S	E	O	S	M	O	S	I	S
H	E	Y	■	D	I	A	L	■	■	O	N	T	O	P
E	W	E	R	■	P	L	E	B	E	■	G	E	N	E
D	O	L	O	R	■	■	C	A	M	S	■	A	E	R
D	R	I	V	E	U	P	T	H	E	W	A	L	L	■
A	D	D	E	D	T	O	■	R	A	N	■	■	■	■
■	■	■	■	P	A	R	K	R	A	N	G	E	R	S
A	T	A	R	I	■	T	E	A	L	■	O	K	I	E
L	O	G	O	N	■	E	N	I	D	■	R	E	S	T
B	O	O	Z	E	■	R	O	D	S	■	A	S	K	S

57

U	K	E	S	■	E	M	M	E	■	C	O	M	F	Y
S	E	X	Y	■	N	E	A	L	■	A	D	O	R	E
E	M	I	R	■	Z	A	G	S	■	D	E	L	I	A
R	O	T	A	R	Y	D	I	A	L	■	S	T	E	T
■	■	C	U	M	E	■	A	S	S	E	S	S	■	■
I	N	J	U	N	E	■	B	E	M	O	A	N	■	■
S	E	A	S	■	S	K	E	W	E	R	■	L	I	P
N	A	M	E	S	■	A	G	E	■	T	R	A	D	E
T	R	E	■	A	R	T	U	R	O	■	A	V	O	W
■	S	A	L	O	O	N	■	A	P	P	A	L	S	■
C	R	I	M	E	A	■	S	K	I	S	■	■	■	■
R	A	V	E	■	M	U	S	C	L	E	T	O	N	E
O	Z	O	N	E	■	N	O	R	A	■	A	R	C	A
F	O	R	D	S	■	I	S	O	N	■	R	E	A	R
T	R	Y	S	T	■	T	O	D	D	■	S	O	A	P

58

A	T	B	A	T	■	G	O	L	F	S	■	I	C	E
M	O	O	L	A	■	A	W	E	E	K	■	S	O	D
B	R	A	I	N	F	R	E	E	Z	E	■	O	L	D
E	S	T	■	G	I	R	D	S	■	T	O	S	A	Y
R	O	S	E	L	L	E	■	■	A	C	D	C	■	■
■	■	M	E	L	T	E	D	C	H	E	E	S	E	■
W	H	A	M	S	■	A	I	R	Y	■	L	I	D	■
R	O	B	E	■	M	A	S	S	E	■	D	E	L	I
A	U	S	■	S	A	L	E	■	A	I	S	L	E	■
P	R	E	T	T	Y	P	L	E	A	S	E	■	■	■
■	■	N	O	R	A	■	S	C	H	M	E	A	R	■
G	O	T	T	A	■	T	O	P	I	C	■	L	S	U
A	P	E	■	F	L	O	R	I	D	A	K	E	Y	S
Z	E	E	■	E	A	G	L	E	■	N	O	N	E	T
E	L	S	■	S	T	A	Y	S	■	S	P	A	T	S

59

A	S	F	A	R	■	L	S	A	T	S	■	F	I	G
L	A	R	G	O	■	E	P	C	O	T	■	I	R	A
K	I	E	R	K	E	G	A	A	R	D	■	N	O	R
A	N	S	E	■	T	A	R	D	E	■	D	E	N	Y
■	T	H	E	A	C	T	■	I	S	N	T	■	■	■
■	■	S	C	H	O	P	E	N	H	A	U	E	R	■
S	M	O	T	E	■	R	O	T	E	■	N	C	O	■
H	A	L	O	■	D	R	A	N	O	■	R	E	O	S
A	M	Y	■	F	I	N	N	■	S	A	D	L	Y	■
H	A	M	M	A	R	S	K	J	O	L	D	■	■	■
■	P	E	N	T	■	E	R	R	A	T	A	■	■	■
T	W	I	N	■	P	L	A	T	S	■	R	A	R	E
E	R	A	■	M	O	U	S	S	O	R	G	S	K	Y
R	A	D	■	G	O	A	P	E	■	O	U	T	I	E
M	P	S	■	T	R	U	S	T	■	O	N	E	N	D

60

B	R	A	S	S	■	S	T	E	N	O	■	S	A	P
E	A	T	U	P	■	P	I	N	E	A	P	P	L	E
A	R	O	M	A	■	E	N	T	E	R	T	A	I	N
R	E	P	O	R	T	C	A	R	D	■	E	R	A	S
■	■	■	■	S	I	S	S	Y	■	P	R	E	S	■
S	T	A	M	E	N	■	■	S	A	O	■	■	■	■
L	O	V	E	■	C	O	R	K	E	R	■	P	E	W
A	A	A	A	A	A	A	A	A	A	A	A	A	A	A
M	T	S	■	I	N	T	E	N	T	■	L	I	V	Y
■	■	D	R	S	■	■	T	R	A	D	E	S	■	■
■	A	L	E	S	■	S	C	A	L	A	■	■	■	■
F	D	I	C	■	P	E	R	F	E	C	T	G	P	A
A	L	M	A	M	A	T	E	R	■	E	R	R	O	L
T	E	A	F	O	R	T	W	O	■	R	E	A	D	E
S	R	S	■	D	R	E	S	S	■	S	E	N	S	E

61

C	B	S		C	R	O	C		M	A	L	A	W	I
R	E	A		H	A	L	L		E	D	I	T	E	D
I	C	U		U	S	D	A		S	H	A	M	E	S
N	O	N	E	T	H	E	W	I	S	E	R			
G	O	A	T	E	E			C	U	R		S	E	W
E	L	S	A		S	O	M	E	P	E	O	P	L	E
			A	T	N	O		S	N	E	A	K	S	
A	I	M	E	R		A	I	L		T	R	Y	S	T
C	R	I	S	C	O		S	E	E	S				
M	O	S	T	W	A	N	T	E	D		D	U	A	L
E	N	T		E	R	A		U	G	A	N	D	A	
			A	L	L	Y	O	U	C	A	N	E	A	T
U	P	S	I	D	E		G	N	A	T		A	G	E
S	T	A	R	E	S		L	I	T	E		S	E	N
S	A	T	Y	R	S		E	X	E	S		E	S	S

62

A	I	N	T		P	L	E	A		A	D	M	A	N
S	N	O	O	T	I	E	S	T		R	A	I	S	E
T	H	E	K	I	N	G	S	T	O	N	T	R	I	O
R	E	V	E	L	S			P	I	E				
I	R	I	S		S	P	R	E	E		A	R	T	
D	E	L		P	E	A	L	E	D		A	C	I	D
			C	A	T	N	A	P		E	T	H	O	S
	T	H	E	R	A	J	Q	U	A	R	T	E	T	
F	R	O	N	T		O	U	T	M	A	N			
E	A	S	T		I	S	E	E	I	T		N	I	A
E	Y	E		A	M	E	S	S		G	E	N	S	
			E	I	N		D	R	E	A	D	S		
T	H	E	T	R	O	U	T	Q	U	I	N	T	E	T
W	A	S	T	E		R	A	R	E	B	R	E	E	D
A	L	T	A	R		N	E	S	T		E	R	D	A

63

S	A	H	I	B		O	P	E	R	A		B	A	R
A	M	I	N	O		W	A	L	T	S		O	N	O
P	I	C	K	Y	P	I	C	K	E	T		N	I	B
			C	E	N	T	S		A	U	N	T	Y	
R	A	P	S	O	N	G	S		L	I	B	Y	A	N
E	R	U	P	T	S		C	A	R	I	B			
S	T	P	A	T		B	O	O	Z	E		O	O	F
T	O	P	S		S	A	R	G	E		E	N	T	R
S	O	Y		B	A	R	B	S		P	E	N	T	A
			P	U	L	S	E		H	I	R	E	O	N
T	A	U	R	U	S		A	N	A	L	Y	T	I	C
A	P	P	L	E		E	R	O	D	E				
L	A	P		J	U	N	K	Y	J	U	N	K	E	T
I	R	E		A	N	G	I	E		P	I	A	N	O
A	T	T		Y	A	R	N	S		S	A	N	D	Y

64

O	A	H	U		G	O	O	P		D	A	R	N	S
O	L	A	N		A	C	R	E		E	L	I	O	T
M	I	D	D	L	E	E	A	R		P	L	A	T	A
P	B	S		A	L	A	N		L	O	O	S	E	N
H	I	T	C	H	I	N	G	P	O	S	T			
			L	O	C		L	Y	E	S	O	A	P	
A	D	E	E	R		S	H	E	A		M	N	O	
C	O	F	F	E	E	T	A	B	L	E	B	O	O	K
E	S	T		L	A	T	E		L	O	O	N	Y	
D	E	S	P	A	I	R		A	D	S				
			E	N	T	R	A	N	C	E	H	A	L	L
M	I	L	L	I	E		T	E	C	S		W	O	O
A	R	I	L	S		F	R	E	E	T	R	A	D	E
R	A	R	E	E		A	I	D	S		O	R	E	S
K	E	A	T	S		B	A	S	S		T	E	N	S

65

E	R	I	C		L	I	L	A	C		A	M	E	N
D	A	D	O		A	B	O	I	L		P	I	L	E
T	H	O	M	A	S	M	O	R	E		A	S	I	S
			B	U	T	S		A	O	R	T	A	S	
O	B	L	I	G	E		D	O	N	A	T	E		
L	E	A	N	E	D		R	U	S	T		R	T	E
D	A	T	E	R		M	A	T	E	S		C	E	L
I	T	I	S		J	A	P	E	S		C	H	A	D
E	E	N		H	U	G	E	R		R	A	I	S	E
S	N	L		A	M	O	R		H	A	R	P	E	R
			O	L	D	B	O	Y		O	D	I	S	T	S
N	A	V	A	J	O		A	R	I	L				
A	L	E	C		J	O	H	N	M	I	L	T	O	N
S	E	R	E		E	L	A	T	E		O	K	I	E
H	E	S	S		T	A	M	I	L		N	O	L	O

66

O	C	U	L	I		H	A	R	P		A	D	D	S
W	A	T	E	R		A	G	H	A		N	O	O	K
L	L	A	N	O		V	E	E	R		T	O	N	Y
	C	H	A	N	G	E	S	A	T	T	I	R	E	
			B	A	N			T	A	C	K			
M	I	A	T	A	S		E	D	I	T		E	S	T
A	N	G	E	R		E	X	A	M		V	E	T	O
T	U	R	N	S	O	N	T	H	E	V	I	P	E	R
T	I	E	S		P	O	O	L		A	V	E	R	T
E	T	A		Y	E	L	L		B	L	A	R	E	S
			T	O	O	N		E	A	U				
	A	D	J	U	S	T	S	T	H	E	M	I	R	
A	R	E	A		L	A	T	H		D	O	R	I	S
S	L	A	Y		O	R	E	O		A	D	A	G	E
P	O	L	S		T	O	P	S		T	E	N	S	E

67

P	L	U	M	P		S	T	E	W		D	I	V	A
G	A	T	E	S		T	O	D	O		O	L	I	N
A	M	I	T	Y		E	R	G	O		Z	I	N	G
	B	L	A	C	K	E	Y	E	D	P	E	A	C	E
		H	O	P			S	A	N	D	E	R		
J	E	S	T	E	R		S	K	Y	E				
E	B	A	Y		A	D	I	N		A	M	P	E	D
D	O	W	N	O	N	O	N	E	S	N	I	E	C	E
I	N	N	E	R		S	U	E	T		L	O	O	N
			I	C	E	S		E	V	E	N	L	Y	
S	T	E	R	N	O			N	A	E				
M	Y	D	O	G	H	A	S	F	L	E	E	C	E	
A	L	D	O		E	V	I	L		J	I	H	A	D
R	E	I	N		R	O	T	E		A	R	I	S	E
T	R	E	E		E	W	E	R		Y	E	N	T	L

68

D	W	E	E	B		A	J	A	R		C	F	O	S
O	H	A	R	E		R	E	D	O		S	E	N	T
L	A	R	G	E	B	I	R	D	O	F	P	R	E	Y
E	M	S		G	O	O	K		M	E	A	N	I	E
		E	E	L	S		O	M	A	N				
T	W	O	B	E	L	O	W	P	A	R		T	O	M
I	A	M	B	S		E	A	T		W	I	F	E	
T	R	E	E		E	A	G	L	E		H	E	F	T
L	E	N	D		G	L	O			B	A	U	E	R
E	S	S		F	O	O	T	B	A	L	L	P	R	O
		F	A	M	E		A	G	E	E				
S	H	E	I	L	A		E	N	O	S		N	B	A
T	O	P	R	A	N	K	I	N	G	S	C	O	U	T
U	S	E	S		I	O	N	E		E	A	R	L	E
B	E	E	T		A	P	E	D		D	R	A	K	E

69

M	A	K	E		A	L	O	O	F		I	H	O	P
A	V	I	V		M	E	L	B	A		N	U	D	E
G	A	R	A	G	E	S	A	L	E		S	M	O	G
M	I	O	S	I	S			O	R	A	T	O	R	S
A	L	V	I	N		I	G	N	I	T	E	R		
		V	O	L	T	A	G	E	S	P	I	K	E	
A	P	S	E		E	L	M		E	S	S	A	Y	
A	L	P		M	I	L	I	T	I	A		T	R	E
R	E	E	S	E		E	A	T		S	S	T	S	
P	A	C	K	A	G	E	S	T	O	R	E			
		T	E	N	A	N	T	S		A	R	I	S	E
A	N	A	L	Y	S	T			E	Z	I	N	E	S
M	I	T	T		M	I	D	D	L	E	A	G	E	S
O	T	O	E		E	R	R	O	L		L	O	D	E
K	E	R	R		N	E	S	T	S		S	T	Y	X

70

R	E	B	A		A	D	M	A	N		M	O	L	S
I	C	O	N		D	O	O	Z	Y		A	R	A	T
B	O	B	K	E	E	S	H	A	N		R	A	R	E
		B	L	T	S		A	L	Y		S	T	E	R
A	S	Y	E	T		O	W	E		A	B	O	D	E
C	A	P	T	A	I	N	K	A	N	G	A	R	O	O
L	U	I	S		R	E	S		A	R	R			
U	R	N		F	I	G		M	C	A		F	O	P
			T	I	S		A	A	H		O	E	N	O
C	L	O	W	N	H	A	L	L	O	F	F	A	M	E
Z	A	X	I	S		U	L	T		E	F	R	E	M
E	B	B	S		C	R	O		O	U	R	S		
C	R	I	T		H	O	W	D	Y	D	O	O	D	Y
H	E	R	E		A	R	I	S	E		A	M	O	S
S	A	D	R		N	A	N	T	Z		D	E	A	L

71

A	T	O	L	L		W	O	N		E	X	P	O	
J	O	N	E	S		H	A	Y		U	N	M	A	N
A	N	Y	I	D	I	O	T	C	A	N	F	A	C	E
R	E	X			R	A	H		C	E	A	S	E	D
			W	H	I	M		J	U	A	N			
	A	C	R	I	S	I	S	I	T	S	T	H	I	S
W	R	A	I	T	H		O	B	E	Y		E	C	O
O	U	S	T		D	O	S			G	R	I	N	
O	B	E		G	A	I	T		S	A	R	O	N	G
D	A	Y	T	O	D	A	Y	L	I	V	I	N	G	
		O	D	D	S		A	X	E	D				
S	C	H	O	O	L		A	P	T		G	A	S	
T	H	A	T	W	E	A	R	S	Y	O	U	O	U	T
A	A	R	O	N		W	E	E		W	R	O	T	E
B	R	I	O		L	A	D		E	N	D	O	W	

72

H	I	M	O	M		B	B	C		R	E	B	U	S
O	S	A	K	A		L	E	O		A	G	A	S	P
C	A	R	D	S	H	A	R	P		T	O	T	E	R
			H	A	Z	M	A	T		I	T	R	Y	
E	B	W	H	I	T	E		P	O	S	S	E		
T	E	H	E	E	S		E	L	E	C	T	R	I	C
C	A	I	N			A	E	R	O		Y	A	Y	
H	T	S		P	O	P	T	A	R	T		A	M	B
E	E	K		A	R	I	A			E	C	T	O	
S	N	E	E	R	S	A	T		S	E	N	I	O	R
		Y	U	K	O	N		H	A	N	G	D	O	G
U	S	S	R		N	O	V	E	L	S				
S	H	O	O	T		B	I	T	T	E	R	E	N	D
C	O	U	P	E		A	B	U		A	O	L	E	R
G	O	R	E	D		R	E	P		L	E	F	T	Y

73

```
HAFT ■ SHIV ■ SISAL
ARIA ■ HARE ■ IRANI
BEETHOVEN ■ LAUDE
INSTATE ■ TOAST ■
TOTEMS ■ FEDS ■ ELY
STARS ■ GIDE ■ FREE
■ ■ TROD ■ TBONES
■ MADEOVERTURES ■
LABORS ■ LEAF ■
ONUS ■ ISIS ■ FERMI
PEN ■ ONTO ■ SAVEAS
■ DALAI ■ CELESTE
ELAND ■ TOLEONORE
PENNE ■ CRAM ■ ELOI
ATTAR ■ HEMS ■ DENT
```

74

```
SCAN ■ SPOT ■ PLATE
ALOE ■ WADE ■ EUROS
MENU ■ ASIA ■ RAILS
■ FERRYTERMINAL ■
■ OOZE ■ ION ■
TIPTOE ■ BAND ■ SHY
ONEIS ■ MULE ■ ELOI
PUNCTUATIONMARK
ARCS ■ RATE ■ ABIDE
ZEE ■ GAME ■ SCENES
■ POL ■ POHL ■
■ THATSALLFOLKS ■
MOORE ■ GOUT ■ INCH
POLKA ■ ROME ■ SEAM
GLEAM ■ AMEN ■ HERO
```

75

```
PAD ■ FAWN ■ BASALT
ESE ■ ILIE ■ ELIXIR
ALL ■ JANE ■ FINELY
READINGROOM ■
LENO ■ ■ RUBBISH
SPONGE ■ OIL ■ ISLE
■ ORING ■ ALTAR
EVERLASTINGLOVE
GAPED ■ RANCH ■
ASIA ■ CAP ■ OATERS
DECLARE ■ ALAI
■ FALLINGRAIN
ADROIT ■ ONEA ■ INK
SECURE ■ ATOZ ■ NEE
HEATER ■ NONE ■ ERR
```

76

```
TEAPOT ■ BANS ■ LIP
INDOOR ■ ETNA ■ ESE
MURPHYBROWN ■ SOL
ERE ■ SARAN ■ SETTO
RING ■ TATAS ■ ROOT
SNAPS ■ KELLYRIPA
■ GLOATED ■ AISLES
■ LED ■ EVE ■
THRIVE ■ MISLEAD
RYANONEAL ■ DRIER
AGIN ■ YATES ■ ORCA
WINOS ■ SHEET ■ PIN
LEM ■ SWEENEYTODD
ENA ■ TOUR ■ DEARER
DEN ■ SOPS ■ SENTRY
```

77

```
SPAM ■ MASSE ■ KOLA
OAHU ■ OWNER ■ ENOS
CLOD ■ SAILS ■ PERK
KEYBOARDFEATURE
■ ABIDE ■ LOPED
MYSTIC ■ GAIN ■
OATH ■ MAINE ■ IRA
CLOSETORGANIZER
SEW ■ RAMPS ■ NONE
■ GAGA ■ GRADEA
POSIT ■ QUIET ■
ASTRONAUTSCRAFT
SCAD ■ OPIUM ■ IDEA
TALL ■ METRO ■ CALM
ERLE ■ EDENS ■ EMTS
```

78

```
ATOM ■ INALL ■ IDOL
LIVE ■ ROLEO ■ BIRL
TEETOTALER ■ ISNO
ARROW ■ HAZARDPAY
■ CONE ■ HANA ■ ETD
SOO ■ UPI ■ ISLES
TRAPPISTMONK ■
PETE ■ STAIR ■ ISPY
■ ARCHIEBUNKER
PARKA ■ SIS ■ EIS
APE ■ SABE ■ TILE
ROUGHNECK ■ NOTSO
ELBA ■ SALADGREEN
NLER ■ ELATE ■ CREE
TONY ■ LETON ■ ASKS
```

79

O	M	A	H	A	■	D	U	M	B	■	A	D	D	S
S	Y	B	I	L	■	E	L	I	A	■	C	R	U	E
C	R	E	D	I	T	C	A	R	D	■	H	U	M	P
A	N	A	■	M	O	R	N	■	P	R	O	M	P	T
R	A	M	H	O	M	E	■	B	R	O	O	M	■	■
■	■	I	N	S	E	C	R	E	T	■	A	T	M	■
D	E	C	R	Y	■	C	U	S	H	Y	J	O	B	■
U	C	L	A	■	P	E	L	T	S	■	O	O	N	A
S	T	A	M	P	E	D	E	■	B	U	R	G	S	■
K	O	S	■	S	N	I	F	F	L	E	R	■	■	■
■	S	P	A	T	E	■	L	A	T	E	F	E	E	■
S	P	A	R	T	A	■	S	U	I	T	■	O	D	D
T	A	C	O	■	G	O	L	F	C	O	U	R	S	E
O	N	T	V	■	O	L	A	F	■	R	A	M	E	N
P	E	S	O	■	N	E	W	S	■	S	E	A	L	S

80

C	A	N	E	■	R	E	M	I	X	■	S	P	E	C
A	N	A	T	■	I	R	A	N	I	■	C	U	R	L
P	I	T	C	H	F	O	R	K	S	■	A	G	R	A
E	M	U	■	E	L	S	A	■	U	L	N	A	S	■
M	A	R	P	L	E	■	T	O	S	S	P	O	T	S
A	T	E	U	P	■	U	N	I	■	S	U	E	■	■
Y	E	S	T	■	P	H	O	T	O	N	■	E	M	S
■	■	T	H	R	O	W	R	U	G	S	■	■	■	■
P	I	N	■	A	U	K	L	E	T	■	T	A	R	A
O	N	O	■	C	D	E	■	■	B	A	N	A	L	■
P	A	S	S	K	E	Y	S	■	S	A	N	C	T	A
S	H	I	P	S	■	Q	U	A	Y	■	I	R	S	■
T	O	R	E	■	C	H	U	C	K	S	T	E	A	K
A	L	E	E	■	H	A	I	L	E	■	I	N	C	A
R	E	E	D	■	E	D	D	A	S	■	S	T	E	N

81

C	H	O	W	■	B	A	H	■	D	O	T	C	O	M
S	E	N	D	■	E	X	O	■	T	A	H	I	N	I
P	A	S	S	F	A	I	L	■	S	T	O	N	E	D
O	R	A	■	I	N	L	A	W	■	N	E	A	T	■
T	Y	L	E	N	O	L	■	E	K	E	■	A	C	E
S	E	E	Y	A	■	A	T	L	A	S	■	S	T	R
■	■	E	L	M	■	A	S	P	S	■	T	E	M	■
■	R	E	S	E	A	R	C	H	P	A	P	E	R	■
P	E	R	■	X	X	I	I	■	A	Y	E	■	■	■
O	N	O	■	A	I	M	T	O	■	T	A	X	E	S
P	O	T	■	M	M	E	■	H	E	E	L	T	A	P
Q	U	I	P	■	D	A	W	N	S	■	E	S	O	■
U	N	Z	I	P	S	■	L	E	C	T	U	R	E	R
I	C	E	T	E	A	■	A	L	L	■	G	R	I	T
Z	E	S	T	E	D	■	R	L	S	■	H	A	N	S

82

M	A	G	I	C	■	T	O	W	N	■	T	O	E	D
E	L	E	N	A	■	A	R	E	A	■	I	P	S	E
A	G	N	E	S	■	P	O	I	S	■	N	I	T	A
L	A	E	R	T	E	S	■	L	A	C	T	E	A	L
■	■	■	T	U	T	■	A	L	L	O	Y	■	■	■
T	R	A	I	P	S	E	S	■	S	U	P	E	R	B
I	O	T	A	■	E	A	T	■	P	E	N	A	L	■
M	L	I	■	S	Q	U	A	R	E	S	■	O	V	O
E	L	L	I	N	■	R	O	N	■	E	L	E	C	■
S	O	T	T	E	D	■	T	I	D	E	M	A	R	K
■	■	S	L	O	P	E	■	U	T	E	■	■	■	■
F	E	E	B	L	E	R	■	R	E	C	R	O	O	M
O	N	Z	E	■	S	A	F	E	■	H	I	N	D	I
U	Z	I	S	■	O	W	L	S	■	E	T	A	I	L
R	O	O	T	■	K	N	O	T	■	D	A	N	C	E

83

E	T	H	I	C	■	T	A	D	S	■	B	E	D	S
B	E	A	M	E	■	G	U	R	U	■	A	X	E	L
W	A	R	A	D	M	I	R	A	L	■	R	A	K	E
■	M	A	G	I	C	■	A	F	F	I	R	M	E	D
■	■	E	L	M	S	■	T	A	R	O	■	■	■	■
W	H	I	R	L	A	W	A	Y	■	M	O	M	M	A
I	A	N	■	A	H	A	B	■	F	A	M	O	U	S
N	O	T	I	■	O	M	A	H	A	■	S	I	N	K
E	L	E	V	E	N	■	C	E	N	T	■	S	R	I
D	E	L	E	D	■	S	I	R	B	A	R	T	O	N
■	■	H	I	R	T	■	A	E	R	O	■	■	■	■
C	I	T	A	T	I	O	N	■	L	I	L	T	S	■
O	V	I	D	■	C	O	U	N	T	F	L	E	E	T
R	A	V	I	■	O	G	L	E	■	F	O	R	E	S
K	N	O	T	■	H	E	L	D	■	S	N	I	D	E

84

S	C	T	V	■	E	S	S	O	■	D	U	C	T	S
H	O	R	A	■	L	O	C	K	■	A	G	R	E	E
A	V	O	N	■	A	G	A	R	■	W	H	I	N	E
W	E	D	D	I	Ⓝ	G	B	A	N	D	■	M	O	P
■	■	■	A	T	T	Y	■	A	L	D	E	R	S	■
A	M	B	L	E	R	■	S	E	B	E	R	Ⓖ	■	■
C	E	O	■	M	A	D	A	M	S	■	A	R	M	S
T	E	X	T	S	■	E	L	M	■	S	W	O	O	P
S	T	I	R	■	L	A	T	E	S	T	■	U	R	I
■	■	N	I	C	E	L	Y	■	W	E	A	P	O	N
L	A	G	O	O	N	■	■	H	A	M	M	■	■	■
I	T	S	■	C	O	L	L	A	Ⓡ	S	T	A	I	N
F	R	Ⓘ	S	K	■	P	A	R	T	■	R	U	D	E
T	I	T	H	E	■	G	O	S	H	■	A	D	O	S
S	P	E	E	D	■	A	S	H	Y	■	K	I	L	T

85

```
C L A N   E D A M   L A P A Z
R I T E   N O S E   O L I V E
A L A R   D O I N   W A X E D
S A L V E T R A D E R   Y R S
S C L E R A     E W O K
      O B T U S E A N G E L
B O D Y S L A M   D I E G O
L A R A   E D E M A   S T E N
A H A L F     K A L A H A R I
B U T T E R F I L E S
    A T K A     H A I R D O
A D J   C O L D H O P P E R S
Q U O T H   L I E U   A M O K
U N T I E   I V E S   N A N A
A S S A D   N A P E   A P E R
```

86

```
S A L I C   S H A Q   A B E T
E R I T U   P E L E   T A R O
Q U E E N M A R Y 2   T S A R
S T U   A A R     S A S S Y
      I R K   L O O K I E
B L O N D E   O R I E N T A L
L I C K   H A N D L E   E W E
U N E   L A R G E S T   R A N
R D A   A S S E R T   A R I D
B A N D I T O S   O W L E T S
    L A T E N T   N I L
B R I N Y     R E D   S E E
R I N G   C R U I S E S H I P
O P E L   A I R S   S H O R E
W E R E   T O N E   T E P E E
```

87

```
J A B B A   N A V E   A P B S
A B O I L   A M E R   W A R P
B U D G E T C U T S   E L I A
    H A I L   T A P   A C T
U P C A S T   P E T R O C K S
N O H I T T E R   Z O N E
S L U R   E R I K   N A G A T
E L M   B R O M I D E   U T A
R O P E R   S A T E   W A S P
    C L A P   R E S T A R E A
M A H O G A N Y   P A N D A S
A D A   S R O   P O R T
M E N U   F I R S T M A T E S
B U G S   U S E S   A D O R E
A X E S   M E A T   C S P A N
```

88

```
A T S E A   P L O W   J O G S
S I T A R   R A V I   E R I E
S M I R K   O M E N   S A V E
    F L A B B E R G A S T E D
S P F   N E E   L E E R S
H O N E S T   Q T I P S
E L E N A   B U O N   A T O
D I S E N F R A N C H I S E D
S O S   L A R K   A L T H O
    F O U N T   I S S U E R
T I A R A   E R A   D E S
I N D E F A T I G A B L E
R U D E   X I N G   A U N T S
E R O S   E L L E   L A T E R
D E N T   D E A D   L U S T S
```

89

```
  R A T   D A M E   J A M E S
P A R R   A B E D   A L I S T
L I M O   M U N I   M O L L Y
A D A Y I N D U B L I N
N E D   A S H   L I N E A G E
B R A G G   A T E N   S O L
    A R U B A   D R E S S Y
  J U N E S I X T E E N T H
B U N G E E   C O N V Y
A L L   D R O P   E A S E L
D E V I A T E   P E R   O V A
    L E O P O L D B L O O M
T A P I R   A L I I   A T K A
A D L A I   S E N T   C H E R
J O Y C E   T O G S   Y E S
```

90

```
P A C S   S L U R   D E F A T
I G O T   E I R E   A D E L E
T U B A   A L G A   N I N E S
H A B L A S I E D E U T S C H
    K N O T     A B S
A S H   I N H A S T E   A B E
S H A F T   R U E   E R A T
P A R L A T H E E N G L I S H
I N D Y   O U T   O S S I E
C A Y   S P E E D E R   E E R
    S P A     O D E S
P A R L E Z V O U S N O R S K
A L I E N   E R S E   D E A N
L O P E D   R E E L   A N T I
M E E T S   B O S S   S T E T
```

91

M	S	N	B	C	█	R	E	I	D	█	E	W	A	N
U	H	A	U	L	█	E	D	N	A	█	R	A	T	E
C	A	N	Y	O	U	H	E	A	R	M	E	N	O	W
H	M	O	█	S	P	A	N	S	█	I	N	E	P	T
█	█	A	E	O	N	█	█	E	N	T	O	█	█	█
T	E	S	T	I	N	G	O	N	E	T	W	O	█	█
A	V	I	A	N	█	I	S	A	Y	█	R	N	A	█
M	E	N	D	█	J	A	N	E	T	█	Z	I	O	N
E	R	A	█	S	O	C	K	█	█	B	O	N	G	O
█	█	I	S	T	H	I	S	T	H	I	N	G	O	N
█	T	E	N	D	█	W	A	G	E	█	█	█	█	█
C	H	A	I	N	█	T	A	I	L	S	█	A	F	T
H	E	L	L	O	H	E	L	L	O	H	E	L	L	O
A	R	A	L	█	A	S	T	I	█	O	N	E	A	M
D	O	N	S	█	S	T	A	T	█	T	E	X	T	S

92

M	E	N	S	A	█	A	C	A	D	█	D	I	S	C
P	A	N	T	S	█	L	O	G	E	█	O	B	O	E
S	T	E	E	P	█	E	L	I	A	█	D	I	B	S
█	█	█	W	I	N	K	A	N	D	R	O	S	E	S
A	H	A	█	R	U	E	█	█	E	A	S	E	I	N
P	A	R	K	I	N	G	F	I	N	K	█	S	T	A
B	R	I	A	N	█	█	L	O	D	E	S	█	█	█
S	P	A	M	█	C	L	A	N	S	█	A	D	A	M
█	█	A	S	H	E	N	█	█	P	R	I	C	E	█
S	P	A	█	L	I	N	K	O	F	S	I	G	H	T
A	R	T	F	U	L	█	S	R	A	█	S	E	E	█
M	A	K	E	M	I	N	E	M	I	N	K	█	█	█
I	N	I	T	█	D	E	V	O	█	D	I	N	G	Y
A	C	N	E	█	O	M	E	N	█	Q	T	I	P	S
M	E	S	S	█	G	O	L	D	█	S	E	P	A	L

93

B	O	S	H	█	B	A	S	R	A	█	S	A	D	A
A	R	C	O	█	E	M	A	I	L	█	U	X	O	R
L	I	R	R	█	T	U	R	T	L	E	N	E	C	K
L	O	U	N	G	E	L	I	Z	A	R	D	█	█	█
A	L	F	█	O	L	E	S	█	█	M	R	M	O	M
D	E	F	R	O	S	T	█	A	L	I	E	N	E	E
E	S	S	E	█	█	S	P	O	N	S	O	R	S	█
█	█	S	N	A	K	E	E	Y	E	S	█	█	█	█
M	E	C	H	A	N	I	C	█	█	E	S	M	E	█
D	E	P	O	N	E	D	█	B	R	I	S	T	O	L
S	N	O	U	T	█	█	A	E	O	N	█	R	O	E
█	█	L	E	A	P	E	R	O	G	G	I	N	G	█
T	O	A	D	S	T	O	O	L	S	█	A	P	I	A
A	N	N	E	█	M	E	R	I	T	█	P	E	E	N
G	E	A	R	█	O	M	E	N	S	█	E	R	S	T

94

M	A	H	I	█	P	A	L	E	S	█	B	A	T	S
A	S	I	F	█	O	F	A	R	T	█	E	D	I	E
B	I	G	F	A	T	L	Y	R	E	█	A	L	A	P
█	█	H	I	D	█	█	L	O	N	█	M	I	R	A
█	C	H	E	M	I	C	A	L	C	Y	M	B	A	L
F	L	O	R	I	D	A	█	█	H	E	E	█	█	█
O	A	R	█	T	O	R	C	H	█	A	U	D	I	S
R	I	S	E	█	S	T	R	U	M	█	P	E	N	A
E	M	E	N	D	█	A	T	B	A	T	█	C	D	I
█	█	█	T	O	M	█	█	B	R	O	I	L	E	D
Q	U	A	R	T	E	R	B	A	C	K	S	A	X	█
U	N	C	A	█	N	E	O	█	█	E	A	R	█	█
A	S	O	N	█	█	S	T	O	L	E	N	B	A	S	S
D	A	R	C	█	C	R	E	O	N	█	E	N	T	O
S	Y	N	E	█	H	O	D	A	D	█	L	T	R	S

95

F	E	T	E	█	A	B	O	V	E	█	A	M	A	T
U	L	A	N	█	C	U	B	I	T	█	V	A	R	Y
J	A	C	Q	U	E	L	I	N	E	█	I	R	O	N
I	L	I	U	M	█	K	E	Y	█	S	A	L	M	A
█	█	T	I	P	█	█	L	A	O	T	I	A	N	█
H	O	U	R	█	I	N	D	█	M	O	O	N	S	█
A	W	R	Y	█	B	O	U	V	I	E	R	█	█	█
L	E	N	█	K	E	N	N	E	D	Y	█	S	T	U
█	█	O	N	A	S	S	I	S	█	█	H	M	O	S
█	R	O	R	E	M	█	T	N	T	█	E	O	N	S
S	A	D	D	E	S	T	█	█	S	L	O	█	█	█
A	I	D	E	S	█	W	P	A	█	R	I	T	T	S
U	S	M	A	█	P	I	L	L	B	O	X	H	A	T
D	I	A	L	█	O	X	I	D	E	█	E	L	S	A
I	N	N	S	█	S	T	E	A	L	█	S	Y	S	T

96

D	O	B	R	O	█	T	R	O	D	█	Z	A	P	S
I	S	L	E	T	█	R	O	L	E	█	A	M	I	E
P	L	A	N	E	█	O	P	E	C	█	G	I	L	L
S	O	H	E	L	P	M	E	G	O	D	█	N	O	M
█	█	█	G	L	O	P	█	█	D	A	K	O	T	A
W	E	R	E	O	V	E	R	H	E	R	E	█	█	█
A	L	I	█	█	█	E	A	S	I	N	E	S	S	█
I	L	O	V	E	█	A	N	T	█	N	O	L	I	E
L	A	T	I	T	U	D	E	█	█	█	I	L	L	█
█	█	T	H	R	O	W	T	H	E	B	A	L	L	█
M	O	S	A	I	C	█	█	A	U	E	R	█	█	█
O	U	I	█	C	H	E	C	K	P	L	E	A	S	E
R	I	T	A	█	I	R	A	E	█	I	N	I	N	K
A	J	A	R	█	N	O	T	I	█	E	D	D	I	E
L	A	R	K	█	S	O	O	N	█	R	A	S	P	S

97

98

99

100

101

102

103

S	A	W	S		I	P	S	O		M	A	S	S	E
A	R	I	E		L	O	A	M		A	L	T	O	S
N	E	N	E		L	O	R	E		N	O	I	S	E
C	A	N	Y	O	U	F	I	N	D	T	E	N		
T	W	E	A	K	S			S	U	R		K	O	S
U	A	R		A	I	D	E		B	A	D	B	E	T
M	Y		S	P	O	I	L	T			A	U	R	A
		T	H	I	N	G	S	W	R	O	N	G		
L	I	E	U			S	E	E	I	N	G		P	I
S	W	A	T	C	H		S	E	N	T		G	U	N
D	O	M		A	A	A			G	O	C	A	R	T
	W	I	T	H	T	H	I	S	P	U	Z	L	E	
S	H	O	D		A	T	A	R	I		P	E	O	N
L	O	R	E		H	A	L	E	D		I	B	I	S
A	N	K	A		A	R	O	S	E		D	O	N	E

104

R	A	P		S	L	A	Y	S		S	T	E	I	N
A	C	E		T	O	S	E	A		I	G	L	O	O
L	T	R		A	C	T	A	S		L	I	K	U	D
S	U	I	T	Y	O	U	R	S	E	L	F			
T	A	S	K	S		D	O	E	R	S		C	N	N
O	T	H	O		R	E	F	R	Y		Z	H	O	U
N	E	A		B	E	N	T		B	O	A	S	T	
	B	A	R	S	T	H	E	D	O	O	R			
A	A	L	T	O		E	R	I	N		L	A	W	
K	I	E	V		S	O	M	N	I		P	E	L	E
A	R	S		S	O	D	O	I		A	I	M	E	E
	B	U	S	I	N	E	S	S	C	A	R	D		
A	T	A	R	I		S	K	E	I	N		G	T	O
D	I	G	I	N		T	E	L	L	A		N	E	U
Z	E	R	O	G		S	Y	S	O	P		E	D	T

105

	H	I	R	A	B	L	E		W	A	S	I
	S	O	R	E	N	S	E	N		O	F	A	N
	T	H	E	B	E	H	A	V	I	O	R	O	F
E	R	O	S		A	N	Y	A		A	P	O	P
A	A	H		C	T	R		L	A	M	A	R	R
T	W	O	P	E	O	P	L	E		L	E	U	M	I
	I	L	K		O	R	A	L		L	O	M
J	O	C	K	E	Y	I	N	G	F	O	R	O	N	E
I	V	O		B	O	R	E		I	V	E	
H	E	S	S	E		A	R	M	R	E	S	T	I	N
A	R	T	I	S	T		E	E	R		O	N	O
D	R	U	M		A	L	I	T		S	L	U	G
	A	M	O	V	I	E	T	H	E	A	T	E	R
	T	E	N	S		D	A	Y	T	R	A	D	E
	E	S	S	O		A	L	L	E	G	R	O

106

K	E	R	R		N	O	T	C	H		O	O	Z	E
E	L	I	E		A	D	O	R	E		B	R	E	N
L	A	M	P		G	E	N	O	A		R	E	A	D
P	N	E	U	M	A	T	I	C	D	R	I	L	L	S
		B	U	N	S			G	R	E				
A	P	O	L	L	O		E	T	E	R	N	I	T	Y
S	O	N	I	C		A	T	R	A		R	A	E	
P	S	Y	C	H	O	T	H	E	R	A	P	I	S	T
E	T	O		U	R	I	S		P	O	N	T	I	
N	E	U	R	O	T	I	C		D	E	L	A	Y	S
		E	L	S			S	U	R	E				
P	T	O	L	E	M	A	I	C	S	Y	S	T	E	M
R	A	G	A		A	R	G	O	T		T	A	R	A
O	P	R	Y		R	O	O	N	E		A	D	I	N
P	E	E	S		T	O	T	E	R		R	A	C	Y

107

J	A	M	B		S	M	A	S	H		S	G	T	S
U	B	E	R		A	T	S	E	A		T	A	R	A
N	B	A	A	L	L	S	T	A	R		A	L	A	S
K	A	N	S	A	S		O	L	D	F	L	A	M	E
		I	T	A	L		S	E	R	I	A			
T	A	B	L	E	S	A	W		N	O	N	F	A	T
A	L	A	I	N		M	O	D	E	M		F	D	R
M	I	R	A		J	A	R	O	D		S	A	D	E
E	B	B		H	U	R	T	S		S	T	I	L	E
D	I	A	D	E	M		H	E	C	T	A	R	E	S
		R	U	M	B	A		D	A	R	N			
B	E	A	N	P	O	L	E		N	O	D	I	C	E
I	M	A	C		J	A	V	A	A	P	P	L	E	T
D	I	N	E		E	M	E	N	D		A	S	S	N
S	T	N	S		T	O	S	C	A		T	A	T	A

108

P	I	C		G	A	S	P		X	I	M	M	E	E
I	T	A		A	G	U	A		E	C	A	R	T	E
X	A	N	D	T	E	L	L		D	E	N	I	A	L
E	L	O	I		S	T	A	R		M	O	S	S	Y
L	O	E	S	S		A	V	A	T	A	R			
			L	E	A	N	E	D	O	N		E	A	R
A	E	R	I	E	S		R	I	P		A	L	B	A
X	M	E	K	A	T	E		X	I	N	G	K	I	N
L	I	N	E		R	S	T		C	O	R	S	E	T
E	L	O		C	A	T	E	R	S	T	O			
	L	O	Y	O	L	A		A	U	R	A	L		
S	N	A	I	L		P	E	N	T		N	O	S	E
F	I	N	A	L	S		X	G	O	O	D	B	Y	E
A	D	O	N	I	S		E	E	R	O		O	L	D
X	I	N	G	E	R		D	R	O	P		T	A	S

109

S	T	A	C		C	P	A	S		G	R	I	M	M
O	A	T	H		L	A	N	E		R	U	P	E	E
D	I	V	I	N	I	N	G	R	O	O	M	S	E	T
		C	A	M	E	L		S	C	O	O	T	S	
D	I	V	A	N	B	L	O	C	K	E	R			
A	R	E	N	A	S		H	A	R		S	Y	D	
G	A	T	O	S		D	R	U	R	Y		K	A	I
G	I	T	S		F	O	U	R	S		N	I	K	E
E	S	E		B	A	G	E	L		T	O	H	I	S
R	E	D		R	U	M			B	Y	N	A	M	E
			D	I	V	A	S	K	A	P	I	T	A	L
A	V	E	R	S	E		A	I	D	E	S			
D	I	V	O	T	S	A	N	D	D	A	S	H	E	S
A	T	A	L	L		L	E	D	A		U	E	Y	S
M	A	N	L	Y		T	R	O	Y		E	D	E	N

110

H	A	N	A		S	L	I	M		A	C	H	O	O
I	D	O	L		L	A	V	A		M	A	O	R	I
P	O	L	I	T	I	C	A	L		A	D	M	E	N
P	R	E	S	I	D	E	N	T	S		D	E	S	K
I	N	S	T	S			E	T	H	Y	L			
E	S	S		B	E	A	D	L	E		A	R	T	
			T	I	T	A	N			R	A	N	C	H
I	N	A	U	G	U	R	A	T	I	O	N	D	A	Y
C	O	M	B	O			C	I	N	D	Y			
E	W	E		R	A	T	T	L	E		A	H	A	
		R	O	S	I	E			A	R	R	I	D	
W	A	I	F		M	A	R	C	H	F	O/OU	R	T	H
I	N	C	A	N		B	I	P	A	R	T	I	T	E
S	T	A	G	E		A	G	A	S		E	V	E	R
P	I	N	E	D		G	A	S	P		S	E	R	E

Note: The circled square has two answers.

111

C	C	C	P		B	A	S			P	A	T	T	Y
R	O	L	E		A	L	T	A		S	Q	U	A	D
U	N	I	T	A	R	I	A	N		A	U	T	O	S
D	E	P	E	N	D	E	N	T	C	L	A	U	S	
		A	T	O	N		E	L	M	S				
	Y	A	C	H	T		A	D	A	S		E	E	G
F	I	C	H	E		R	I	A	S		A	N	D	I
R	E	M	E	M	B	E	R	T	H	E	M	A	I	N
A	L	E	R		I	D	E	E		X	A	C	T	O
T	D	S		S	K	I	D		P	E	R	T	H	
		B	E	E	R		A	R	M	Y				
	S	A	Y	P	R	E	T	T	Y	P	L	E	A	S
D	E	L	T	A		C	O	U	N	T	L	E	S	S
E	A	S	E	L		T	E	N	N		I	R	I	S
F	L	O	S	S		S	E	E		S	O	N	S	

112

A	M	A	S	S		A	D	O	B	E		S	T	Y
D	O	G	I	E		R	E	N	E	E		T	O	O
D	R	O	M	E		N	A	T	A	L	P	A	R	K
L	E	G	O	F	H	O	N	O	R		E	T	T	E
			L	I	E			P	D	J	A	M	E	S
L	O	S	E	T	I	M	E			A	K	A		
A	L	P	O		N	U	M	B	E	R		S	T	P
N	E	O	N		I	D	I	O	M		O	T	O	E
D	O	R		P	E	S	T	L	E		P	E	T	E
		T	B	S			S	O	R	C	E	R	E	R
D	E	S	O	T	O	S		I	O	N				
I	T	S	O		P	U	R	P	L	E	P	A	S	S
T	H	E	B	I	C	M	A	N		R	O	G	U	E
T	I	C		D	I	E	G	O		C	R	U	E	T
O	C	T		S	T	R	U	M		E	T	A	T	S

113

P	A	P	A		S	H	A	S	T	A		I	V	Y
O	P	U	S		T	O	R	P	O	R		F	A	A
W	I	R	Y		A	E	R	A	T	E		N	C	O
W	E	S	L	E	(yin-yang)	R	A	D	U	A	T	E		
O	C	E	A	N		Y	E	P		R	E	B	A	
W	E	D		D	N	A		F	I	D	E	L		
		A	L	Y	S	S	A		R	A	B	B	I	
	D	I	R	E	C	T	E	D	B	(yin-yang)	L	E	E	
S	I	M	M	S		I	N	R	A	G	S			
A	R	I	A	S		Y	A	P		T	R	E		
P	E	N	N		T	H	A		A	S	H	E	N	
	L	I	B	(yin-yang)	O	V	E	R	N	M	E	N	T	
A	D	O		I	G	N	O	R	E		A	F	A	R
N	O	V		N	U	D	I	S	M		C	A	M	E
T	E	E		S	P	A	R	E	S		K	N	E	E

114

G	N	U		M	A	M	B	O		N	A	T	A	L
N	A	P		O	N	L	O	W		E	R	O	D	E
A	B	S		N	O	I	S	S	I	W	N	O	O	W
W	S	I	N	O	X	I	N		S	C	E	N	T	
		D	O	D	I		L	T	R	S				
A	N	E	M	I	C		O	I	H	O	S	S	I	W
H	A	D	A	C		V	A	M	P		P	S	I	
E	B	O	N		H	S	I	M	I		H	U	R	L
R	O	W		T	O	O	T		T	E	N	E	T	
N	O	N	I	W	O	O	Z		F	A	R	A	D	S
		C	O	H	N		U	X	O	R				
	A	C	H	O	O		N	O	M	I	N	O	M	I
S	N	O	I	N	O	N	I	X	I	W		U	R	N
A	T	O	N	E		O	P	E	N	A		N	E	G
W	I	N	G	S		T	A	N	G	Y		D	D	E

115

```
E F G . S P O T . L A U R A S
S E R I A L N O . A L L O U T
P L A N T O B E . N A T U R E
. I N S I T U . J A N I T O R
A C T O N . D V I I . M E R E
T I O . . T G I F . P A R A S
M A R S H I E R . D R T . . .
. . S P O N T A N E O U S . .
. . E R G . G U N S M I T H .
A S H E N . T O M S . . D E A
T E E D . B O S E . S P E L L
O N A D I E T . . R E P U T E
M E D I A N . T O M O R R O W
I C E A G E . H U M O R I S T
C A R L O S . Y S E R . P T S
```

116

```
. H M S . B A T S . I N T A K E
O A K . E C H O . S T O N E D .
S T R I N G T E L E P H O N E S
A T O N E S . P I T Y . L O P .
L E O N E . B I D S . L A Y I T
K A N E . I R A S . P E T I T E
. . D O N E N . R E V E N U E .
M T A . O N E O N O N E . G P S
I O D I Z E D . C O N E S . . .
F O R C E R . L A K E . M A W S
F L I E S . B I A S . D O N E E
. R E B . S A N G . S O O N E R
L O N E L Y H E A R T S C L U B
G O N E O N . A M O I . H E N .
E M E R G E . L E E R . Y E S .
```

117

```
A R C O . R A S . S E S A M E
C H E F . E N T R E N C H E D
T I C T A C T O E I S A M I D
U N I . I L I A D . O P E R A
P O L A R I S . D A R E . . .
. . . A T M . E F S . S H A Q
. G E A R B O X O I L . A L E
B A L S A . X X X . A P H I D
U Z I . P R O O X I D A N T .
M A S T . A N N . C D S . . .
. . . O M N I . O H I O A N S
S T O L E . A B C D E . G O O
W O R D S I N T H I S G R I D
A R E Y O U S U R E . M E S A
B Y L A N D . S E N . T E E S
```

118

```
P C B S . S A P S . A D E L A
I O U S . P U R L . R E V E L
C C C T H E D A Y . C L E A T
A O K . E N I D . S H A R K S
. A W O R D T O T H E Y Y Y .
. . H A M S . R A R E . . . .
W H E R E . H A I R . D R E W
B O A . S N O W P P P . E G O
A N T I . E W E S . L E D G E
. . G N A T . P I E R . . . .
. U U U I T O R L O S E I T .
A T T A C H . A I L S . B I T
L E T N O . K I L L E R B B B
A R E A L . I S L E . L O I S
N O R S E . T E E N . S N A P
```

119

```
A B A C I . P A S A . C H E .
D O N O R . I M I N . L U I Z
O L D M A N A N D T H E S E A
. . . M E A N I E . O A S I S
L A M E . G O O D F O R Y O U
T R E N D S . . U T E . . . .
C O N D E . B E A D . D U A L
O S S . F R I E N D S . B R A
L E A D . U G L Y . U C O N N
. . . E L I . . A M A L I E .
B E S T I N S H O W . S T E S
U L C E R . C A R H O P . . .
C L O S E B U T N O C I G A R
S I L T . I D E O . T A E B O
. E D S . P S S T . O N E A M
```

120

```
S S E E . A L A M O . B A D S
L A V A . L A M A R . O L E A
I B I S . I N E R T . G O E R
N E A T . S E X T E T . N R A
E R N E S T S . G A D G E T .
. . . R I A . U S A G E S . .
T R A N S I E N T . S W I F T
I O N . R E T E R . D I D
P E T I T . R E M E M B E R S
. . . I S O P O D . F O E . .
O S P R E Y . D E M A G O G .
P T A . S L I C E R . R E M O
E R S T . O L D I E . I N A T
N I T A . N I E C E . S O R A
H A I D . S A F E S . H A S T
```

Note: Corner squares clockwise from upper left: S = sight; S = smell; T = taste; H = hearing
Center square: T = touch.

121

R	A	F	T		T	U	S	K		S	C	A	L	E
A	M	A	H		A	N	T	I		L	A	S	E	R
J	U	N	E	A	U	O	I	L	T	A	N	K	E	R
A	R	G	O	N				R	O	O	S	T		
		R	O	O	M	S		W	H	A	T	I	F	
H	O	L	E		S	O	U	R			T	O	N	I
O	N	O	M	A	T	O	P	O	E	I	A	U	S	E
T	E	T		C	E	L		B	L	T		C	A	N
A	D	I	E	U	O	A	H	U	I	S	L	A	N	D
I	G	O	R			H	O	S	S		O	N	E	S
R	E	N	A	M	E		S	T	E	P	S			
		S	O	L	T	I		T	E	M	P	T		
S	E	Q	U	O	I	A	E	M	P	L	O	Y	E	E
A	D	O	R	N		P	R	O	S		U	R	N	S
D	O	M	E	S		E	Y	E	S		T	A	T	S

122

P	E	R	E	Z		M	A	S	T		C	H	I	A
A	L	A	M	O		O	S	L	O		R	U	N	S
S	L	I	P	O	U	T	F	O	R	L	U	N	C	H
T	A	N		N	I	A			E	S	S	A	Y	
		S	H	I	F	T	I	N	T	O				
	L	A	P	A	T			L	A	T	E	F	E	E
E	I	D	E	R		C	U	E	S			J	U	L
S	L	A	C	K	S	O	F	F	A	T	W	O	R	K
S	A	P		H	O	O	T		H	E	R	O	S	
O	C	T	A	G	O	N		B	E	A	D	S		
		F	I	R	S	T	G	E	A	R				
S	N	A	R	L		E	A	T			C	C	S	
H	O	S	E	D	O	W	N	T	H	E	W	A	L	K
I	R	I	S		V	A	S	E		S	I	N	A	I
N	A	S	H		A	X	E	D		Q	T	I	P	S

123

P	A	C	T		I	T	C	H		C	H	O	P	S
A	T	O	I		S	O	H	O		H	A	B	I	T
C	O	N	V	E	N	T	I	O	N	A	L	I	T	Y
		T	O	T	O		P	E	R					
A	P	R		S	T	D	S		A	L	P	A	C	A
T	I	A		M	A	T	S		O	L	I	O	S	
T	E	R	M		O	T	O	E		T	A	R	A	S
E	R	I	E		R	A	R	E		T	I	E	T	O
S	C	A	N		A	S	Y	M	M	E	T	R	I	C
T	E	N	A	B	L	E		S	I	B				
		T	R	I	T	E		D	R	I	V	E	R	
N	I	T	W	I	T		D	E	M	O	T	A	P	E
O	N	I	O	N	Y		I	R	O	N	E	D	O	N
S	C	O	R	E			T	E	S	T	R	I	D	E
H	A	N	K	S			S	I	T	E		S	E	W

124

J	A	P	E		V	A	N	Y	A		N	U	T	S
E	W	A	N		E	S	T	E	R		O	N	C	E
F	O	R	G	E	T	T	H	E	P	A	S	T	E	L
F	L	A		D	O	A			W	E	I	L	L	
	M	A	D	E	B	Y	H	A	N	D	E	L		
C	L	O	R	I	S		O	O	Z	E				
H	A	U	T	E		C	L	O	U	D	N	I	N	E
A	I	R	S		B	A	K	E	R		O	V	E	N
I	T	S	Y	B	I	T	S	Y		S	L	A	N	G
		E	T	T	A		R	E	I	N	E	R		
	M	O	T	L	E	Y	C	R	E	W	E	L		
P	E	R	E	C		E	D	U		E	R	A		
F	L	A	S	H	I	N	T	H	E	P	A	N	E	L
F	E	L	T		S	P	R	A	Y		I	D	E	A
T	E	S	S		T	R	I	B	E		L	L	D	S

125

S	O	L	D		W	A	R	M		M	O	T	E	S
E	V	E	R		A	L	I	A		T	O	O	T	H
R	E	V	E	N	G	E	O	N		A	L	P	H	A
A	R	I	S	E	O	U	T	O	F		A	B	E	L
		S	E	N	T		F	E	E	L	I	L	L	
D	E	T	E	R	S		M	I	T	R	A	L		
O	C	H	S		S	O	R	E	S		L	E	T	
C	H	E		G	E	T	L	O	S	T		I	D	O
S	O	L		A	L	E	A	N		P	N	I	N	
	E	A	S	I	E	R		S	E	R	G	E	I	
T	E	A	S	H	O	P		A	C	R	E			
E	N	D	S		T	H	E	M	E	S	S	A	G	E
A	V	O	I	D		I	N	O	N	E	S	W	A	Y
M	O	U	S	E		L	Y	R	E		O	O	Z	E
S	I	T	I	N		L	A	T	S		N	L	E	R

126

P	A	G	O		A	P	E	S		S	U	G	A	R
E	R	I	K		P	A	V	E		C	N	O	T	E
P	A	R	A	M	E	T	E	R		R	S	V	P	S
O	L	L	Y	O	X	E	N	F	R	E	E			
			S	V	E	N			O	A	R	I	N	G
Z	S	A		E	S	T		H	M	M		C	A	R
E	P	C	O	T			T	E	E		R	I	V	A
S	H	E	L	O	V	E	S	Y	O	U	Y	E	A	H
T	E	T	E		I	T	E		P	A	S	H	A	
E	R	E		P	A	C		C	R	T		T	O	M
D	E	N	T	A	L		L	E	O	N				
			I	T	S	A	M	A	D	W	O	R	L	D
D	O	N	D	I		R	A	C	O	N	T	E	U	R
A	V	I	A	N		A	N	K	A		E	D	N	A
W	A	L	L	A		B	A	S	K		S	I	N	G

127

```
A T E U P ■ M O N A ■ T A M P
B A S S O ■ O B I S ■ O G E E
C L A S S ■ L I M B ■ R E N T
S K I R T E D T H E I S S U E
■ ■ ■ I R E ■ ■ S R O ■ ■ ■
■ B E L T E D O U T A S O N G
N O V A S ■ C M O N ■ D Y E
O W E D ■ S E E P S ■ C O M A
T I N ■ G I L A ■ ■ P U R E R
V E S T E D I N T E R E S T ■
■ ■ O N E ■ ■ U T E ■ ■ ■ ■
S O C K E D I N T H E N O S E
A X L E ■ I S E E ■ M A U L S
F E I N ■ S L O E ■ P T R A P
E N O S ■ H E N S ■ T E S T Y
```

128

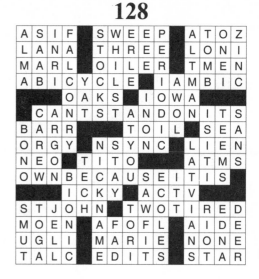

```
A S I F ■ S W E E P ■ A T O Z
L A N A ■ T H R E E ■ L O N I
M A R L ■ O I L E R ■ T M E N
A B I C Y C L E ■ I A M B I C
■ ■ O A K S ■ I O W A ■ ■
C A N T S T A N D O N I T S
B A R R ■ T O I L ■ S E A
O R G Y ■ N S Y N C ■ L I E N
N E O ■ T I T O ■ ■ A T M S
O W N B E C A U S E I T I S
■ ■ I C K Y ■ A C T V ■ ■
S T J O H N ■ T W O T I R E D
M O E N ■ A F O F L ■ A I D E
U G L I ■ M A R I E ■ N O N E
T A L C ■ E D I T S ■ S T A R
```

129

```
M A R C ■ S H E L V E ■ W W W
O L E O ■ M U D E E L ■ I R E
H I N D U U T O P I A ■ L Y E
S I D E S ■ ■ U N N A M E D
■ I S U Z U U S E D C A R S
A R T ■ R O M P ■ D S T ■
M O I ■ P L A S M ■ O M E N
I D O L ■ A S T O R ■ R O T E
D E N Y ■ S A R A H ■ N O W
■ N B A ■ T A T A ■ A N T
F O N D U U T E N S I L S ■
E S T E L L E ■ K I T E S
T O E ■ O A H U U K U L E L E
E L S ■ V I E N N A ■ A R I A
S E T ■ A T E O U T ■ C Y S T
```

130

```
L A B S ■ I N S ■ S E A C O W
O L E O ■ H O P ■ N E V A D A
G L A U C O M A ■ I R O N E D
J U M P U P A N D D O W N ■
A R E S T ■ D I R E ■ I M P
M E D ■ O I S E ■ I B A R
■ M A R C H I N P L A C E
A S L O P E ■ O A K L E Y
F L A P B O T H A R M S ■
R O W E ■ M E N D ■ A F L
O W N ■ T E A T ■ C A L L A
■ S I M O N D I D N T S A Y
G O A W A Y ■ S W A N L A K E
P O L I T E ■ E A T ■ A C E R
O P E N E D ■ T R A ■ S E S S
```

131

```
B O L O ■ J A G S ■ S T A L L
A V I A ■ U S E S ■ A N N I E
J E F F E R S O N ■ V O I L A
A R T ■ P I E ■ J E T T A S
■ W H E N Y O U R E A C H
S R T A ■ S T E A L ■ ■
W E A V E ■ T H E E N D O F
A L B E R T A ■ U P S T A T E
Y O U R R O P E ■ S E T I N
■ O S A K A ■ S A S S
T I E A K N O T I N I T ■
E V A D E S ■ N C R ■ A H A
P A G A N ■ A N D H A N G O N
I N E P T ■ P O L O ■ B E L T
D A R T S ■ E V E R ■ A D D S
```

132

```
G L O B E ■ A S E A ■ T E A
R A N A T ■ D E A L ■ M O N T
O V E R A N D O U T ■ O A T H
A R C ■ F L U ■ A U N T I E
T O E ■ C E L ■ I N T E R N
S O U L ■ S S E ■ F R E E S
A R N O L D ■ O N C U E ■
S Y D N E Y A U S T R A L I A
■ A N E S T ■ A L L O T S
G R O S S ■ P H D ■ C O C K
R A S P E D ■ K I T ■ A K A
E N C A S E ■ O N O ■ N I N
E S A I ■ C A R G O P A N T S
C O R N ■ O G E E ■ A D O B E
E M S ■ Y E A R ■ M A N E T
```

133

```
A C R E   S P U D   A C T O R
D I E U   T E R I   C H O R E
D I S C R E D I T   I R M A S
    T H E W I C K E D I T C H
W H E R E S   H A N   S I L O
B O D E D       D O T T E D
A P O   A T A T I M E
  I N T E R N R E V E N U E
  W A R T I M E     N R A
M A R I N E     W A L D O
O D O R   A O L   S H R I E K
D O L L A R S T O N U T S
E R L E S   O C C I P I T A L
L E E R Y   L O A D   E E R O
T E R S E   E L S E   R D A S
```

134

```
R I F E   P R A T T   B R A N
E N O S   R I C H E   I O N A
E R R S   O C E A N S T A T E
V O T E S F O R W O M E N
E A R N S       S R A
D D E   T Y K E   R A C E R
  S U S A N B A N T H O N Y
M A S C   D O O N E   M U S E
A M E L I A B L O O M E R
H A S A T   A N N A   T N T
      A T F     U S H E R
  J U L I A W A R D H O W E
P H O N O G R A P H   R U M P
H E L D   R A D I O   E S A I
I N T O   E D E N S   W E N D
```

135

```
M A T   O L O F     A P R O N
A T E   S A M O A   L O O N Y
R O N   S I N G L E P L A C E
I N A M E R I C A W H E R E
S E M I     I D E A S
    N I P A T       I S I S
  B E A U T Y C O N T E S T
N O R   I P O   A N O   W H Y
T H E A M A Z I N M E T S
H O W L     S T Y L E
    L A V A L       R Y E S
  F O U R S T A T E S M E E T
F O U R C O R N E R S   A L A
R A Z E D   A D M I T   S E C
I L O S E   S A C S   T R Y
```

136

```
B L O T   C A L M S   M O T H
B E C K   U B O A T   E C H O
K A T T S P A U S E   T H E N
I N A S N I T   S W O O S H
N O V   E D E R   N O T U P
G N O M E   R E A C T   A L P
  I Z E   D W I   E L K S
  B A E R S C L A U S E
S P Y S   M O O   O P T
N O R   P A W A T   S H A W L
O L D I E   T R E E   P H I
  E S P R I T   O N T O P O F
N C A A   C R O W E S F E A T
P A Y S   B U Y E R   F A M E
R T E S   M E L L O   S L I D
```

137

```
D I R G E   S E C S   L C D S
I N E E D   E T U I   E L A L
S T A N D G U A R D   N O M E
C E L L A R S   L E T S S E E
H R E   A S S I S I   E N V
A N S E L M   A C T E   B E E
R A T S O   G L U E   T U L L
G L A C I E R   E P I S T L E
E R T E   V A L S   C A N I S
P E E   D A N E   T H R O E S
A V A   O L D S A W   C M D
P E G A S U S   M I L K I E R
E N E S   A L L A T I N G L E
R U N E   T A O S   S A A B S
S E T A   E M T S   A R R A S
```

138

```
A S O L D A S T H E H I L L S
W O R D O N T H E S T R E E T
I N A L L D I R E C T I O N S
N A T   L Y N E   E P S
G R E G   G A P   H A A S
    I S R   D R A M   B L T
G I F T C E R T I F I C A T E
I V E G O T A H E A D A C H E
G A S O L I N E S T A T I O N
O N T   D E A N   E S E
T A S S   T E A   R A G A
  T A D   E L K E   M O S
D A V I D A N D G O L I A T H
O N C E I N A L I F E T I M E
H E R B A L M E D I C I N E S
```

139

```
S N A P S A T ■ W I N E B A R
L I M E A D E ■ H O U D I N I
I C E C U B E ■ O W N U P T O
M E R ■ K I N S M A N ■ L O T
J O I N ■ Z I P P Y ■ H A N A
I N C U S ■ D O S ■ G E N I C
M E A T H O O K ■ F I R E A T
■ ■ T I T L E R O L E ■ ■
S T E R E O ■ N E X T T I M E
A O L E R ■ P F C ■ S I L E X
R O M E ■ B R O O D ■ C O D A
O S U ■ Q U E R I E S ■ V I C
N O N J U R Y ■ L E T S E A T
G O D L I K E ■ E R U D I T E
S N O O Z E D ■ D E B I T E D
```

140

```
S A N T A F E ■ A R T S H O W
U R G E S O N ■ D A Y T O N A
C L A S S I C ■ L I N E M E N
K E I T E L ■ G A T E L E G ■
S N O R E ■ W R I T ■ A M A T
■ U N T I E ■ I R A T E
I C O N O C L A S T S ■ K I N
R E L ■ N H L T E A M ■ E V E
A L D ■ T R A D E S E C R E T
N E G E V ■ A I S L E ■
I B E X ■ F O N T ■ L A M P S
■ R E C E I V E ■ M A S A L A
G A Z E L L E ■ P U R I T A N
A T E L I E R ■ A T A N E N D
T E R S E S T ■ L E T G O B Y
```

141

```
H A C K ■ P O G O ■ C O P E D
O D I E ■ I W O N ■ A L A M O
H A T E T O E A T A N D R U N
O P E N A N D S H U T C A S E
S T R O K E ■ K E L S O ■
■ N E E D Y ■ D E I G N S
B O B ■ R O O T ■ E N D O W
A L E C ■ S L U R S ■ S A G A
R E A L M ■ E R I E ■ Y O N
N O M A A M ■ M O A T S ■
■ P R O M O ■ C H E A T S
T O O T T O O T T O O T S I E
S O R R Y T O H E A R T H A T
A N E A R ■ R E M S ■ E B R O
R A M P S ■ E R A T ■ R Y A N
```

142

```
B I G A P E ■ F A L L O P E N
A M O S O Z ■ I D E E F I X E
R A T H E R ■ R O A S T P I G
E L L ■ T A V E R N S ■ P T A
A L O S S ■ E D E N ■ M E E T
R O O T ■ L I U ■ S A N D E
M U S E ■ O N P A P E R ■
S T E E P L E ■ T I E C L I P
■ L E A D O R E ■ O O N A
S H R E W ■ R E D ■ N O D S
H E A R ■ R A G S ■ M I K E S
O R G ■ R E G A T T A ■ I M P
G E T S A T A N ■ A T O N A L
U T A H J A Z Z ■ M T E T N A
N O G O A R E A ■ P A R O D Y
```

143

```
S C A M A R T I S T ■ G I F T
N O T A C H A N C E ■ A S I A
A C T T H E P A R T ■ F U N K
R O I ■ E A S I E R ■ F R E E
L O C H ■ D E A R ■ E T A
S N A I L E D ■ N S A ■ C U B
■ G E A R S ■ P I A N O
S O W H A T E L S E I S N E W
C R O C K ■ R A V E L ■
H A R ■ E S P ■ S E R I E S E
E L K ■ D A R T ■ P L E D
M E S S ■ D O O D A D ■ P A W
E X I T ■ I N D E L I C A C Y
R A T E ■ S T O N E M A S O N
S M E W ■ T O S S E S D O W N
```

144

```
B R A K E F L U I D ■ U S T A
R E S I L I E N C E ■ N E E T
A P P R E N T I C E ■ J E S T
I T I ■ M I S S ■ S H A S T A
D I R T ■ D O N ■ U M E K I
E L I O T ■ O N E P M ■ Y I N
R E N E W A L ■ W I D G E T S
■ Y A L U ■ S E R I ■
F I X E D O N ■ P R U N I N G
I N S ■ D E C C A ■ M U R A L
F L A I L ■ H U P ■ P O R E
T A N D E M ■ D E F T ■ N R A
E R D E ■ D E G R E E P L A N
E G O S ■ C L E A N S L A T E
N E S T ■ C O L D S H O W E R
```

145

M	U	N	C	H	K	I	N	S	■	M	E	M	O	S
A	S	I	A	M	I	N	O	R	■	A	M	I	N	O
H	O	T	P	O	T	A	T	O	■	N	I	N	E	R
A	P	R	■	S	E	P	T	■	F	I	N	I	T	E
L	E	I	S	■	S	E	R	V	I	C	E	M	E	N
O	N	C	U	E	■	T	U	E	S	■	M	A	N	E
■	■	M	M	E	■	E	A	T	S	■	R	T	S	■
T	I	M	P	A	N	I	■	L	E	N	G	T	H	S
E	N	T	■	G	A	N	G	■	D	O	A	■	■	■
A	P	A	T	■	B	R	A	D	■	B	L	I	S	S
M	I	R	A	C	L	E	B	R	A	■	S	T	A	T
M	E	A	L	I	E	■	F	E	L	T	■	S	L	Y
A	C	R	E	D	■	D	E	A	L	A	M	E	A	L
T	E	A	S	E	■	E	S	M	E	R	A	L	D	A
E	S	T	E	R	■	I	T	S	N	O	T	F	A	R

146

C	A	F	E	R	E	S	T	A	U	R	A	N	T	S
A	N	A	L	O	G	C	O	M	P	U	T	E	R	S
M	I	L	I	T	A	R	Y	O	F	F	I	C	E	R
P	O	D	■	S	D	I	■	■	O	U	S	T	■	■
S	N	O	W	■	■	M	O	O	R	S	■	A	R	G
■	■	■	H	O	P	P	I	N	G	■	A	R	E	A
D	E	L	A	N	O	■	D	O	R	■	F	I	B	S
E	V	E	R	E	S	T	■	R	A	V	I	N	E	S
L	E	A	F	■	T	R	A	■	B	A	R	E	L	Y
E	N	D	S	■	M	O	L	E	S	T	S	■	■	■
S	T	P	■	C	O	D	E	X	■	T	A	M	S	■
■	■	I	Z	O	D	■	A	M	B	■	N	O	T	■
J	A	P	A	N	E	S	E	C	U	I	S	I	N	E
E	L	E	C	T	R	I	C	T	O	A	S	T	E	R
W	A	S	H	I	N	G	T	O	N	S	T	A	T	E

147

M	R	C	O	F	F	E	E	■	S	O	R	D	I	D
Y	E	A	R	L	I	N	G	■	P	U	E	R	T	O
F	A	L	S	E	T	T	O	■	A	C	C	O	S	T
O	L	A	■	D	I	R	T	■	S	H	O	P	S	■
O	T	I	C	■	N	O	R	M	■	O	N	O	R	■
T	Y	S	O	N	■	P	I	A	N	O	K	E	Y	S
■	■	C	A	L	Y	P	S	O	S	■	T	O	V	■
F	I	G	A	R	O	■	L	A	P	S	U	P	■	■
A	G	A	■	C	O	V	E	R	A	G	E	■	■	■
T	U	R	N	S	T	I	L	E	■	E	R	N	I	E
E	E	R	O	■	M	E	M	O	■	M	I	N	N	■
■	S	I	N	E	S	■	C	O	N	N	■	N	B	C
A	S	S	A	Y	S	■	T	V	C	A	M	E	R	A
I	S	O	M	E	R	■	R	E	U	N	I	T	E	S
L	O	N	E	R	S	■	A	R	E	A	C	O	D	E

148

A	N	K	A	R	A	■	I	N	A	F	L	A	S	H
N	I	N	J	A	S	■	W	A	D	E	I	N	T	O
O	C	E	A	N	S	■	I	N	D	E	N	I	A	L
T	O	E	■	G	E	T	S	O	U	T	■	M	I	L
H	I	P	P	E	T	Y	H	O	P	■	L	A	N	E
E	S	A	U	■	P	I	K	■	H	A	T	E	R	■
R	E	D	F	A	C	E	D	■	S	A	B	E	R	S
■	■	■	F	L	I	E	S	S	O	L	O	■	■	■
A	D	F	E	E	S	■	A	U	T	O	R	A	C	E
W	E	A	R	S	■	L	I	L	■	E	G	A	D	■
E	M	L	Y	■	G	O	D	F	E	A	R	I	N	G
S	O	L	■	O	U	T	T	A	L	K	■	T	A	I
O	L	D	I	R	I	S	H	■	S	E	R	A	P	E
M	A	U	N	A	L	O	A	■	E	L	I	T	E	S
E	Y	E	S	L	E	F	T	■	S	A	G	E	S	T

149

U	N	S	T	A	C	K	■	S	A	V	E	S	U	P
B	A	L	I	H	A	I	■	P	R	E	D	A	T	E
O	N	E	C	A	L	L	■	R	E	I	N	T	E	R
A	C	E	■	B	I	L	L	I	O	N	A	I	R	E
T	Y	P	E	■	J	O	E	L	■	E	O	S	■	■
■	■	L	I	T	H	O	G	R	A	P	H	■	■	■
E	Y	E	T	O	E	Y	E	■	R	O	S	S	I	■
N	O	S	H	O	W	S	■	S	O	Y	B	E	A	N
O	N	S	E	T	■	C	O	L	O	N	E	L	S	■
■	■	R	H	I	N	O	C	E	R	O	S	■	■	■
B	A	T	■	L	E	A	K	■	B	A	N	E	■	■
A	L	I	T	T	L	E	L	A	M	B	■	W	I	N
B	E	P	R	O	U	D	■	W	E	A	R	I	E	D
A	P	P	E	A	S	E	■	A	S	K	A	N	C	E
S	H	I	F	T	E	D	■	Y	O	U	N	G	E	R

150

C	O	S	T	E	L	L	O	■	A	B	B	O	T	T
I	N	T	E	R	I	O	R	■	D	R	A	W	E	R
R	O	A	D	R	A	G	E	■	D	I	N	E	R	O
■	■	D	I	M	A	G	G	I	O	■	D	E	W	■
B	A	B	Y	S	■	N	A	R	C	■	O	S	E	■
A	R	A	B	■	U	S	N	A	T	I	O	N	A	L
M	C	L	E	A	N	■	O	N	I	O	N	■	■	■
S	O	M	A	L	I	A	■	D	O	N	O	T	G	O
■	■	■	R	A	N	K	S	■	N	A	C	H	O	S
C	L	A	S	S	T	I	M	E	S	■	C	A	L	I
R	E	G	■	■	E	N	I	D	■	B	A	R	D	S
I	V	E	■	E	N	D	T	I	M	E	S	■	■	■
M	I	N	D	E	D	■	I	T	A	L	I	A	N	O
E	N	D	U	R	E	■	N	O	N	L	O	C	A	L
S	E	A	G	O	D	■	G	R	E	E	N	T	E	A

151

```
S K I M A S K   H A S A T I T
I N F O R C E   E X P L O R E
N O S W E A T   L E A P T O N
A C T   A T O L L S   S E N T
T K O S   S N U B     B A B
R E N A L   E X E S   S A G E
A D E L I E   U N H I N G E D
      U N D E R T O N E
W H A T A D A Y   O N E D G E
H A L E   A R B S   O R I O N
A V E     C O M B   S A N D
N E W S   M A X O U T   D E O
G O I N G I N   O N A T E A R
E N F I E L D   C C L A M P S
D E E P S K Y   H O L Y S E E
```

152

```
M I S D I R E C T   A V I L A
A L L O C A T O R   N A D I R
Y O U M U S T B E   I G E T A
E N N A   E A S Y S T R E E T
R A G I N       E R A
      N O D E S   N A N T E S
I P O   D E L T A S   C O T E
S A T I S F I E D O R Y O U R
E R I C   A S P I R E   T I T
E T C E T C   S A Y E R
      S O T     L I L L I
B A C K P O C K E T   B E A N
O P R A H   H O N E Y B A C K
R E A T A   A L T A M O N T E
E X M E T   W A R R A N T O R
```

153

```
A C C R U A L S   G O G G L E
C O P A P L E A   A M O R A L
R O A D S I G N   B A H A M A
E L S   A R A L   N O V E L
    L O S E N O T I M E
O H M A N   E D G E   E L K O
S E A D O G   R O N A   P A T
M A K E F R I E N D S W I T H
I V E   F A V A   S O O T H E
C E S S   F I S T   N O S I R
    W H I T E F A C E D
A L O U S   S A L A   N O W
C A R T E R   U L T I M A T A
I N S U R E   L E T S I N O N
D E E P E N   T R Y A C A S E
```

154

```
N O T A   D I D   S P I D E R
I N A C T I O N   A A C E L L
T O K U G A W A   B R E A K S
  R E T I N A   P E A R L S
    S A F E   T E R M S
S A A B   E A S E   R I D
E R D O S   C A N A D I A N A
D R I V E T H R U W I N D O W
G A V E A H O O T   C A I N E
E Y E   W O O S   M O E S
    S O U S E   M E O W
  E M E R G E   N O R M A L
D E A R T H   M E D I E V A L
A R I G H T   T H E E N E M Y
M O N E Y S   S I S   T S P S
```

155

```
A D H E R E   A S G O O D A S
B E E M E R   S Q U A R E L Y
E N A M O R   Q U I T C O L D
R I D E S   Q U A S H   D O N
D E B T   S U I T E   M A T E
E D U   S T I E S   H O R S Y
E T T A K E T T   S O N
N O T G I V E A H O O T F O R
    I L E   S A P P H I R E
I W I L L   R A M P S   N A S
N O M E   Y U M M Y   P E L T
D O G   H O B O S   H O T E L
I L O V E Y O U   D E L U X E
G E N E R O U S   A R E N A S
O N E T A S T E   M O D E M S
```

156

```
Z I P C O D E   C H A I N S
A L L U D E T O   H O W N O W
F L A R E S U P   E N L A C E
T U N A   D E D E E   S H E
I S O T O P E   O S S   N A T
G E N E V A   U R E T H A N E
      I R O N S   E R G S
A C R O S S T H E S T R E E T
S H U N   T I T H E
S I D E S T E P   I N C H E S
E V E   E R R   O N T H E Q T
S A W   R E S O D   A G U A
S L O V E N   D I A L S O A P
E R R A N D   A N N O T A T E
S Y D N E Y   G A M E T E S
```

157

```
A N D R O C L E S █ M A H A L
F O O D C O U R T █ A G O R A
T R E A S U R E R █ M R M O M
E T S █ P E S E T A █ E M I
R O S I N S █ T I E █ S A N
S N O W E D █ U S M C █ P T A
█ E V E R █ A P E S U I T
S T O R A G E █ N O T O N C E
P H A E D R A █ D R E D █
E E K █ A A R E █ A R O U N D
C I R █ C E N █ L A I N I E
I D I █ M E N S A L █ S E N
A I D E D █ D I S O R I E N T
L O G E S █ E L A B O R A T E
S T E L E █ R E S E T T L E D
```

158

```
S I T C O M █ I S I T S A F E
O R I O L E █ S T R A I N E D
D A M N E D █ T R A C T O R S
A L E K █ I T H I N K █ D U E
J E T █ V C H I P █ P E L L
E V O K E █ E S S O █ U S E S
R I G O R O U S █ D U N █
K N O W S O N E S O N I O N S
█ T E N █ A I R M E D A L
I D E O █ A L T O █ A R E N A
N O R W █ U T U R N █ T A P
A S I █ I C E A X E █ P O N S
J I V E T A L K █ E L I J A H
A D A M S A L E █ K I M O N O
M O N T A N A N █ S T A Y A T
```

159

```
R A M O N E S █ M A I L B A G
E P I S O D E █ E S T E L L E
D O N T R O C K T H E B O A T
F L I E D █ O N E O N █ T M S
L O C O █ S N E R T █ L O O M
A G A █ W A D E S █ G O U D A
G Y M S H O E S █ T O U T E D
█ L A N D L O R D S █
S P R I T E █ A N A L Y S T S
T H A T S █ A P T L Y █ H I E
R O W S █ A L P H A █ T Y N E
I N D █ A L L E E █ S U S H I
K E E P Y O U R S H I R T O N
E M A I L E D █ L A M B E R T
R E L E A S E █ Y E S O R N O
```

160

```
A N T E S U P █ W R A P P E D
T E R M I N I █ H I T T U N E
T R I E S T E █ I N R A N G E
A V E R █ A T I T █ A S C A P
C I D █ I C I N E S S █ H R S
K N I C K K N A C K █ D E D E
S E T O N █ M A I N I D E A
█ C O R R U P T E D █
L O C O W E E D █ T A P E S
E L L A █ P A D D Y W H A C K
A D E █ R O L L O U T █ S H Y
P L A T A █ T E R P █ S T E M
F I T I N T O █ S P A T U L A
O N E S T A R █ A I R D R O P
R E D H O T S █ L E S S E N S
```

161

```
J U M A N J I █ L I O N I Z E
O P I N I O N █ A C R O N Y M
G A T E L E G █ Y A N G T Z E
G T O █ E Y E S O R E █ E Z R
E R S E █ S A L V E █ K A Y S
R E I N S █ R Y E █ S E R V O
S E S A M E █ A R K A N S A N
█ M I N U S S I G N █
S T T E R E S A █ D E E P E R
C H A L K █ A F C █ S T O N E
R E G S █ A T O L L █ H O L A
E R L █ E P O X I E S █ R A D
A M I S T A D █ M A E S T R I
M I N U T I A █ A V E R A G E
S C E N E R Y █ X E R O X E S
```

162

```
B L A T A N T █ I N T A K E S
O I L Y G O O █ C A I R E N E
W A L K I N A P A R T M E N T
L I K E N █ T O N E S █ P O T
I S I S █ F E L T S █ B A B E
N O D █ A R E A S █ B A S L E
E N D U R E █ R E H A S H E S
█ I D L E D █ E A T S A █
W A N D E R E D █ T H I R S T
H A G E N █ L I M E S █ P O R
O M A R █ O T T O S █ D E S I
I I S █ S M A S H █ B U Y U P
S L I P P E R Y A S A N E E L
I N D I A N A █ W E L C O M E
T E E N T S Y █ K L E E N E X
```

163

TROTTER · MACHETE
RIVIERA · ESSAYER
ICELAND · SLAVING
CERT · SIAM · ENTO
KAL · STAGEFRIGHT
KRONE · TURRET · ·
NOREASON · ELMIRA
ENDOWER · IDEAMEN
EISNER · STANDPAT
· · LEVIES · TERSE
INCIDENTALS · ESA
DOUG · LAMA · SCUT
TOSHIBA · ENSNARE
ASHTRAY · SCOOTER
GEYSERS · · SEABEDS

164

QUEEREYE · MARCEL
UPINARMS · APERCU
ANNERICE · DOTELL
· MICA · OEDIPAL
CAPITA · HUP · TET
HALEY · MITRAL ·
IRAS · MISSOREGON
LON · RUNSOUT · UNE
INTHEFIELD · GROW
· UNFOLD · MOUNT
FAR · INF · RAISES
POLLENS · TENN ·
ENLIST · WINDGUST
ADONAI · AVEMARIA
RAYGUN · DOESTIME

165

THRU · SICKASADOG
WEEP · ATANYPRICE
ALAS · NATURALGAS
SPRINGLET · DEALT
· ZEROS · YENTAS
ASSISI · TORE ·
SAINTALBANS · TWO
HUNG · OIL · MOON
ELK · PRINCEHARRY
· FAUN · VERTEX
SPLINT · FLEAS ·
TIARA · PAINTBALL
OPTICNERVE · ALIA
OPENHOUSES · ROAD
LARGEPRINT · SPRY

166

DETROITMICHIGAN
ITSAFREECOUNTRY
MAKEAMENTALNOTE
ELS · NAS · USC · SET
· ESTES ·
AST · STAN · HAIM
CHARLOTTEBRONTE
TAKEITORLEAVEIT
ACEUPONESSLEEVE
SKIP · EASE · LED
· SKEDS ·
AMI · INE · BAM · ASU
SATELLITESTATES
ATEENAGERINLOVE
STARSINONESEYES

167

BANKGUARD · ALERT
ONONESWAY · AIMEE
BONEHEADS · ABABA
SNEER · YIP · CRIER
· ALIT · OHREALLY
ANTIGEN · EELS ·
MOAN · NORMAL · MIL
BELG · STOIC · CEDE
ILL · HITEST · HMOS
· ROTH · MELROSE
NYAHNYAH · DOOR ·
BOGIE · TOM · SMASH
OWENS · BUILTINTO
MINOT · ARTSTUDIO
BETSY · DITTOMARK

168

FBIFILE · TABASCO
RECROOM · ONESTOP
ATEINTO · PALEALE
GOB · ATTEST · ANON
IKEA · SEAT · DRT
LEERS · DROP · ATTO
ENROOT · TRUELOVE
· MURPHYBED ·
ONSALEAT · SKIBIB
LOPS · ENOS · SNIDE
DCI · GNUS · ERST
POND · SLEEPS · DAW
RUNUPTO · DEADEYE
ONEROUS · ENDORSE
STRAINS · STETSON

169

```
W I N S   S I G M A   S P A M
A S E A   P L E A D   M A X I
L O W↓  S R I N G S   A G E D
T U T O R I A L     A R E
  R O U T E D   D O N T↓  E R
      T A R   D A L I   B E E
P O L S     W A N E S   A R N
A B E   J O H N D O E   C I D
R E F   A M I T Y     E K E S
E S T   P E T E   S Y N
R E↓  L A N E   U T A H A N
    T O N   O P E R A H A T
T H O U   N O C↓  E D N O S E
A M O S   O N T A P   C O T E
D O Z E   D E A L S   E T Y M
```

170

```
C N B C       T R Y S T E D
H E A R S T   S E E A L O N E
O N S A L E   H A S W O R D S
Y E S W E R E O P E N   R O I
  S O L E M N V O W   S I R S
        P I N E Y   M I D S T
      C N O T E S   R A N E E S
    B R A V E S   P E R U S E
  I R I D E S   M O D E S T
M I M E R   M O R N S
P A I R   C A N T O N E S E
A N N   M E T R O S E X U A L
L E A D I N T O   E S T A T E
E N L I S T E E   S T O V E S
R O S E O I L     L E N S
```

171

```
S W E E T G U M   P A D D L E
M A L E A L T O   O T H M A R
O V E R S E E N   P R A V D A
R E C I T E S   S C A R
E S T E E   C P O   M A C S
    S T A S H I N G A W A Y
M A N T E L P I E C E   A I D
O L E   S P E N S E R   S R O
M I C   T H E N O R M S H O W
M A K E S A D E N T I N
A S S N   B E D   N A R C S
    D E E R   G R A P H I C
R E S U L T   D I E T S O D A
A G A S S I   U N L E A D E D
H O M E E C   D A Y S T A R S
```

172

```
    F R U S T R A T I N G
  S E A S I D E R E S O R T
S T E V E N S P I E L B E R G
T U L E S   U S N A   G A R
A D I N   W E L T Y   V O C E
B I N   S A L S A   P A R E E
L O G   K A L E   D A M I E N
E R O T I C A   P E N P A L S
D E N I E S   C A N S   N E A
O M E N S   N U T S Y   C M L
O A S T   G O S E E   S H E A
R K O   B A T T   S T A N D
S E A T O F Y O U R P A N T S
  S T U F F E D S H I R T S
  S A F E T Y C O N E S
```

173

```
U M M Q A S R   P A T I N A S
T R O U N C E   A B I L E N E
A H E A D O F   R A N L A T E
H Y S T E R I A S   T Y P E D
A D H E R E N C E   T A L
N E A R S   E R R S   S I T E
    N O I R E   A B O D E S
S A V A N T S   T W O F E R S
A V E R S E   S H A L T
V E R Y   M U T E   S E G U E
E M S   P O S I T R O N S
T A I G A   S P A C E S O U T
I R O N A G E   R E R I N S E
M I N A R E T   G A U D I E R
E A S T E R S   E X P E N D S
```

174

```
C H I P P E D I N   G A L O P
H O M E A L O N E   A L I B I
A T A N Y C O S T   P A B S T
M T G   S H R I L L S   R E S
P I E T   E S P O O   W E S T
S E R E N A   I S T H A T S O
    R A P I D S   O N T O P
F I S S I O N   E D I T O R S
A C H E S   A S S E S S
T E E S H I R T   S T I R P S
A S S T   C R E P T   N O R T
L O G   C H E E R I O   O F A
I V O R Y   A L A N A R K I N
S E N D S   R I D E S H E R D
T R E A T   S E A S T O R M S
```

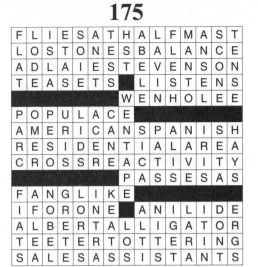

175

```
F L I E S A T H A L F M A S T
L O S T O N E S B A L A N C E
A D L A I E S T E V E N S O N
T E A S E T S ■ L I S T E N S
■ ■ ■ ■ ■ W E N H O L E E
P O P U L A C E ■ ■ ■ ■ ■ ■ ■
A M E R I C A N S P A N I S H
R E S I D E N T I A L A R E A
C R O S S R E A C T I V I T Y
■ ■ ■ ■ P A S S E S A S
F A N G L I K E ■ ■ ■ ■ ■ ■ ■
I F O R O N E ■ A N I L I D E
A L B E R T A L L I G A T O R
T E E T E R T O T T E R I N G
S A L E S A S S I S T A N T S
```

176

```
A G O R A ■ ■ ■ S H A L A L A
B O N E U P ■ P H O T O L A B
A D E S T E ■ I R R I G A T E
S I M E O N ■ T I N T ■ M E R
E V A N P I C O N E ■ S A N D
■ A N T I T A N K ■ M O N T E
■ ■ ■ L E G S ■ C I R C L E
G O O D O N E ■ F O N T E Y N
A R N E T T ■ L I L I ■ ■ ■
M A R E S ■ F I N D A W A Y
E T E S ■ P I L A S T E R E D
L O P ■ D A N A ■ N U B I L E
A R O M A T I C ■ A R E O L A
W I R E L E S S ■ P E R S O N
S O T T I S H ■ ■ S N O W S
```

177

```
M I X N M A T C H ■ U P F O R
I N F I R M A R Y ■ S E I N E
S T I C K E M U P ■ M O N E Y
D E L E O N ■ S E W I N G O N
I N E R T ■ M A R I N ■ E N O
D T S ■ T O E D ■ S T E R O L
■ ■ D E P L E T E ■ V E N D
R E F E R E E ■ U M P I R E S
A V O N ■ N E T B A L L ■ ■
M A R T H E ■ R A N A ■ S O I
A C T ■ A R G U S ■ S P A N S
L U K E W A R M ■ S T O N E D
L A N I S ■ A P P L I E D T O
A T O N E ■ S E E A C T I O N
H E X E S ■ S T A Y S S A N E
```

178

```
C A M I L L O ■ B O O K B A G
A C A D I A N ■ E N C L O S E
T E R E N C E R A T T I G A N
A R R A Y ■ P A M ■ S E A L E
L O I S ■ C A P E K ■ G R A S
A S A ■ E R I T R E A ■ T R I
N E G A T O R ■ S T R E A K S
■ E I N S ■ ■ C M O N ■
B A L L A S T ■ T H E E D G E
E L I ■ S E E T H E D ■ B E Y
C A C O ■ S N O W S ■ V A N E
A M E B A ■ D A H ■ P A C E S
L E N O Z Z E D I F I G A R O
M I S T I E R ■ T I T U L A R
S N E E Z E S ■ E S T E L L E
```

179

```
A P P A R A T ■ A D H E R E S
B E E H I V E ■ D O O D A D S
R E P A P E R ■ E N L A C E S
A L A B A M A S L A M M E R S
■ ■ ■ A W I L L ■ ■ ■
E L A B O R A T E D E T A I L
M A S O N I T E ■ ■ L I L L E
M Y T R E A T ■ D U M P S O N
A I R E R ■ ■ M I L E P O S T
S T A R S A N D S T R I P E S
■ ■ D A L A I ■ ■
D I A G N O S I S M U R D E R
U S U R E R S ■ T A N T A R A
S A R A L E E ■ E T I E N N E
E N A B L E R ■ R A S S L E S
```

180

```
S P H E R E S ■ B L O N D E R
T R I T E S T ■ L I N E O N E
R E L E A S E ■ A S T A R T E
A L L ■ P E N N S T A T I O N
P U T T ■ X O U T ■ P E T I T
O D O R S ■ S M U T ■ R O L E
N E P A L I ■ B L A H ■ S S R
■ ■ C O B B S A L A D ■ ■
B A D ■ P E R K ■ C L I M A X
O D E R ■ T A U S ■ S E I Z E
A A M E S ■ I L K A ■ T S A R
S W A N N I N L O V E ■ F L O
T A N N A T E ■ P I N K I E S
O R D E R E R ■ J A I A L A I
F E S T E R S ■ E N D L E S S
```

181

C	H	A	S	M	A	L	■	A	T	A	C	L	I	P
D	E	S	P	I	N	A	■	C	A	T	H	O	D	E
A	M	B	U	L	A	N	C	E	C	H	A	S	E	R
L	L	A	M	A	■	D	A	T	E	S	■	T	A	T
B	I	D	E	■	G	F	L	A	T	■	M	O	T	E
U	N	A	■	G	R	I	L	L	■	D	Y	N	E	S
M	E	S	S	H	A	L	L	■	A	R	R	E	S	T
■	B	O	O	T	L	E	G	G	E	R	S	■		
S	P	A	R	S	E	■	T	R	A	S	H	B	A	G
C	A	D	E	T	■	S	T	A	R	S	■	A	M	A
R	I	C	S	■	S	T	E	N	S	■	O	L	E	S
O	D	A	■	S	P	O	R	T	■	G	N	A	R	L
O	F	N	O	C	O	N	S	E	Q	U	E	N	C	E
G	O	B	R	O	K	E	■	E	U	N	I	C	E	S
E	R	E	C	T	E	D	■	S	I	N	L	E	S	S

182

C	H	A	W	■	T	H	E	E	■	B	E	F	O	G
R	A	G	A	■	R	I	L	L	■	I	G	I	V	E
O	V	E	R	■	I	S	M	E	L	L	A	R	A	T
W	E	N	C	E	S	■	S	C	A	L	D	S	■	
E	N	T	R	E	E	S	■	T	R	I	S	T	A	N
■			I	N	C	H	A	R	G	E	■	G	L	O
F	I	L	M	S	T	U	D	I	O	■	L	E	E	S
I	R	A	E	■	T	O	C	■	E	A	V	E		
T	A	U	S	■	S	T	R	E	S	S	F	R	E	E
I	T	N	■	A	L	L	E	Y	C	A	T	■		
N	E	C	K	T	I	E	■	E	R	R	A	N	D	S
■	H	I	T	E	C	H	■	I	G	L	O	O	S	
B	O	I	L	E	R	R	O	O	M	■	O	L	E	G
R	E	N	T	S	■	E	A	R	P	■	N	A	S	T
A	N	G	S	T	■	W	R	A	Y	■	E	N	T	S

183

■	B	I	T	P	A	R	T	■	■	P	E	A	T
■	C	A	P	S	U	L	A	R	■	M	A	N	T	A
F	L	Y	O	U	T	T	H	E	W	I	N	D	O	W
L	O	W	■	A	S	K	A	R	O	U	N	D		
I	S	A	A	C	S	■	S	C	O	U	R	E	R	
P	E	T	S	H	O	P	S	■	S	T	O	R	Y	
■	S	C	H	E	D	U	L	E	A	■				
T	H	E	M	A	N	O	F	S	T	E	E	L		
		S	T	O	O	P	E	D	T	O				
E	A	M	E	S	■	P	R	I	C	I	E	S	T	
S	T	O	U	T	E	N	■	C	H	E	R	T	Y	
P	O	R	C	E	L	A	I	N	■	N	A	P		
I	N	T	H	E	L	I	N	E	O	F	F	I	R	E
E	C	A	R	D	■	S	K	E	R	R	I	T	T	
D	E	L	E	■	H	Y	D	R	O	X	Y			

184

D	I	S	B	A	R	■	S	E	M	I	R	A	R	E
E	N	T	E	R	O	■	E	L	I	C	I	T	E	D
B	L	A	N	C	S	■	N	I	N	E	F	O	L	D
B	U	T	T	H	A	T	S	J	U	S	T	M	E	
I	C	U	■	I	N	H	E	A	T	■	I	A	M	
E	K	E	■	M	N	O	■	H	I	E	■	Z	S	A
■			W	E	A	R	Y	■	A	X	S	E	E	D
S	K	I	E	D	■	N	E	O	■	T	E	R	S	E
P	U	L	S	E	S	■	S	H	A	R	E			
U	R	L	■	S	I	D	■	W	P	A	■	M	I	S
D	O	H	■	E	U	R	O	P	E	■	E	N	T	
■	S	U	P	E	R	B	O	W	L	X	X	X	V	I
N	A	M	E	D	R	O	P	■	A	T	R	I	A	L
T	W	O	P	H	A	S	E	■	U	R	A	C	I	L
H	A	R	A	S	S	E	D	■	D	A	Y	O	N	E

185

A	P	E	■	S	E	R	F	■	S	H	A	R	D	S
S	H	R	A	P	N	E	L	■	E	A	S	E	I	N
T	E	A	C	A	D	D	Y	■	A	M	S	T	E	L
U	N	S	A	Y	■	C	L	A	M	O	R	S	■	
T	O	E	D	■	S	P	A	I	N	■	C	O	I	L
E	L	D	E	R	H	O	S	T	E	L	■	F	R	Y
■	M	E	A	L	T	I	M	E	■	I	A	N		
A	L	R	E	A	D	Y	■	G	O	R	E	T	E	X
H	I	E	■	P	O	M	P	A	N	O	S	■		
A	M	I	■	S	W	E	E	N	E	Y	T	O	D	D
B	E	N	Z	■	B	R	A	T	S	■	E	L	I	E
■	T	H	E	M	O	S	T	■	C	E	D	E	S	
P	R	O	L	I	X	■	B	I	G	A	M	I	S	T
B	E	L	I	Z	E	■	O	V	E	R	S	E	E	R
S	E	D	G	E	S	■	G	Y	M	S	■	S	L	Y

186

L	O	S	T	I	T	■	B	A	R	B	■	L	S	T
O	P	P	O	S	I	T	E	W	A	Y	■	A	A	A
B	U	R	K	I	N	A	F	A	S	O	■	T	I	C
B	L	U	E	■	G	R	A	D	E	B	M	I	L	K
Y	E	N	■	G	E	T	Z	■	I	N	T	O		
I	N	G	O	O	D	■	E	M	E	R	S	I	O	N
S	C	O	F	F	■	A	D	A	G	E	S	■		
T	E	N	F	E	E	T	■	P	O	P	E	A	F	B
■	B	R	E	T	T	S	■	E	N	T	R	E		
C	O	L	E	S	L	A	W	■	M	A	T	T	E	A
R	H	E	A	■	O	B	I	T	■	H	E	R		
I	D	A	T	A	R	B	E	L	L	■	C	E	L	S
T	A	D	■	O	U	A	G	A	D	O	U	G	O	U
I	R	E	■	K	I	N	G	H	E	N	R	Y	V	I
C	N	N	■	I	N	K	S	■	W	A	S	M	E	T

187

```
T R A D E S H O W ■ A R R I S
H I R O S H I M A ■ M I A M I
E S T A T E T A X ■ A P P A L
B E I N ■ A I R P A S S A G E
E S S ■ D R T ■ O C S ■ N I N
S T A S I S ■ T E L ■ D U S T
T O N E D ■ P U T U P W I T H
■ ■ ■ C U B A L I B R E ■ ■ ■
D O N T P A N I C ■ M E T E D
A C I S ■ S T P ■ D E B O N E
S E P ■ D I S ■ R E N ■ S D S
H A P P E N U P O N ■ B T U S
O N E O N ■ I L L A T E A S E
F I R S T ■ T A L L O R D E R
F A S T S ■ S T E I N M A R T
```

188

```
C O O K P O T ■ S T M A R Y S
U N D E R D O ■ T H E R E S A
S T O N I E R ■ R E N A M E D
P O R T M A N T E A U W O R D
■ ■ ■ ■ ■ ■ A R E S ■ ■ ■ ■ ■
G U S S I E D U P ■ C A S C A
O P T I N G I N ■ M A S H U P
F O O T L O C K E R S T O R E
O N L O A N ■ F R E T O V E R
R A I N Y ■ H I N D E R E R S
■ ■ ■ ■ ■ C O S I ■ ■ ■ ■ ■ ■
C A S E O F T H E C R E E P S
A M I A B L E ■ E R I T R E A
R E T R I A L ■ L E F T A R M
P R E S E T S ■ S W E E T I E
```

189

```
T V Q U I Z S H O W ■ A B C S
Y O U A R E H E R E ■ L R O N
S C O R E B O A R D ■ T U N A
O A T ■ D U E T ■ G D A N S K
N L E R ■ L E P E R ■ H E E
■ ■ ■ H E T E R O ■ O P I N E
M E N O M O S S O ■ P A L S Y
E V A D E R S ■ R E S I D U E
R A V E R ■ J E R K I N E S S
C L A S S ■ O R I E N T ■ ■ ■
Y U L ■ O L E I C ■ S C A M
S A B I N E ■ C H O O ■ O R O
E B A N ■ N A S A L B O N E S
A L S O ■ I N O R D I N A T E
T E E N ■ S A N D S T O N E S
```

190

```
B U B B L E B A T H ■ S H U T
O P E R A S E R I A ■ N O N E
A D V A N C E M E N ■ O L I N
T O Y S T O R Y ■ D A W D L E
■ ■ ■ H E R S ■ C A R P S A T
E L B E R T ■ F O X I E S T ■
L E A R N ■ F O R E D A T E D
S A D ■ F O L D S ■ ■ I R E
E D G E T O O L S ■ L A L A W
■ P E N A L T Y ■ F O U L L Y
F E R T I L E ■ B O O T ■ ■
A N G E L O ■ H A L F O P E N
S C A R ■ W H A C K A M O L E
T I M E ■ M I L K S H A K E S
S L E D ■ E C O S Y S T E M S
```

191

```
E N A M O R S ■ M O P P E T S
R I L E S U P ■ A R E A M A P
O N E M O M E N T I N T I M E
T E X ■ ■ C O R O N E T E D
I M A ■ M U S H I N E S S ■
C O N L O N ■ ■ ■ ■ ■ ■ ■
I N D I V I D U A L I S T I C
S T R A I T O F M E S S I N A
T H E R E S N O I I N T E A M
■ ■ ■ ■ ■ ■ ■ T O S S U P
■ ■ B A T W E I G H T ■ A D O
R E A C H I N T O ■ ■ K I R
A S S T U P I D A S C A N B E
S P I E L E D ■ P I E H O L E
H O L D E R S ■ E S T A T E S
```

192

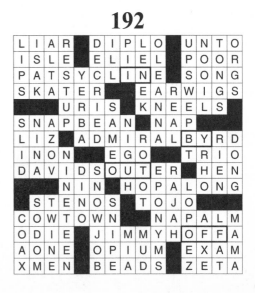

```
L I A R ■ D I P L O ■ U N T O
I S L E ■ E L I E L ■ P O O R
P A T S Y C L I N E ■ S O N G
S K A T E R ■ E A R W I G S
■ ■ ■ U R I S ■ K N E E L S
S N A P B E A N ■ N A P ■ ■
L I Z ■ A D M I R A L B Y R D
I N O N ■ E G O ■ ■ T R I O
D A V I D S O U T E R ■ H E N
■ ■ N I N ■ H O P A L O N G
■ S T E N O S ■ T O J O ■ ■
C O W T O W N ■ N A P A L M
O D I E ■ J I M M Y H O F F A
A O N E ■ O P I U M ■ E X A M
X M E N ■ B E A D S ■ Z E T A
```

193

```
B I J O U . S E I K O . I R S
L O A M S . H A Z E L . V I E
U N M A N . A T O N E T I M E
. I E R . P R A D O . H E E D
M A S . C E E . R E D D Y .
A N D . H A W G . F E R .
I S A W E S A U H E S A W M E
D E L A W A R E P R O P H E T
S A Y S O N E S P R A Y E R S
. H U T . T R E K . E R E
E B E R T . I T S . L I Q
G A L A . A X O N S . J E N
B R A G A B O U T . J A D E D
D R T . M E U S E . A V I S O
F E E . P E T E R . M A N S E
```

194

```
M O V E S A S I D E . A L E S
I N E R T G A S E S . L O T T
D A N G E R L I N E . P A R E
S I T . L E A S T . R A N U P
T R I M M E R . P A C E R S
. R O S Y S C E N A R I O
H O B S . C H O R D . C A N
A H A . R E A U M U R . A N T
N I L . A P P L E . O R S O
G O A C R O S S T O W N .
A R C H E S . O V A T I O N
R I L E D . L E P E R . O N O
I V A N . C O V A R I A N C E
N E V E . T R I P L E B I L L
G R A Y . R E L A Y R A C E S
```

195

```
S C A M S . G L A D . C O M A
P U R E E . R O B E . A U L D
I T I N A . O N L Y C H I L D
K I T T R E D G E . R O S E S
E T H I O P I A . L O O
. M O V I N G P I C T U R E
T H E N E T . O A K . S N I T
R O T . R H O . D E F . A G A
E M I T . E S P . W O M B A T
S E C R E T A D M I R E R .
. A L S . J U S T M I S S
C L A I M . C A T E R E D T O
C Y C L O R A M A . E N G E L
E R T E . E V E N . S T E N T
D E E R . F E S T . S O D O I
```

196

```
S P O R T S B R A . E L I H U
W I N E T H I E F . T E N O N
O P E N O R D E R . S I L L S
R E B . P E E N . B E S I D E
E D Y S . D R A M A Q U E E N
T O O L E . S C A B . R U N T
O W N E R S . T R I B E .
. N E E D E D . V E R S E S
. P E P U P . S A U N A S
C C V I . I N I T . T I T L E
R A I N M A K E R S . T I E S
O M E G A S . R O A R . C S T
W E N C H . D R I V E T I M E
D I N A R . P O K E F U N A T
S N A R E . S T A R S I G N S
```

197

```
R E N T A C A R . F L A W E D
O V E R R I C E . I O D I N E
N O B I G G I E . G U A R D S
A L B S . A D D E N D . E W E
L V I . A R R I V E . S T I R
D E S K S . A N E W . H A S T
. S H I N D I G . T A U P E S
. T E R N . W O R T .
C A S T R O . C A N D I C E
R A K E . P R O S . E N E R O
I M A N . S I M I A N . L A D
C I T . S H T E T L . S E S E
K L E P T O . S Y L L A B U S
E N R O O T . T O A S T E R S
T E S L A S . O U T T O S E A
```

198

```
B R U T . F E T A . C L I V E
R O P E . E T O N . L I T E R
A T T N . A U C T I O N E E R
G E O D E S I C . S T E M S .
. N E X T . A L O H A .
A B O R T S . T O L E R A N T
P A G E R . B A R D S . P I A
P R O R A T E . R E H I R E S
L O O . V A L S E . O N I C E
E N D T A B L E . B R A C E R
. A G A I N . E S T O .
. B E H A R . D E S E R T E D
P A L I N D R O M E . I P S O
F R A N Z . O F I T . C I T E
C E L I A . E F T S . E T E S
```

199

J	I	L	L	S	T	J	O	H	N	■	E	D	A	M
O	R	E	O	C	O	O	K	I	E	■	C	O	P	E
C	O	T	T	O	N	E	D	T	O	■	H	O	P	I
K	N	I	T	T	E	D	■	■	S	P	O	R	E	S
E	S	T	■	T	R	I	P	P	■	A	I	M	A	T
Y	O	G	A	■	S	M	A	L	L	S	C	A	L	E
S	N	O	B	S	■	A	N	A	C	T	■	T	S	R
■	■	S	H	A	G	G	Y	D	O	G	■	■		
T	A	E	■	A	L	G	A	E	■	R	E	W	E	T
H	I	G	H	F	L	I	E	R	S	■	E	R	N	E
E	R	G	O	T	■	O	A	S	T	S	■	I	C	E
A	C	R	O	S	S	■	■	C	R	O	P	T	O	P
T	O	O	K	■	P	U	L	L	I	N	H	E	R	E
R	O	L	E	■	A	N	O	U	K	A	I	M	E	E
E	L	L	Y	■	N	U	M	B	E	R	L	E	S	S

200

C	A	C	T	U	S	■	A	S	K	S	F	O	R
O	N	L	I	N	E	■	C	R	E	A	T	I	V	E
U	G	A	N	D	A	■	L	I	T	T	E	R	E	D
P	L	U	S	E	S	■	A	S	I	T	W	E	R	E
L	E	D	E	R	H	O	S	E	N	■	A	B	L	E
E	D	E	L	W	E	I	S	S	■	P	R	O	A	M
■	■	A	L	L	Y	■	T	O	D	A	Y	S		
■	R	A	T	T	L	Y	■	H	O	I	S	T	S	■
M	E	L	E	E	S	■	V	E	I	N	■			
A	M	B	E	R	■	T	E	L	L	T	A	L	E	S
F	I	A	T	■	R	E	S	P	E	C	T	I	V	E
I	N	C	I	D	E	N	T	■	T	O	O	L	E	D
O	D	O	M	E	T	E	R	■	T	U	N	I	N	G
S	E	R	E	N	I	T	Y	■	E	N	C	A	S	E
O	R	E	S	T	E	S	■	S	T	E	N	O	S

The New York Times

Crossword Puzzles

The #1 Name in Crosswords

Available at your local bookstore or online at nytimes.com/nytstore

St. Martin's Griffin